Entrepreneurship Education and Training
Programs around the World

DIRECTIONS IN DEVELOPMENT
Human Development

Entrepreneurship Education and Training Programs around the World
Dimensions for Success

Alexandria Valerio, Brent Parton, and Alicia Robb

THE WORLD BANK
Washington, D.C.

© 2014 International Bank for Reconstruction and Development / The World Bank
1818 H Street NW, Washington DC 20433
Telephone: 202-473-1000; Internet: www.worldbank.org

Some rights reserved

1 2 3 4   17 16 15 14

This work is a product of the staff of The World Bank with external contributions. Note that The World Bank does not necessarily own each component of the content included in the work. The World Bank therefore does not warrant that the use of the content contained in the work will not infringe on the rights of third parties. The risk of claims resulting from such infringement rests solely with you.

The findings, interpretations, and conclusions expressed in this work do not necessarily reflect the views of The World Bank, its Board of Executive Directors, or the governments they represent. The World Bank does not guarantee the accuracy of the data included in this work. The boundaries, colors, denominations, and other information shown on any map in this work do not imply any judgment on the part of The World Bank concerning the legal status of any territory or the endorsement or acceptance of such boundaries.

Nothing herein shall constitute or be considered to be a limitation upon or waiver of the privileges and immunities of The World Bank, all of which are specifically reserved.

Rights and Permissions

This work is available under the Creative Commons Attribution 3.0 IGO license (CC BY 3.0 IGO) http://creativecommons.org/licenses/by/3.0/igo. Under the Creative Commons Attribution license, you are free to copy, distribute, transmit, and adapt this work, including for commercial purposes, under the following conditions:

Attribution—Please cite the work as follows: Valerio, Alexandria, Brent Parton, and Alicia Robb. 2014. *Entrepreneurship Education and Training Programs around the World: Dimensions for Success*. Washington, DC: World Bank. doi: 10.1596/978-1-4648-0202-7. License: Creative Commons Attribution CC BY 3.0 IGO

Translations—If you create a translation of this work, please add the following disclaimer along with the attribution: *This translation was not created by The World Bank and should not be considered an official World Bank translation. The World Bank shall not be liable for any content or error in this translation.*

Third-party content—The World Bank does not necessarily own each component of the content contained within the work. The World Bank therefore does not warrant that the use of any third-party-owned individual component or part contained in the work will not infringe on the rights of those third parties. The risk of claims resulting from such infringement rests solely with you. If you wish to re-use a component of the work, it is your responsibility to determine whether permission is needed for that re-use and to obtain permission from the copyright owner. Examples of components can include, but are not limited to, tables, figures, or images.

All queries on rights and licenses should be addressed to the Publishing and Knowledge Division, The World Bank, 1818 H Street NW, Washington, DC 20433, USA; fax: 202-522-2625; e-mail: pubrights@worldbank.org.

ISBN (paper): 978-1-4648-0202-7
ISBN (electronic): 978-1-4648-0203-4
DOI: 10.1596/978-1-4648-0202-7

Cover photo: © Getty Images/Blend Images—Ariel Skelley. Used with permission. Further permission may be required for reuse.

Library of Congress Cataloging-in-Publication data.

Valerio, Alexandria, 1968–
 Entrepreneurship education and training programs around the world: dimensions for success / Alexandria Valerio, Brent Parton and Alicia Robb.
    pages cm. — (Directions in Development)
  Includes bibliographical references.
  ISBN 978-1-4648-0202-7 (alk. paper) — ISBN 978-1-4648-0203-4 (electronic)
  1. Entrepreneurship—Study and teaching. 2. Educational assistance—Evaluation. I. Parton, Brent. II. Robb, Alicia. III. Title.
   HB615.V3485 2014
   658.4'21071—dc23   2014008439

Contents

Preface		*ix*
Acknowledgments		*xi*
About the Authors		*xiii*
Abbreviations		*xv*

	Overview	1
	Entrepreneurship Promotion	1
	Entrepreneurship Education and Training	1
	About the Study	2
	Typology for EET Programs	2
	Conceptual Framework for EET	3
	EET Program Landscape Analysis	5
	Implications for EET Program Design and Implementation	8
	Implications for Policy	9
Chapter 1	**About the Study**	11
	Motivation	11
	Objective	12
	Methodology	12
	Structure of the Study	15
	Audience	15
	Note	15
	Bibliography	16
Chapter 2	**Literature Review**	17
	On Entrepreneurship	17
	On Entrepreneurship Education and Training	20
	Implications for Policy	25
	Bibliography	26
Chapter 3	**Conceptual Framework**	33
	Types of EET Programs	33
	Developing a Conceptual Framework for EET	35
	Describing the Framework by Dimension	36

	Note	51
	Bibliography	51
Chapter 4	**EET Program Landscape and Analysis**	**57**
	Entrepreneurship Education—Secondary Education Students (EESE)	58
	Analyzing EESE Programs	60
	Entrepreneurship Education—Higher Education Students (EEHE)	70
	Analyzing EEHE Programs	71
	Entrepreneurship Training—Potential Entrepreneurs (ETPo)	82
	Analyzing ETPo Programs	84
	Entrepreneurship Training—Practicing Entrepreneurs (ETPr)	98
	Analyzing ETPr Programs	101
	Notes	117
	Bibliography	118
Chapter 5	**Implications for Program Design and Implementation**	**123**
	Summary of Findings	123
	Implications for Program Design	126
	Policy Implications	128
	Conclusion	129
	Bibliography	130
Appendix A	**Program Outcomes**	**133**
Appendix B	**Program Characteristics**	**137**
	Note	141
	Bibliography	141
Appendix C	**Moderating Factors**	**143**
	Note	144
	Bibliography	144
Appendix D	**Program Narratives**	**147**
	BizWorld	The Netherlands	148
	Network for Teaching Entrepreneurship (NFTE)	Boston Chapter, United States	152
	Bødo Entrepreneurship Program	Norway	156
	Business Plan Thesis Competition	Tunisia	160
	McGuire Center for Entrepreneurship Program	United States	164
	Entrepreneurship Development Centre	Bosnia and Herzegovina	169

	Economic Empowerment of Adolescent Girls and	
	Young Women | Liberia	172
	TechnoServe | El Salvador	176
	FINCA Entrepreneurship Program | Peru	180
	National Rural Savings Programme | Pakistan	184
	Interise | United States	188
	Notes	191
	References	192
Appendix E	**Program Descriptions**	**195**
	References	260

Boxes

3.1	Building Socio-Emotional Skills: BizWorld (the Netherlands)	37
3.2	Improving Entrepreneurial Capabilities: FINCA (Peru)	38
3.3	Becoming Entrepreneurs: Student Training for Promoting Entrepreneurship (Uganda)	39
3.4	Enhancing Firm Performance: Interise (United States)	40
3.5	Political Support through Partnership: Start and Improve Your Business (Vietnam)	42
3.6	The Gender Effect: National Rural Savings Programme (Pakistan)	44
3.7	Entrepreneurial Intentions: Entrepreneurship Development Center (Bosnia and Herzegovina)	46
3.8	Training the Trainers: Network for Teaching Entrepreneurship (United States)	48
3.9	Coaching as Follow-Up: Business Plan Thesis Competition (Tunisia)	49
4.1	Examining the Formation of Human Capital in Entrepreneurship	78
4.2	What Are We Learning from Business Training and Entrepreneurship Evaluations around the Developing World?	86
4.3	Human Capital and Entrepreneurial Success	104
4.4	Effects of Entrepreneurship Training in Developing Countries	105

Figures

O.1	Classifying Entrepreneurship Education and Training Programs	3
O.2	Conceptual Framework	4
2.1	Entrepreneurship Versus Business Management Education	22
3.1	Classifying Entrepreneurship Education and Training Programs	34
3.2	Conceptual Framework	35
3.3	Outcome Domains	37
3.4	Contextual Factors	41
3.5	Participant Characteristics	43
3.6	Program Characteristics	47
3.7	Conceptual Framework: Detailed Structure	50

4.1	Entrepreneurship Education—Secondary Education	60
4.2	Entrepreneurship Education—Higher Education	71
4.3	Entrepreneurship Training—Potential Entrepreneurs	84
4.4	Entrepreneurship Training—Practicing Entrepreneurs	101
5.1	Summary of EET Program Analyses	127

Tables

4.1	Entrepreneurship Education—Secondary Education Students (EESE) | List of Evaluations	59
4.2	Entrepreneurship Education—Secondary Education Students (EESE) | Key Information	61
4.3	Entrepreneurship Education—Higher Education Students (EEHE) | List of Evaluations	70
4.4	Entrepreneurship Education—Higher Education (EEHE) | Key Information	72
4.5	Program List: Entrepreneurship Training—Potential Entrepreneurs (ETPo) | List of Evaluations	83
4.6	Available Information on Costs | ETPo Programs	89
4.7	Entrepreneurship Training—Potential Entrepreneurs (ETPo) | Key Information	90
4.8	Entrepreneurship Training—Practicing Entrepreneurs (ETPr)	100
4.9	Available Information on Costs | ETPr Programs	106
4.10	Entrepreneurship Training—Practicing Entrepreneurs (ETPr) | Key Information	107
E.1	Entrepreneurship Education—Secondary Education Students (EESE)	196
E.2	Entrepreneurship Education—Higher Education Students (EEHE)	206
E.3	Entrepreneurship Training—Potential Entrepreneurs (ETPo)	217
E.4	Entrepreneurship Training—Practicing Entrepreneurs (ETPr)	234

Preface

Over the last 20 years, entrepreneurship education and training (EET) programs have mushroomed, given their promise and potential to promote entrepreneurial skills and attitudes. While the number of such programs continues to expand worldwide, global knowledge about these programs' impact remains thin. The objective of this study is to identify and catalog the range of EET program types as well as the program dimensions that shape program outcomes, including program characteristics, participant characteristics, and program context. Informed by a body of EET research, this study presents a Conceptual Framework for EET programs and applies the framework to conduct an analysis of both EET research and a global sample of program evaluations. Building on the observations of the analysis, this study describes a set of practical insights about EET program design and implementation across target groups, intended outcomes, and contexts.

The importance of this topic is reflected within the World Bank's *Education Sector Strategy 2020, Learning for All: Investing in People's Knowledge and Skills to Promote Development*[1] and responds directly to Step Four of the Skills Toward Employment and Productivity (STEP) Framework. Specifically, this study corresponds to the goal of encouraging entrepreneurship and innovation.[2] This study also aligns with the Bank's Social Protection and Labor Strategy for 2012–22,[3] and complements a new multi-sector work program being led by the Bank's Social Protection Network (HDNSP)—Supporting Self-Employment and Small-Scale Entrepreneurship: Creating and Improving Alternatives to Wage Employment. This study builds upon the existing multi-sector effort that examines the broader population of entrepreneurship promotion programs, including but not limited to EET, and is financed by a Trust Fund from the Bank-Netherlands Partnership Program (BNPP).

Notes

1. Washington, DC: World Bank, 2011.
2. World Bank, *Stepping Up Skills: For More Jobs and Higher Productivity* (Washington, DC: World Bank, 2010).
3. World Bank, *Resilience, Equity and Opportunity: The World Bank 2012–22 Social Protection and Labor Strategy* (Washington, DC: World Bank, 2012).

Acknowledgments

This study was prepared by a team led by Alexandria Valerio (World Bank) and composed of Brent Parton (World Bank) and Alicia Robb (Kauffman Foundation) with support from Maria Ariano (World Bank), Shiranthi Gnanaselvam (World Bank), Teal Pennebaker (World Bank), and Sebastian Monroy Taborda (World Bank). The study was developed in close collaboration with a team of experts from the Thunderbird School of Global Management led by Amanda Bullough (Assistant Professor of Entrepreneurship and Leadership, Thunderbird School of Global Management) and composed of Dina Abdel Zaher (Assistant Professor of Management, University of Houston-Clear Lake), Berkley Roberts (Client Director of Strategic Projects and Impact Division, Thunderbird School of Global Management), and Laura Libman (consultant at Tech Talk Ink and CEO of Tia Foundation). We appreciate the overall support of Elizabeth King (Sector Director, Human Development Network) and Harry Patrinos (Sector Manager, Human Development Network) of the World Bank.

Helpful peer review comments were provided by the following World Bank colleagues: Louise Fox, Margo Hoftijzer, Mattias Lundberg, Michel Welmond, and Evan Burfield (Chairman, Startup DC of the Start-up America Partnership). The team appreciates the thoughtful advice and guidance of a number of colleagues, including: Diego Angel Urdinola, Stefanie Brodmann, Pedro Cerdan Infantes, Yoonyoung Cho, Robin Horn, Helen Craig, Wendy Cunningham, Peter Darvas, Keiko Inoue, Esperanza Lasagabaster, David Margolis, Francisco Marmolejo, Victor Macias, Ana Ruth Menezes, Marta Milkowska, Maria Paulina Mogollon, Matteo Morgandi, David Robalino, Maria Laura Sanchez Puerta, Halsey Rogers, Jee-Peng Tan, Emine Velidedeoglu, Quentin Wodon, and Cecilia Zanetta, all from the World Bank; Carlos Herran from the Inter-American Development Bank; Vanessa Beary (Harvard University) and Victor del Rio (Consultant). The team is also thankful for the overall assistance received from Marie Madeleine Ndaw, Elise Egoume-Bossogo, and Lorelei Lacdao. The written pieces contained within this study were edited by Marc DeFrancis (DeFrancis Writing & Editing).

The study benefited from comments received from the research team that prepared a series of country case studies using the methodology developed for this study. They include: Akua Ofori-Ampofo, Wilberforce Owusu-Ansah, and Kofi Poku (Ghana); Jutta Franz, Wairimu Kiambuthi, and Dave Muthaka (Kenya); and Constantino Marrengula, Zeferino Martins, and Manolo Sanchez (Mozambique).

The team would like to thank all of the members and organizations on the Advisory Council set up to review the study, comprised of experts on entrepreneurship education and training from both industry and academia. The following members have contributed significant knowledge, feedback, and expertise to this study: Peter Bamkole (Director, EDC Pan-African University, Enterprise Development Center); Debbi Brock (Assistant Professor of Entrepreneurship and Marketing, Wingate University of Charlotte, North Carolina); Jaime Casap (Education Evangelist, Google, Inc.); Shelly Esque (Vice President in the Legal and Corporate Affairs Group and Director of Corporate Affairs, Intel); Rich Leimsider (Director of Fellowship and Alumni Programs, Echoing Green); Alyse Nelson (President and Chief Executive Officer, Vital Voices Global Partnership); Bob Nelson (Professor Emeritus, College of Education, University of Illinois); Guy Pfefferman (Founder and Chief Executive Officer, Global Business School Network); Minet Schindehutte (Associate Professor of Entrepreneurship, Entrepreneurship and Emerging Enterprises, Whitman School of Management, Syracuse University); and George Solomon (Associate Professor and Co-Director of Center for Entrepreneurial Excellence, George Washington University).

Finally, the team would also like to thank the leaders of organizations featured in the Program Narratives. The following have contributed significant knowledge, feedback, and expertise to these narratives: BizWorld's Catherine Markwell (CEO); Pauline van Dulken (Commercial Director, Jong Ondernemen, BizWorld Licensee); Bodø Graduate School of Business's Gry Agnete Alsos (Associate Professor, University of Nordland); Business Plan Thesis Competition's Stefanie Brodmann (Economist, World Bank); Economic Empowerment of Adolescent Girls and Young Women's Sarah Elizabeth Haddock (Knowledge Management Officer, World Bank) and Peter Darvas (Senior Education Economist, World Bank); Entrepreneurship Development Centre's Selma Cilimkovic (Market Research Officer, Partner Microcredit Foundation) and Miriam Bruhn (Economist, World Bank); FINCA-Peru's Iris Lanao Flores (CEO) and Viviana Salinas (Regional Director for Ayacucho); Interise's Jean Horstman (CEO); McGuire Entrepreneurship Program's[1] Patty Sias (Director, University of Arizona's Eller College of Management); National Rural Savings Programme's Rashid Bajwa (CEO); Network for Teaching Entrepreneurship's Tracy Mehu-Hammonds (Program Manager), Alyssa Miller (Public Relations Consultant), and Jennifer Green (Executive Director, NFTE New England); Start and Improve Your Business's Merten Sievers (Global Coordinator/Specialist, ILO) and Eva Majurin (Monitoring Officer, ILO); and TechnoServe's Andrew Eder (Marketing and Communications Manager) and Oscar Artiga (Central American Regional Director).

---

[1] Formerly Berger Entrepreneurship Program.

About the Authors

Alexandria Valerio is a senior economist in the Education Department at the World Bank. Alexandria is currently leading global research agendas focused on identifying the characteristics of effective entrepreneurship education and training programs and implementing large-scale surveys to measure adult skills sets and their impact on a range of outcomes. Before joining the Education Department, she led the policy dialogue and project portfolios in Argentina, Brazil, Chile, Nicaragua, Panama, and Paraguay in the Latin America and the Caribbean region and in Angola and Mozambique in the Africa region. Her published work includes peer-reviewed papers on the cost and financing of early childhood development, impacts of school fees, technical vocational education and training, workforce development, and school-based health programs. She holds a PhD in Comparative and International Education from Columbia University and a master's degree in Public Administration from the Maxwell School of Citizenship and Public Affairs at Syracuse University.

Brent Parton is an education consultant for the World Bank. He has research, technical, and writing experience across a range of education, workforce, and health issues. With the World Bank, in addition to his work on the linkages between entrepreneurship, education, and economic development, he supported a global program benchmarking workforce development systems, and a research project investigating the political economy of education reform in developing countries. He has also served in various capacities working to shape U.S. healthcare policy as a communications and advocacy professional, and currently holds an appointment as an adjunct professor at Vanderbilt University. He holds both an MEd in international education policy as well as a BA in history, both from Vanderbilt University.

Alicia Robb is a senior fellow with the Kauffman Foundation. She is also a visiting scholar with the University of California in Berkeley, the Basque Institute for Competitiveness in San Sebastian, Spain, and the Federal Reserve Bank of Atlanta. She is the founder and past executive director and board chair of the Foundation for Sustainable Development, an international development organization working in Africa, India, and Latin America (www.fsdinternational.org). Alicia received her MS and PhD in economics from the University of North

Carolina at Chapel Hill. She has previously worked with the Office of Economic Research in the Small Business Administration and the Federal Reserve Board of Governors. She is also a prolific author on the topic of entrepreneurship. In addition to numerous journal articles and book chapters, she is the co-author of *Race and Entrepreneurial Success*, published by MIT Press, and A *Rising Tide: Financing Strategies for Women-Owned Businesses*, published by Stanford University Press. She serves on the board of the National Advisory Council for Minority Business Enterprise and on the advisory board for Global Entrepreneurship Week, and is a guest contributor to outlets such as Huffington Post and *Forbes*.

Abbreviations

10KW	10,000 Women Program (Indian School of Business—ISB)
AAC	*Atención a Crisis* (Ministry of the Family, Nicaragua)
ACTiVATE	Achieving the Commercialization of Technology in Ventures through Applied Training for Entrepreneurs (University of Maryland, USA)
APSB	Auchi Polytechnic School of Business (Nigeria)
BACIP	Building and Construction Improvement Programme (Aga Khan, Pakistan)
BEP	Berger Entrepreneurship Program (McGuire Entrepreneurship Program, University of Arizona, Eller College, USA)
BIZ	BizWorld (Netherlands)
Bødo	Bødo Graduate School of Business (Norway)
BPTC	Business Plan Thesis Competition (Ministries of Education, Tunisia)
CCOE	College Carve-Out Education (China)
CEM	Certificate in Entrepreneurial Management (Nigeria)
CO	community organization
CREA	Capacitación y Reclutamiento Empresarial Americana (CREA Mexico)
DCEI	Dade County Entrepreneurial Institute (Miami, FL, USA)
DDFET	Dutch Dairy Farmers Entrepreneurship Training (Netherlands)
DFCU	Development Finance Company of Uganda
EAC	entrepreneurial action capability
EB	entrepreneurial behavior
EDC	Entrepreneurship Development Center (Bosnia and Herzegovina)
EE	entrepreneurship education
EET	entrepreneurship education and training

ELP	Executive Leadership Programme (IDP, Northern Ireland)
EMPRETEC	EMPRETEC Programme (in 32 countries)
ENBDP	Entrepreneurship and New Business Development Programme (Sweden)
END	Endeavor (South Africa)
EOEAS	Entrepreneurial Orientation and Education in Austrian Secondary Schools (Austria)
EPAG	Economic Empowerment of Adolescent Girls and Young Women (Liberia)
ET	entrepreneurship training
ETPo	entrepreneurship education—potential entrepreneurs
ETPr	entrepreneurship education—practicing entrepreneurs
FBO	farm-based organization
FEE	Finland Entrepreneurial Education (Finland)
FINCA	FINCA-Peru
FTDAP	Farmer Training Development Assistance Program (Honduras)
GATE	Growing America through Entrepreneurship Project (United States)
GDP	gross domestic product
GE	*Grande École* (France)
GED Index	Global Entrepreneurship and Development Index
GNAG	Ghana National Association of Garages (Ghana)
GOWE	Growth-Oriented Women Entrepreneurs (Kenya)
INJAZ	Junior Achievement for Youth in Middle East (Middle East)
INT	Interise (USA)
JACP	Junior Achievement Company Program (Sweden)
JAN	Junior Achievement (Namibia)
JE	*Juventud y Empleo* (Youth Development Project, Dominican Republic)
JEA	*Jóvenes en Acción* (Colombia)
KAB	Know about Business (Syria)
MEP	*Microemprendimientos Productivos* (government workforce program, Argentina)
MiDA-FBO	Millennium Development Authority—Farm-Based Organization (Ghana)
MIT	Massachusetts Institute of Technology Engineering Students (USA)
MSE	micro and small enterprises
MSETTP	Micro and Small Enterprise Training and Technology Project (Kenya)

NFTE	Network for Teaching Entrepreneurship (Previously National Foundation for Teaching Entrepreneurship) (USA)
NGO	nongovernmental organization
NRSP	National Rural Support Program (Pakistan)
PAVCOPA	Agricultural Trading and Processing Promotion Pilot Project (Mali)
PBS	Production and Business Services (El Salvador)
PRIDE	PRIDE Bank (Tanzania)
PSM	propensity score matching
ROT	Rules of Thumb (Dominican Republic)
s.d.	standard deviation
SAIE	South African Institute for Entrepreneurship (South Africa)
SEWA	SEWA Banks (India)
SIYB	Start and Improve Your Business program (Vietnam)
SIYB-SL	ILO's Start and Improve Your Business (Sri Lanka)
SME	small and medium enterprise
STEP	Student Training for Promoting Entrepreneurship (Uganda)
TECH	TechnoServe (Central America)
TVET	technical vocational education and training
ULTP	Urban Land Titling Program (Peru)
UTES	University Training for Entrepreneurs (Sweden)
WEMTOP	Women's Enterprise Management Training Opportunity Program (India)
WEP	Women Entrepreneurship Program (South Africa)
WETVBI	Women's Virtual Business Incubator (Tanzania)
WINGS	Women's Income Generating Support Program (Uganda)
WSBP/MBDP	Women's Small Business Program and Micro Business Development Program (USA)
YE	Young Enterprise (Denmark)
YOP	Youth Opportunities Program (Uganda)

Overview

Entrepreneurship Promotion

There is a growing interest in the role that entrepreneurship can play as a catalyst to achieve economic and social development objectives, including growth, innovation, employment, and equity. Entrepreneurship can manifest within an economy in a number of ways, and it includes both formal and informal economic activities for the purposes of creating wealth. In turn, entrepreneurship can contribute to economic development through high-growth enterprises or, as in the case of necessity-driven entrepreneurship, through enterprises that can serve as an important source of income and employment for vulnerable populations. The variety of potential beneficial spillovers of entrepreneurship in turn focuses attention on interventions that stimulate individuals' decisions to become and succeed as entrepreneurs. A current focus of entrepreneurship promotion is the role of mindsets and skills in enabling individuals to both recognize and capitalize on entrepreneurial opportunities. Research suggesting that several of these mindsets, types of knowledge, and skills can be learned situates educational institutions and training programs firmly within the broader discussions around entrepreneurship promotion.

Entrepreneurship Education and Training

A number of international, regional, national, and local actors are taking part in the global experiment of entrepreneurship education (EE) and entrepreneurship education and training (EET). Today, EET is recognized as an established field of study, growing in parallel with the interest of policymakers and students. Taken as a whole, EET represents both academic education and formal training interventions that share the broad objective of providing individuals with the entrepreneurial mindsets and skills to support participation and performance in a range of entrepreneurial activities. EET encompasses a heterogeneous array of interventions, including formal academic education programs as well as stand-alone training programs. Both of these may aim to stimulate entrepreneurship as well as support individuals and enterprises already engaged in entrepreneurial activities. EET beneficiaries include both potential and practicing entrepreneurs who are traditional students enrolled in degree programs, early school leavers, adult learners, individuals with doctoral degrees, minority groups, women, and rural as well as urban populations.

About the Study

Despite a global interest in education and training for entrepreneurship, many (if not most) high-profile efforts have not been rigorously evaluated, and global knowledge about these programs' impact remains thin. Responding to this need, this study sets out to identify and organize the landscape of EET program types as well as the dimensions that shape program outcomes, including program characteristics, participant characteristics, and program context. Informed by a body of EET research, this study proposes a Conceptual Framework, which it then applies to conduct an analysis of both EET research and a global sample of program evaluations. The study is guided by four key questions about the global landscape of EET programs: *(a) Who do EET programs target? (b) What outcomes do EET programs aim to achieve? (c) What dimensions shape these outcomes?* and *(d) At what cost are outcomes achieved?* Flowing from the observations of this analysis, this study describes a set of practical insights about EET program design and implementation across target groups, intended outcomes, and contexts.

Typology for EET Programs

EET programs can be classified under two related but distinct categories: *education* and *training programs* (see figure O.1). Broadly speaking, both aim to stimulate entrepreneurship, but they are distinguished from one another by their variety of program objectives or outcomes. While differing from program to program, EE programs tend to focus on building knowledge and skills *about* or *for the purpose of* entrepreneurship. Entrepreneurship training (ET) programs, by contrast, tend to focus on building knowledge and skills, explicitly in preparation for starting or operating an enterprise.

Advancing the classification of EET, programs can also be distinguished by their target audiences. The academic nature of EE means these programs target two groups in particular: secondary education students and higher education students, the latter including both graduate and undergraduate students enrolled in formal degree-granting programs. By contrast, ET programs target a range of potential and practicing entrepreneurs who are not part of formal, degree-granting programs. Potential entrepreneurs targeted by ET programs can include, at one end of the range, vulnerable, unemployed, inactive individuals or necessity-driven potential entrepreneurs, and at the other end, highly skilled, innovation-led, or opportunistic potential entrepreneurs. Likewise, the range of practicing entrepreneurs runs from individuals owning informal, micro- and small enterprises (MSEs), all the way to high-growth potential enterprise owners.

Figure O.1 Classifying Entrepreneurship Education and Training Programs

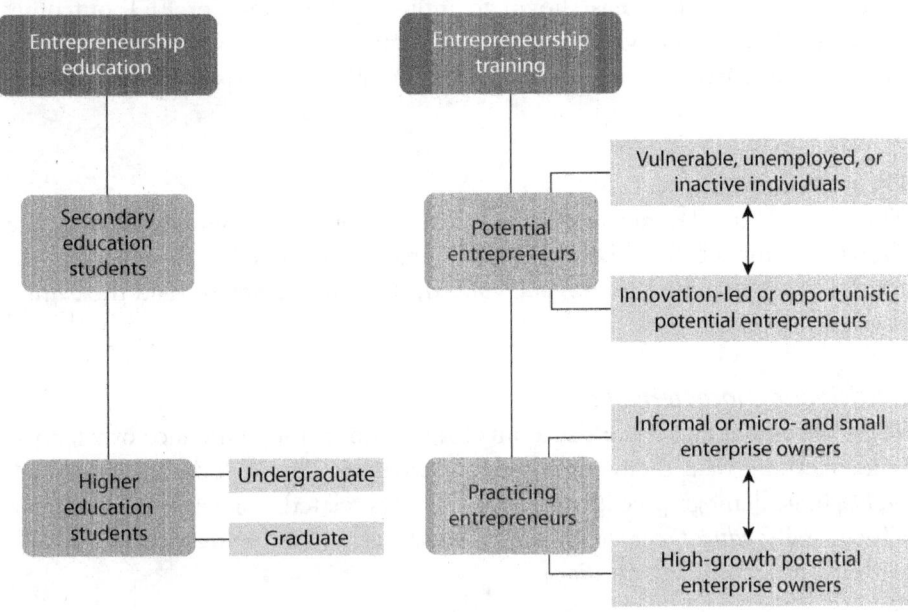

Conceptual Framework for EET

Determining the outcomes of EET programs is a complex and multidimensional challenge, regardless of whom a program targets. The task is complicated in part because the intended outcomes of EET programs can vary substantially from program to program. Therefore, this study draws upon existing EET research to propose a way of conceptualizing both the results EET programs seek and the factors that can shape those outcomes.

The Conceptual Framework categorizes EET outcomes into a series of four domains. The first, *entrepreneurial mindsets*, refers to the socio-emotional skills and overall awareness of entrepreneurship associated with entrepreneurial motivation and future success as an entrepreneur (e.g., self-confidence, leadership, creativity, risk propensity, motivation, resilience, and self-efficacy). The second, *entrepreneurial capabilities*, refers to entrepreneurs' competencies, knowledge, and technical skills associated with their entrepreneurship (e.g., management skills, accounting, marketing, and technical knowledge). The third, *entrepreneurial status*, refers to the temporal state of a program beneficiary as measured through entrepreneurial activities and beyond (e.g., starting a business, becoming employed, and achieving a higher income). Lastly, the fourth domain, *entrepreneurial performance*, refers explicitly to how indicators of a venture's performance have changed as a result of an intervention (e.g., higher profits, increased sales, greater employment of others, higher survival rates).

The Conceptual Framework (see figure O.2) also outlines three dimensions that available research has shown to influence the range of EET outcomes: (a) the context within which programs are implemented, (b) the characteristics of individual participants, and (c) the functional characteristics of the program itself.

Program Context
The Conceptual Framework accounts for a series of contextual influences shown to impact the likelihood of a program's capacity to generate outcomes. These include the *economic context*, the *political context*, and the *cultural context*.

Participant Characteristics
The Conceptual Framework accounts for the moderating influence of what participants bring with them coming into a program. This includes an individual's *profile*, basic demographic identifiers and factors related to a participant's personality or traits; *education*; *interest and intentions*; as well as *behaviors* while enrolled within a program (e.g., *attrition*).

Program Characteristics
The Conceptual Framework distinguishes among four major categories of program characteristics: program design, trainers and delivery, content and curriculum, and wrap-around services.

Figure O.2 Conceptual Framework

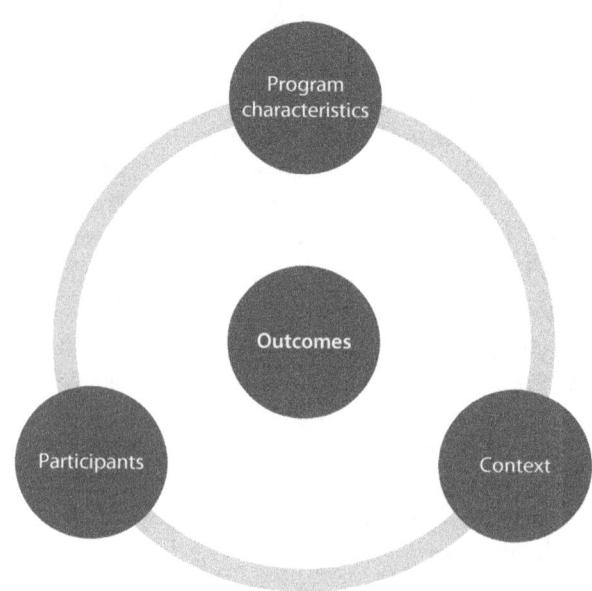

EET Program Landscape Analysis

The Conceptual Framework was applied to conduct an analysis of a global sample of EET programs, based on available evaluations. Given the heterogeneity of the EET landscape, the analysis was conducted by target group to enable a more focused discussion. It breaks down the sample of programs as follows: Entrepreneurship Education—Secondary Education (EESE) students, Entrepreneurship Education—Higher Education (EEHE) students, ET for potential entrepreneurs, and ET for practicing entrepreneurs.

Entrepreneurship Education—Secondary Education Students

This study identified and examined a total of nine EE programs targeted at secondary education students. Unfortunately, for these nine programs, the only impact evaluation available targeted children in the final grade of primary school, indicating a significant lack of rigorous evaluations on secondary education programs. That evaluation demonstrated moderate positive and significant effects on the development of non-cognitive skills (such as self-efficacy, the need for achievement, risk-taking propensity, persistence, analyzing, creativity, and proactivity) among the students who received the intervention when compared to the control group. Across the landscape of EESE programs, measured outcomes were concentrated in the entrepreneurial mindset domain. Evaluations indicated that these programs can achieve positive changes in outcomes associated primarily with foundational entrepreneurial mindsets and the range of socio-emotional skills that literature associates with entrepreneurship, such as self-confidence, locus of control, leadership, creativity, risk propensity, motivation, resilience, and self-efficacy.

EESE program characteristics are influenced by the fact that these programs are already within secondary schools. As such, many of them demonstrate a degree of functional collaboration with schools themselves or with the broader education system through program integration into standard curricula. Furthermore, an EESE program can also be part of a broader or more national rollout, in which the program is being adopted into curricula on a mass scale. EESE program evaluations focus on the need for teachers trained in the specific pedagogies and content of EESE programs. In terms of contextual factors potentially influencing mindset and skills acquisition, program evaluations cite the socioeconomic level of community and school as well as the relative quality of instruction, which are issues not uncommon to broader discussions of contextual influences on student learning in education research.

Entrepreneurship Education—Higher Education Students

This study identified and examined a total of 10 EE programs targeted at higher education students. An additional meta-analysis indicated that there is a relationship between entrepreneurship outcomes and academic-focused EET interventions. Of the 10 programs, impact evaluations were available for

2 programs. Both impact evaluations provide compelling results for the capacity of EEHE programs to foster positive effects in mindsets and capabilities, but they provide mixed results around entrepreneurial status. One intervention produced strong impacts on participants' self-reported business skills and networking proxies, but indicated only a small positive increase in the probability of being self-employed, and there was no evidence that the program significantly affected overall employment. The evaluations of the other EEHE programs also appear to reflect promising results in the mindsets and capabilities domains. Findings from these other evaluations are heavily concentrated in the mindsets and capabilities domains and indicate promising results in these domains. On the whole, the evaluations of EEHE programs provide less robust insight on which programs influence indicators in the entrepreneurial status and performance domains.

Across EEHE programs, general business education, entrepreneurship awareness, marketing, and accounting are common areas of curricular focus. A number of the evaluated programs place emphasis on the knowledge and skills required to develop a business plan as well as contribute to the strategic development of an enterprise. To facilitate this learning, several EEHE programs use business plan competitions and enterprise simulations. Common EEHE wrap-around services include mentoring and coaching, typically from entrepreneurs, as is the case with the Berger Entrepreneurship Program and Business Plan Thesis Competition programs. These types of wrap-around services focus on exposing students to innovation-driven entrepreneurs, suggesting that several EEHE programs are looking to cultivate high-growth potential entrepreneurs and enterprises. Self-selection and selectivity are at the center of participant behavior dynamics for EEHE programs.

Entrepreneurship Training—Potential Entrepreneurs (ETPo)

This study identified and examined a total of 16 ET programs targeted at potential entrepreneurs. Of these 16 programs, impact evaluations were available for 7 programs, and in addition, the analysis was informed by insights from relevant meta-analyses and systematic reviews. One such review indicated that some of the stronger effects of Entrepreneurship Training–Potential Entrepreneurs (ETPo) programs relate to helping potential owners launch new businesses more quickly. The targeted outcomes of the other evaluated ETPo programs are primarily concentrated in the entrepreneurial status domain and to a lesser extent in the entrepreneurial performance, capabilities, and mindsets domains. With regard to entrepreneurial status, several of the evaluations demonstrate mixed but promising results around the capacity of these programs to improve employment, income, and savings for beneficiaries. While few evaluations looked explicitly at rates of new business start-ups, many used proxies for business start-up, such as self-employment and increased business income.

Among the most promising results in the firm performance domain was the enhancing of business practices, with several program evaluations indicating improved record keeping, formal registration, access to new loans, and a more strategic orientation of the businesses concerned. Nonetheless, there was little evidence that training fostered the creation of high-revenue or high-employment firms in the long run. Lastly, some program evaluations also gave attention to the effects on various socio-emotional skills and entrepreneurial awareness. Several program evaluations cited increases in participants' self-confidence and teamwork, and one impact evaluation found mixed results for a range of indicators related to participants' psychological and social well-being. The focus on such indicators is a reminder that many ETPo program evaluations cover interventions aimed at improving the immediate, material well-being of vulnerable populations.

In line with these objectives, a number of the ETPo programs are designed to target vulnerable groups, including women, unemployed youth, and welfare recipients. The characteristics of ETPo programs in turn reflect the diversity among the individuals these programs target and the outcomes they pursue. In some cases, the training is embedded within a broader support program that may include a number of services in addition to training, including grants, conditional cash transfers, and intensive follow-ups. Across these programs, the content ranges from business knowledge, to entrepreneurial skills, to financial literacy and accounting, to marketing, sales, and general management skills, to vocational and life skills. Most ETPo programs appear to include some wrap-around services. According to available ETPo evaluations, the training components that combine grants with activities such as internships and mentoring services have higher impacts than simple training programs. Program outcomes are cited as being influenced by factors relating to local economic conditions and infrastructure, including access to finance and access to markets.

Entrepreneurship Training—Practicing Entrepreneurs

This study identified and examined a total of 25 ET programs targeted at practicing entrepreneurs. Of these program evaluations, 11 were impact evaluations with an experimental design. In addition to the program evaluations, the Entrepreneurship Training–Practicing Entrepreneur (ETPr) program analysis is informed by insights from relevant literature, including four meta-analyses and systematic reviews. The most common stated objectives of ETPr programs relate to the firm performance outcome domain, which corresponds to the immediate needs of the target audience: practicing entrepreneurs. Common targeted performance objectives include increases in profits, employees, and productivity, as well as business expansion in markets, financing, investment, and the implementation of better business practices and innovations. Despite being the most targeted program objective, ETPr program evaluations indicated mixed results around firm performance. In terms of firm profits or revenues, evaluations found limited effects. For example, one impact evaluation did not demonstrate higher profits or revenues; however, difference-in-difference specifications did find a positive (though small) impact on enterprise revenues. Some evaluations demonstrated more promising results on this indicator depending on the type of training that was delivered. Mixed findings from evaluations on the impact of training on enterprise survivorship reflect the findings of available meta-analyses and systematic review. One program evaluation suggested training raised the probability of enterprise survival by 8 or 9 percentage points, while another evaluation found no impact. A systematic review found relatively modest impacts of training on survivorship among existing firms. Program evaluations and reviews indicated that few studies find significant impacts on profits or sales, but do find modest effects on practicing entrepreneurs' decision to implement better business practices. Several program evaluations and meta-analyses give attention to the promise of ETPr programs to enhance trainees' entrepreneurial capabilities (knowledge and skills), by shedding light on how these capabilities may ultimately contribute to better entrepreneurial performance. One meta-analysis finds a significant relationship between EET and entrepreneurship-related human capital assets and entrepreneurship outcomes, while another indicates that while programs can improve knowledge, this does not necessarily lead to related gains in performance and status outcomes.

As is the case with other EET program types, there is considerable heterogeneity across the characteristics of ETPr programs. Several ETPr programs appear to be linked to particular institutions or commercial banks, and a number of evaluations describe programs with a particular sector or target group focus. The scale and duration of ETPr programs ranges considerably as well, from those that serve the proprietors of nearly 35,000 MSEs to highly selective programs serving four to six beneficiaries per cohort. There is also considerable variation in the common areas of content (financial literacy and accounting, marketing and sales, management skills, and strategic planning). Over half of these program evaluations indicated that the program offered some kind of wrap-around service linked to accessing finance or financial assistance, which proved to be important during program implementation. In some cases, programs offer incentives for participation and retention, and others deploy a highly selective vetting process to attract suitable participants and combat attrition. ETPr programs cited the broader economic environment as an opportunity and a constraint. Additionally, cultural moderators, such as attitudes toward gender, were also identified as influencing outcomes.

Implications for EET Program Design and Implementation

The analysis of programs according to program type and target group reveals a set of insights to consider about what tends to characterize programs within each category.

Target Groups Within Target Groups
Within secondary EE programs, there is a differentiation between programs that target "select" groups of students versus programs that target broader student populations. For higher education participants, students may participate in a program as an elective course or capstone activity; students may participate in a degree/certificate granting entrepreneurship program; or students may participate in EE as an extracurricular activity, such as a business plan competition.

For potential entrepreneurs, entrepreneurship programs aim to recruit a range of participants—from potential high-growth or opportunity-driven entrepreneurs to necessity-driven self-employed entrepreneurs. Among ET programs targeting practicing entrepreneurs, interventions also target a range of participants—from high-growth entrepreneurs to necessity-driven, self-employed entrepreneurs.

A Range of Outcomes

There are a number of objectives that EET programs target within the broader domains of entrepreneurial mindsets and capabilities as well as entrepreneurial status and performance. Across program types, there is an increased emphasis on outcomes in the status and performance domains; and among EE programs, there is also a notable emphasis on mindsets and the associated outcomes of socio-emotional skills and entrepreneurship awareness.

Importance of Context

Both relevant research and EET program evaluations signal the importance of context in the capacity of programs to meet their objectives. The importance of context is even discussed in evaluations that are randomized controlled trials, where it is unclear if similar outcomes would accrue if a program were implemented elsewhere. The analysis also suggests that the prominence of particular contextual factors can depend on the outcomes being measured.

Information on Program Costs and Finance

Within the literature and program evaluations, there is a paucity of information on the costs and financing of EET programs. Further, the information that is available is rarely comparable. In most cases, the costs of EET programs are a function of the institutions responsible for implementation as well as associated principles of cost recovery.

Using the Framework to Guide Design Options

Clarity about target groups and desired outcomes can help focus program design choices that align program design to the needs of participants and their particular context.

Implications for Policy

When reflecting on the policy implications of the study, an initial question to consider is whether the government should be involved in the provision, financing, or promotion of EET programs.

Secondary Education Students

The context demands some government role, at least within public institutions or institutions using national curricula. The relationship between labor market performance and socio-emotional skills is documented in a body of research, thus lending creditability to the assertion that some programs may offer a public good, in turn justifying government intervention and support.

Higher Education Students

Government intervention might be important in some contexts, particularly within public institutions, and one can again return to the issue of how EE can be pointed to as a public good—whether in equipping students with relevant skills and/or providing students with the capacity to innovate or bring innovative products or processes to market.

Potential Entrepreneurs

Government involvement is most commonly characterized as directly funding—or enabling other entities to finance—ET programs. Since these types of programs often target specific (often vulnerable) populations that the government may already be generally interested in supporting, the public good is more closely tied to program objectives such as enhancing equity and reducing poverty. In this sense, the policy implications should be grounded in the efficacy and effectiveness of policy alternatives that are present in these contexts (e.g., conditional cash transfers, fostering wage employment) for furthering these same objectives.

Practicing Entrepreneurs

The policy implications for programs targeting practicing entrepreneurs in vulnerable populations echo considerations for programs geared toward potential entrepreneurs of similar backgrounds. For programs targeting high-growth potential entrepreneurs, despite an interest in economic spillovers such as employment and innovation, the government's role is better reserved for creating the space for the financing, providing private entities to train, and fostering a business environment that enables entrepreneurial activity. Given the practical and political limitations of having government "pick winners," selecting and training participants is a role better filled by the market and the private entities.

Amidst the global interest in education and training for entrepreneurship, available and reliable information on program outcomes is relatively sparse. However, through an analysis of programs, this study is able to offer a focused and structured discussion around what generally characterizes these programs when they target particular groups of beneficiaries, seek to achieve certain objectives, and are delivered in various contexts. The study illustrates the challenge of looking at EET as a one-dimensional, silver-bullet solution when the global landscape of these programs reveals that they are a complex and heterogeneous collection.

CHAPTER 1

About the Study

Motivation

There is a growing interest in the role that entrepreneurship can play as a catalyst to achieve economic and social development objectives, including growth, innovation, employment, and equity. Accordingly, there is an expanding body of literature documenting the potential contributions of entrepreneurship to economic and social development—offering a complex picture of what constitutes entrepreneurship, the societal contributions of entrepreneurial success, and the factors driving or constraining the success of entrepreneurs. An increasing area of interest in this field is how a range of actors—including governments, the private sector, and international organizations—can bolster entrepreneurs' success and progress on broader socioeconomic goals.

The potential beneficial spillovers of entrepreneurship and the potential success of entrepreneurs have garnered attention—provoking interest in interventions that stimulate individuals' decisions to become and succeed as entrepreneurs. Entrepreneurship promotion efforts can include the easing of business environment constraints, enhancing access to finance and credit, as well as the provision of support to strengthen business practices and enterprise management. Embedded within a number of entrepreneurship promotion activities are efforts that aim to develop mindsets, knowledge, and skills associated with entrepreneurial success. Research suggests that several of these mindsets, knowledge, and skills can be learned, thus situating educational institutions and training programs firmly within the broader discussions around entrepreneurship promotion.

Education and training for entrepreneurship encompasses a heterogeneous array of interventions, including formal academic education programs and standalone training programs. Both of the latter may aim to stimulate entrepreneurship as well as support individuals and enterprises already engaged in entrepreneurial activities. These interventions can target a range of individuals and have a variety of program objectives, from enhancing socio-emotional skills (e.g., locus of control and self-confidence among secondary education students), to teaching business plan development to graduate students, to providing training in bookkeeping to subsistence farmers. The diversity of these interventions reflects the variety of those who can be considered "entrepreneurs."

Despite a global interest in education and training for entrepreneurship, many (if not most) high-profile efforts have not been rigorously evaluated. This has left critical gaps in information about the outcomes across interventions and, in particular, what is working and what is not. These gaps flow, in part, from the sheer heterogeneity of entrepreneurship programs. The corresponding lack of comparable data makes gauging the impacts across programs a challenge and complicates understanding their cost and effectiveness. In order to avoid wasted resources, efforts are needed to (a) strengthen the foundation of quality studies through rigorous evaluations of existing entrepreneurship education and training (EET) interventions, and (b) catalogue the global landscape of interventions to enable a coherent and structured discussion of program outcomes and practices.

Objective

This study examines the range of EET interventions, herein referred to as EET. EET includes the activity of transmitting specific mindsets and skills associated with entrepreneurship, as well as education and training programs that seek to engender various entrepreneurship outcomes. As a working definition for this study, EET represents academic education or formal training interventions that share the broad objective of providing individuals with the entrepreneurial mindsets and skills to participate in entrepreneurial activities.

The objective of this study is to identify and organize the landscape of EET program types as well as the dimensions that shape program outcomes. These dimensions include program characteristics, participant characteristics, and program context. Informed by a body of EET research, this study proposes a Conceptual Framework and uses the framework to analyze both EET research and a global sample of program evaluations. Building on the observations of the analysis, the study describes a set of practical insights about the design and implementation of EET programs across groups of interest, intended outcomes, and contexts. In addition to this paper, this study includes a set of supplementary research products:

- A *Database of Programs* that contains a global sample of EET program evaluations; and
- *Program Narratives*[1] that profile selected programs to illustrate the dimensions of EET programs in practice.

Methodology

Four key questions about the global landscape of EET programs guided this initial inquiry into EET research:

- *Who do EET programs target?*
- *What outcomes do EET programs aim to achieve?*

- *What dimensions shape these outcomes?*
- *At what cost are outcomes achieved?*

To respond to these questions, this study draws upon two principal sources of information: (a) a review of available literature and research, including meta-analyses and (b) a review of the specific programs' evaluations. Appendixes B, C, and D provide an in-depth look at the program dimensions that contributed to the development of the Conceptual Framework.

Search Strategy

To identify EET literature in peer-reviewed academic journals, the team conducted systematic searches of electronic databases (including EBESCO, EconPapers, JSTOR, Web of Science, Web of Knowledge, ProQuest, and Google Scholar) using a set of relevant key words and search terms (e.g., entrepreneurship education [EE], entrepreneurship training [ET], self-employment competencies, entrepreneurship, self-employment, entrepreneurial intentions, entrepreneurialism, entrepreneurial attitudes).

The team also conducted web searches to identify organizational and practitioner-oriented reports and articles on relevant research institutions' and international organizations' websites (e.g., Global Entrepreneurship Monitor, Kauffman Foundation, International Labor Organization, regional development banks, Organisation for Economic Co-operation and Development, European Union, World Bank), as well as various EET program websites. Lastly, approximately 16 primary interviews were conducted with members of the Advisory Council to identify noteworthy research and programs. The Advisory Council, which includes practitioners, academics, and thought-leaders in the entrepreneurship field, has helped guide the research team throughout the duration of this project.

Selection of Program Evaluations

The search strategy identified 230 EET program evaluations for more in-depth review. From this collection of programs, 87 were found whose program evaluations met the following criteria:

- Had an explicit definition of its expected outcomes and targeted goals;
- Had outcomes expressed in some measurable manner (e.g., number of business start-ups, higher income); and
- Had collected credible information on participants' outcomes.

The rigor of the available evaluations ranged from weak to strong. This study categorized program evaluations according to three tiers of rigor:

- **Tier 1** evaluations are randomized, controlled experiments with an experimental design;

- **Tier 2** evaluations have a quasi-experimental design; and
- **Tier 3** evaluations are principally surveys of program participants, including tracer studies that vary in the range of time examined, as well as monitoring and evaluation reports that rely largely on administrative data.

It is important to note that the tiers of rigor do not relate to the quality or strength of the program per se, but rather to the method of the program evaluation itself. The literature review and Conceptual Framework drew from both the search strategy's body of research and the 87 EET program evaluations. However, the analysis of EET programs (chapter 4) used 60 of the 87 program evaluations. These 60 evaluations were selected because they explicitly featured an EET program and had sufficient information on program characteristics and outcomes. The remaining 27 evaluations looked at broader entrepreneurship promotion efforts that included EET but not as a central component. Given this study's exclusive focus on EET, these 27 evaluations were ultimately excluded from the analysis section of the study.

Of the 60 EET program evaluations that met the inclusion criteria, there were 21 Tier 1 programs, 10 Tier 2 programs, and 29 Tier 3 programs. Among the 60 program evaluations, 19 were classified as EE programs, while 41 were classified as ET programs. All 60 programs are listed in appendix A.

Some of the evaluations cover programs that are now closed or were time-limited by design. Other evaluations did not examine a program in its entirety, and instead focused on particular outcomes or aspects of a program. Evaluations rarely aligned with the full scope of the program and its outcomes—even in cases where evaluations had a random experimental design that could provide insights about which components of a program worked and which did not.

Limitations

- **Coverage of research.** This study does not claim to provide an exhaustive examination of the considerable research available on entrepreneurship. Furthermore, given the sheer number and scope of EET programs in operation today, the sample of programs cannot be considered comprehensive and is limited to insights emerging from published information about specific programs.

- **Rigor of program evaluations.** The team acknowledges the limited rigor of program evaluations, with few evaluations using randomized controlled experiments and quasi-experimental design. Furthermore, "many evaluations suffer from low statistical power, measure effectiveness only within a year of training, and experience problems with survey attrition" (McKenzie and Woodruff, 2012, 1). Even for those studies employing more rigorous methods, issues exist concerning their validity and applicability across contexts, an issue highlighted by Pritchett and Sandefur (2013).

- **Isolating which program dimension led to success.** Although an evaluation may reveal whether a program has achieved a desired outcome, rarely did evaluations explain what aspect of the program contributed most to the outcomes achieved. In other words, one often cannot trace whether the reason for the outcomes achieved was primarily related to the instructor, the curriculum, the wrap-around services, the participant, or other factors. Most programs and their corresponding evaluations fell into this category.

- **Availability of information on cost and financing.** Information on the cost and financing of EET programs was scarce. In several cases, implementing organizations considered this information to be proprietary in nature. In the cases where information was available, it was rarely comparable across target groups, program types, and implementation contexts. Few evaluations gauged the cost-effectiveness of programs or program elements.

Structure of the Study

The remainder of this study is organized into four chapters:

- Chapter 2 summarizes major findings and trends in EET research, particularly around the rationale for investing in EET and the potential role of government in EET programs.
- Chapter 3 sheds light on the difference between EE and ET and proposes a Conceptual Framework for analysis.
- Chapter 4 analyzes the global landscape of EET programs, using the Conceptual Framework and looking specifically at the achievement of outcomes, specific program characteristics, and the role of contextual factors.
- Chapter 5 summarizes the study's findings and lays out potential implications for policymakers. The chapter also presents a roadmap for informing EET program design and implementation and proposes areas for further research.

Audience

This study is intended to contribute to the international dialogue on entrepreneurship. The desired audience is broad, with a primary focus on policymakers, practitioners, and World Bank staff. This information is meant to broaden understanding of existing EET programs, identify directions for improvement, and inform dialogue around including EET in education and training strategies. The secondary audience for this paper is the public at large.

Note

1. See Program Narratives in appendix D.

Bibliography

McKenzie, D., and C. Woodruff. 2012. "What Are We Learning from Business Training and Entrepreneurship Evaluations Around the Developing World?" Policy Research Working Paper 6202, World Bank, Washington, DC.

Pritchett, L., and J. Sandefur. 2013. "Context Matters for Size: Why External Validity Claims and Development Practice Don't Mix." Working Paper 336, Center for Global Development, Washington, DC.

CHAPTER 2

Literature Review

On Entrepreneurship

Defining Entrepreneurship

Entrepreneurship is a globally recognized phenomenon lacking a single precise definition. Early in the 20th century, Schumpeter (1934) discussed the role of entrepreneurship in promoting innovation and implementing change in an economy by introducing new products or processes. Kirzner (1973) defines entrepreneurship as a process of discovery; the acting upon previously unnoticed—and often marginal—profit opportunities. Some definitions tie entrepreneurship only broadly to specific economic activities, describing a process of opportunity recognition to create value and act upon that opportunity (Schoof 2006). Klapper et al. (2010) describe how, from a practitioner standpoint, entrepreneurship is generally understood as a process of creating new wealth, but for the purpose of measuring entrepreneurship, the definition narrows to the initiation of economic activities in the form of a legal (formal) enterprise. Unbound by the need to empirically measure entrepreneurship activity per se, this study proposes a definition that is inclusive of both formal as well as informal economic activities (including self-employment) for the purposes of creating wealth. This broader definition provides space for a comprehensive investigation of the range of activities and individuals, which the nature of this study demands.

Entrepreneurship as a Panacea?

From employment to poverty reduction to innovation, entrepreneurship is tied to a number of pressing global economic imperatives (Brock and Evans 1989; Acs 1992; Carree and Thurik 2003; Volkmann et al. 2009; ILO 2011; Bandiera et al. 2012). For example, Birch (1979) cites entrepreneurship as a critical driver of job creation and suggests that entrepreneurship is the largest single source of new job growth in both developed and developing economies (Fritsch 2004; Acs and Armington 2006; Schramm and Litan 2009). Additionally, entrepreneurship is identified as a mechanism for achieving stable income flows and increased profits for vulnerable populations (Hermes and Lensink 2007; Karlan and Valdivia 2011). Furthermore, a body of research draws linkages between entrepreneurial activity, innovation, and technological change (Acs and Varga 2005; van Praag and Versloot 2007).

Despite assuming a place in dialogue around job creation, poverty reduction, and innovation, the relationship between entrepreneurship, entrepreneurs, and these various economic objectives is complex. With regard to employment, it is suggested that the bulk of job creation is within microenterprises that experience high failure rates, which can compromise net job creation (World Bank 2012). Moreover, while entrepreneurship may contribute to income generation for the vulnerable, Gindling and Newhouse (2012) indicate that as countries develop, many of these individuals are absorbed into wage and salaried employment—jobs that remain the prominent driver of growth. On the innovation front, large, established firms are typically more innovative, investing more in research and development and in launching new products and services (World Bank 2012).

Entrepreneurship and Economic Development

Despite a more nuanced picture of the relationship between entrepreneurship and various economic objectives, a body of literature investigates the relevance of entrepreneurship to economic development (Wennekers and Thurik 1999; Vyakarnam 2009; Klapper et al. 2010). Acs, Desai, and Hessels (2008) summarize one of the more prominent contributions to this relationship: the "U-shaped" theory. This theory posits that as countries develop from a factor-driven stage of development to an efficiency-driven stage, entrepreneurial activity actually decreases; however, as countries develop further from the efficiency-driven stage to the innovation-driven stage, entrepreneurial activity again increases. While indicating that the U-shaped theory is sound for describing a decline in self-employment as countries develop, Acs, Desai, and Hessels (2008) suggest it is inadequate for understating entrepreneurship more broadly, where it is important to differentiate between "necessity entrepreneurship" (starting a business after being pushed into it) and "opportunity entrepreneurship" (starting a business to exploit a perceived business opportunity).

The imperative of this differentiation aligns with both Kilby (1971), who was among the first to suggest that entrepreneurs manifest within in an economy in a number of ways, and Farstad (2002), who makes a similar distinction between "subsistence entrepreneurs" and "innovative entrepreneurs." This suggests that entrepreneurship's contributions to economic development can accrue differently depending on the type of entrepreneurship. Klapper and Richmond (2009) underscore the importance of entrepreneurship in contributing to economic development through the growth of enterprises. These enterprises can generate employment, spillovers, and structural economic change. By contrast, necessity or subsistence entrepreneurs own micro- and small enterprises (MSEs) that are unlikely to expand beyond a few employees (Nichter and Goldmark 2009). Despite the lack of enterprise growth, this type of entrepreneurship can still contribute to development, since these enterprises are an important source of income and represent a substantial share of production and overall employment in the developing world (Grimm, Knorringa, and Lay 2012). Necessity entrepreneurship and self-employment are terms often used interchangeably. But Levine and Rubinstein (2013) suggest that self-employment itself demands differentiation between the incorporated self-employed (formal sector, tend to earn more than their salaried counterparts) and unincorporated self-employed (informal sector, tend to earn less than their salaried counterparts).

While a body of literature differentiates between necessity and opportunity entrepreneurship, new research suggests that these classifications are not necessarily destiny and that in some cases necessity entrepreneurs share characteristics with growth-oriented entrepreneurs. The Grimm, Knorringa, and Lay (2012) study, based in seven cities across West Africa, indicates that somewhere between successful entrepreneurs (whose enterprises grow) and necessity entrepreneurs (whose enterprises do not) are a number of "constrained gazelles." The "constrained gazelles" share the low-capital and low-profit characteristics of necessity entrepreneurs but have the skills and behaviors of successful entrepreneurs (with enterprises that grow). These findings resonate with Gindling and Newhouse (2012), who also find shared characteristics across successful and less successful entrepreneurs.

Government Enabling Entrepreneurship

There is a wide body of research associated with understanding the constraints to entrepreneurial success. Klapper, Lewin, and Delgado (2009) describe how regulations related to the ease of starting a business can affect entrepreneurial activity. Welter (2011) outlines the contextual dimensions that can shape entrepreneurship, including social contexts (e.g., cultural traditions, gender roles) and spatial contexts (e.g., geography). Levie and Autio (2008) suggest finance access is among the most widely recognized factors influencing the success of entrepreneurs. Against this backdrop, whether driven by youth population bulges in Africa and South Asia (Cho and Honorati 2013) or by the imperative for innovation in Europe (EURYDICE 2012), governments have taken an interest in alleviating constraints and promoting entrepreneurship.

Audretsch (2004) sees a government's action grounded in four types of market failures: network externalities (geographic proximity to complementary firms), knowledge externalities (knowledge spillover), failure externalities (value created for other firms and individuals even if firms fail), and learning externalities (motivation and learning from the demonstration of entrepreneurial activities by others). In addressing these various market failures, Minniti (2008) summarizes the views of Baumol (1990) and North (1990), indicating that governments can act through institutions to channel society's existing entrepreneurial intentions away from undesirable activities (e.g., crime) and towards more desirable activities (e.g., enterprise creation and innovation).

To address the constraints to entrepreneurship, governments can employ a number of policy tools (McKernan 2002; Paulson and Townsend 2004; de Mel, McKenzie, and Woodruff 2009). Policymakers can support entrepreneurship endeavors with policies or programs aimed at modifying regulations, easing business environment constraints, expanding access to credit, promoting value chain integration, strengthening capacity to improve business practices, and establishing incubators to support innovation and business start-ups (McKernan 2002; Paulson and Townsend 2004; de Mel, McKenzie, and Woodruff 2009). To summarize, Stevenson and Lundström (2002) offer a framework for the variety of areas that these policies aim to impact—the promotion of entrepreneurship, the reduction of entry-exit barriers, entrepreneurship education, start-up support, start-up financing, and target group measures.

Entrepreneurship Promotion Beneficiaries

The literature documents entrepreneurship policies targeting a number of groups, including youth, women, the unemployed, the self-employed, rural populations, and welfare recipients (Wu and Pangarkar 2006; GEM 2012). The targeting of young adults appears to reflect policymakers' perception of entrepreneurship as a means for combating urgent social problems, such as persistent youth unemployment and criminal activity (Volkmann et al. 2009). Another key subgroup targeted for entrepreneurship promotion is women. The *Global Entrepreneurship Monitor Women's Report* (GEM 2010b) conducted a survey in 59 economies (representing over 80 percent of global gross domestic product) and estimated that more than 187 million women were engaged in entrepreneurial activities. Research suggests that women are more likely to reinvest their profits in their own families; in their families' or their own education; or in their communities. This bolsters policymakers' interest in targeting entrepreneurship promotion for women (GEM 2010b). Lastly, a number of promotional efforts focus on easing constraints for self-employed individuals operating in the informal economy, including the underemployed and rural populations working in agriculture (Todd and Javalgi 2007; Yaw 2007).

On Entrepreneurship Education and Training

Mindsets and Skills for Entrepreneurship

A focus area of entrepreneurship promotion research is the role of mindsets and skills in enabling individuals to both recognize and capitalize on entrepreneurial opportunities (Nichter and Goldmark 2009). Levie and Autio (2008) summarize a body of literature that highlights how education provides individuals with the cognitive ability to match potential entrepreneurial opportunities with their respective skills and abilities. Furthermore, van der Sluis, van Praag, and Vijverberg (2005) as well as Isaacs et al. (2007) describe literature linking higher levels of education with better entrepreneurial performance as well as higher rates of enterprise formation. These associations resonate with a worldwide survey of entrepreneurs, who cite mindsets and skills as a potential constraint to entrepreneurial opportunity and success (Monitor Consulting Group 2012).

Can Entrepreneurship Be Learned?

Further research explores whether mindsets and skills can be cultivated, taught, or transmitted for the purpose of entrepreneurship promotion (World Bank 2012).

Within an ongoing debate about the extent to which entrepreneurship can be learned (Isaacs et al. 2007), a body of literature indicates that aspects of it indeed can (Timmons and Spinelli 2004; Henry, Hill, and Leitch 2005; Kuratko 2005). Haase and Lautenschläger (2011), however, underscore a series of arguments to the contrary, suggesting that certain aspects cannot be learned. To this point, Akola and Heinonen (2006) separate the "art" and the "science" of entrepreneurship, in which the former (e.g., creativity, innovative thinking) is not teachable, except through practical experience; while the latter (e.g., business and management skills) can be taught. Despite these points to the contrary, research supports that when education and training systems incorporate creative and entrepreneurial skills into teaching methodologies, the mindsets and skills more closely tied to the "art" of entrepreneurship are transmittable (World Bank 2010).

Emergence of Education and Training for Entrepreneurship

Even against the backdrop of debates about whether entrepreneurship can be learned, there is a growing global interest in entrepreneurship education and training (EET), as documented by the growth in course offerings at educational institutions (Kuratko 2003) and by its inclusion in international agendas and programs, such as the European Commission's Oslo Agenda and the Global Entrepreneurship Monitor. Mwasalwiba (2010) suggests that this popularization of EET is in part driven by the mutual self-interests of key stakeholders, including policymakers (the political imperative for job creation), students (more graduates competing for fewer jobs, seeking new opportunities and ways to set themselves apart), and education institutions (to satisfy policymakers as well as the student market through course offerings). Taken together with indications that aspects of entrepreneurship can be taught and learned, education and training systems are emerging as a key component of broader discussions about the promotion of entrepreneurship.

Defining Entrepreneurship Education and Training

A number of international, regional, national, and local actors are taking part in the global experiment of EET. Today, EET is recognized as an established field of study, growing in parallel with the interest of policymakers and students (Mwasalwiba 2010). While a single, generally accepted definition remains elusive, researchers are contributing to an evolving definition (Charney and Libecap 2000; Farstad 2002; Menzies 2003; Isaacs et al. 2007; Dickson, Solomon, and Weaver 2008). Taken together, EET generally reflects both the activity of transmitting specific mindsets and skills associated with entrepreneurship, as well as education and training programs that seek to engender various entrepreneurship outcomes. As a working definition for this study, *EET represents academic education or formal training interventions that share the broad objective of providing individuals with the entrepreneurial mindsets and skills to support participation and performance in a range of entrepreneurial activities.*

Focus of Entrepreneurship Education and Training

Common EET mindsets and skills include socio-emotional skills like self-confidence, leadership, creativity, risk propensity, motivation, resilience, and self-efficacy (Lüthje and Franke 2003; Rauch and Frese 2007; Teixeira and Forte 2009; Hytti et al. 2010; Cloete and Ballard 2011); overall awareness and perceptions of entrepreneurship (Kolvereid and Moen 1997; Peterman and Kennedy 2003; Fayolle, Gailly, and Lassas-Clerc 2006; Souitaris, Zerbinati, and Al-Laham 2007); and the general business knowledge and skills needed for opening and managing a business, like accounting, marketing, risk assessment, and resource mobilization (Curran and Stanworth 1989; Detienne and Chandler 2004; Honig 2004; Russell, Atchisona, and Brooks 2008; Bjorvatn and Tungodden 2010; Karlan and Valdivia 2011).

A prominent theme in EET literature is the differentiation between EET and business management education. While both focus broadly on enterprise development (Zeithaml and Rice 1987; Winslow, Wennekers, and Tarabishy 1999), research suggests that business management education traditionally trains students to operate within existing hierarchies and serve as managers of established firms (Sexton and Bowman 1984). Farstad (2002) acknowledges overlap between EET and business education, but indicates that EET goes beyond business education to address the unique conditions entrepreneurs face. Garavan and O'Cinneide (1994) describe how business schools use models to train students how to analyze large amounts of *credible* information in order to ascertain solutions; while entrepreneurs tend to operate under different time and resource constraints, often with *less credible* information. Furthermore, Vesper and McMullan (1998) differentiate EET by its focus on building awareness of entrepreneurship and developing skills specific to both creating new products or services and to opening or expanding business ventures (see figure 2.1).

Entrepreneurship Education and Training Beneficiaries

While the EET literature gives particular attention to the differentiation from business management education, EET is heterogeneous and can resemble a

Figure 2.1 Entrepreneurship Versus Business Management Education

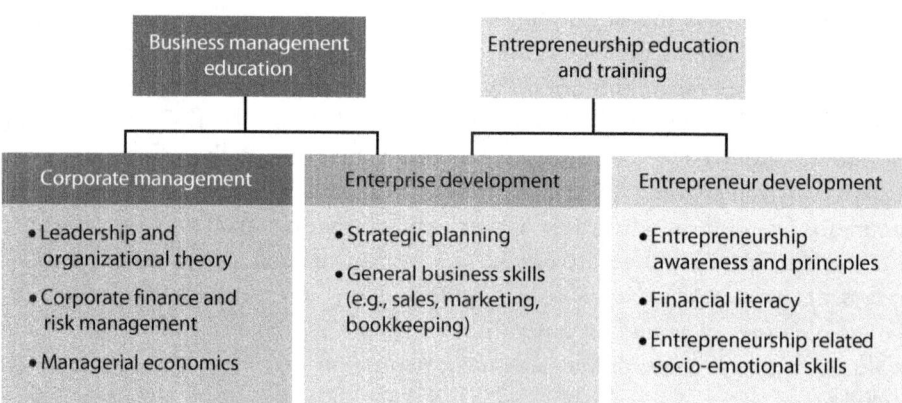

range of other interventions, including general and technical education curricula, second-chance education programs, active labor market programs, and business development services. This variety reflects the range of targeted EET beneficiaries. EET beneficiaries include both potential and practicing entrepreneurs who are traditional students enrolled in degree programs, early school leavers, adult learners, individuals with doctoral degrees, minority groups, women, and rural as well as urban populations. The literature underscores the importance of whether EET programs suit the identities, characteristics, and learning demands of particular beneficiaries (Block and Stumpf 1992; Brockhaus 2001; Henry, Hill, and Leitch 2005; Volkmann et al. 2009; GEM 2010a).

Scope of Entrepreneurship Education and Training

The scope of EET interventions varies by curricula and scale. Some programs are implemented on a global scale, like the International Labor Organization's Know About Business and Start and Improve Your Business programs (Goppers and Coung 2007), or through a global reach, like the Junior Achievement's programs (Mahohoma and Muyambo 2008). By contrast, EET can be specific to an individual school or institution, such as the University of Arizona's McGuire Entrepreneurship Program (Charney and Libecap 2000) or the microfinance institution FINCA Peru (Karlan and Valdivia 2011). Further, EET interventions can represent a blend of global and local—partnerships between global brands and regional or local education ministries and institutions, as exemplified by the INJAZ Al-Arab program (Reimers, Dyer, and Ortega 2012) and BizWorld (Rosendahl-Huber, Sloof, and van Praag 2012). Furthermore, EET can involve a range of public and private stakeholders (Volkmann 2009), including government, educational institutions, businesses, and nongovernmental and international organizations. The roles of these stakeholders can include the development, financing, delivery, and evaluation of EET interventions.

Governments Supporting Entrepreneurship Education and Training

A government's rationale for playing a role in EET is tied to its interest in addressing mindsets, knowledge-based skills, and cultural constraints to entrepreneurship. The World Bank's World Development Report (World Bank 2012) indicates that a government's role in EET is shaped by the potential knowledge spillovers of entrepreneurial-related knowledge and skills (across potential or practicing entrepreneurs in a certain area) as well as by evident market failures when individuals recognize the value of management expertise to their entrepreneurial outcomes.

Governments can be uniquely situated to support EET. For example, at a strategic level, governments can serve as champions for EET through the establishment of national plans and agendas (Peña, Transue, and Riggieri 2010). Governments can set policy frameworks that shape the context of EET delivery within education systems and institutions (Pittaway and Cope 2007).

Governments can directly fund EET interventions (Martin, McNally, and Kay 2013), develop EET curricula, and train instructors to implement curricula in education systems (Nelson and Johnson 1997; Farstad 2002). However, Cho and Honorati (2013) demonstrate that involving the private sector in the delivery of EET is more closely linked to better effects on the participants. This would suggest that governments' role should also include public-private partnerships to provide EET more effectively. Additionally, governments can support the monitoring and evaluation of programs, collaboration, and integration among EET service providers, and they can serve as a convener for sharing good practices across programs (Volkmann 2009). Lastly, Pittaway, and Cope (2007) suggest that research on the government and policy role in EET remains underdeveloped, particularly in understanding the role of regional, national, and supranational polices in shaping EET interventions.

Entrepreneurship Education and Training Research

For governments and practitioners looking for guidance on EET interventions, the body of available research remains relatively limited. Mwasalwiba (2010) highlights literature indicating that despite an agreement on the teachability of aspects of entrepreneurship, critical issues in EET research remain unresolved, including fundamental definitional issues. This may contribute to fragmentation in available research (Garavan and O'Cinneide 1994). Nonetheless, understanding the outcomes of specific EET programs is a growing area of interest for a number of researchers (van der Sluis, van Praag, and Vijverberg 2005; Lautenschläger and Haase 2011; Unger et al. 2011). Glaub and Frese (2011), however, argue that, to date, existing evaluations on the outcomes of EET programs are methodologically weak.

In addition to methodological weakness among the body of evaluations of EET programs, studies find mixed results. For example, some studies examining EET's impact on entrepreneurial intentions indicate a positive short-term influence on (short-term) entrepreneurial intentions (Lüthje and Franke 2003; Lee, Chang, and Lim 2005; Fayolle, Gailly, and Lassas-Clerc 2006; Souitaris, Zerbinati, and Al-Laham 2007); while a set of other studies, as detailed by Lautenschläger and Haase (2011), demonstrate insignificant or negative effects (Oosterbeek, van Praag, and Ijsselstein 2010). Complicating the picture of measuring EET outcomes, Pittaway and Cope (2007) find the connection between one outcome, such as entrepreneurial intentions, and another outcome, such as entrepreneurial activity (e.g., starting a business) to be tenuous. Lastly, most evaluations examine a range of outcomes, but often the results are mixed. As an example, a meta-analysis by McKenzie and Woodruff (2012) demonstrates relatively modest impacts of training on the survivorship of existing firms, but few significant impacts on profits or sales. Furthermore, evaluated EET outcomes can vary across types of training. A meta-analysis by Martin, McNally, and Kay (2013) finds differential effects between academic-focused and training-focused EET interventions.

Areas for Further Entrepreneurship Education and Training Research

Given the growing prevalence of EET, there is a need to better understand what shapes program outcomes. To date, however, few impact evaluations rigorously link EET programs to desired outcomes around entrepreneurial activity or success (Henry, Hill, and Leitch 2005). Furthermore, a dearth of experimental or quasi-experimental studies specifically investigate the impacts of EET programs, and there are few tracer studies tracking graduates of EET programs to see whether they become business owners or go into self-employment (McMullan and Gillin 2001). Moreover, relatively little is known about effective teaching approaches and corresponding learning outcomes (e.g., Gundlach and Zivnuska 2010; Haase and Lautenschläger 2011), how the content of certain programs or learning strategies helps develop skills that result in entrepreneurial activity (Garavan and O'Cinneide 1994), and how wrap-around services (Ibrahaim and Soufani 2002; Volkmann et al. 2009), context, and participant characteristics (e.g., Dana 2001; Lee, Chang, and Lim 2005; Lee et al. 2006) can moderate outcomes. Given the diversity of EET programs, future impact evaluations could make a substantial contribution by testing the relative importance of different combinations of program characteristics. This may bring critical, evidence-based insights to bear on the design and implementation of future EET programs and help to identify what types of programs work for particular beneficiaries to engender particular outcomes, within particular contexts.

Implications for Policy

The literature review raises a number of important issues and provides a glimpse of the ongoing policy questions. There is evidence that governments view entrepreneurship promotion as a policy response to address a number of pressing economic and social issues. As is the case with any public investment, a number of public policy considerations need to be deliberated when formulating interventions.

The questions below, although not exhaustive, illustrate some of the key issues that policymakers may consider when evaluating investments in EET programs:

- **Targeting**—Who should benefit from interventions aimed at encouraging or financing education and training in entrepreneurship?
- **Types of intervention**—Is the intervention addressing market failures such as skills mismatch or access to credit markets, or is it addressing governmental failures such as legal entry/exit barriers or poor business climates for start-ups? Does the intervention generate externalities such as knowledge spillovers, network externalities, and failure externalities?
- **Service providers and delivery**—What is the most effective design to provide successful EET? Should it be provided only via public institutions, the education system, or public-private partnerships?
- **Monitoring and evaluation**—Are there enough rigorous EET evaluations with internal and external validity? What are their findings?

- Fiscal burden and public expenditure—Who should pay for public, interventions? Should they be financed by taxpayers (by payroll or other taxes) or public debt?
- **Role of different governmental levels**—How should the local, regional, national, and supranational levels coordinate to shape EET interventions?

To address all these questions in depth would go beyond the scope of this study. But the discussion in the following chapters touches on these key issues and questions around targeting, types of intervention, and service providers, as well as delivery, monitoring, and evaluation. For the remaining policy implications listed, including fiscal burden, public expenditure, and the role of different governmental levels, more precise guidance on optimal responses in particular contexts must come from future research and analysis.

Bibliography

Acs, Z. J. 1992. "Small Business Economics: A Global Perspective." *Challenge* 35 (6): 38–44.

Acs, Z. J., and C. Armington. 2006. *Entrepreneurship, Geography, and American Economic Growth*. New York: Cambridge University Press.

Acs, Z. J., S. Desai, and J. Hessels. 2008. "Entrepreneurship, Economic Development and Institutions." *Small Business Economics* 31: 219–34.

Acs, Z. J., and A. Varga. 2005. "Entrepreneurship, Agglomeration and Technological Change." *Small Business Economics* 24 (3): 323–34.

Akola, E., and J. Heinonen. 2006. "How to Support Learning of Entrepreneurs? A Study of Training Programmes for Entrepreneurs in Five European Countries." Paper presented at the RENT XX Conference, "Research in Entrepreneurship and Small Business," Brussels, November 22–24.

Audretsch, D. 2004. "Sustaining Innovation and Growth: Public Policy Support for Entrepreneurship." *Industry and Innovation* 11 (3): 167–91.

Audretsch, D., and K. Keilbach. 2004. "Entrepreneurship Capital and Economic Performance." *Regional Studies* 38 (8): 949–59.

Bandiera, O., R. Burgess, S. Guleschi, I. Rasul, and M. Suliman. 2012. "Can Entry-level Entrepreneurship Transform the Economic Lives of the Poor?" Paper originally presented at the Poverty and Applied Micro Seminar Series, World Bank, Washington, DC, March 21. http://ipl.econ.duke.edu/bread/papers/0413conf/bandiera.pdf.

Baumol, W. 1990. "Entrepreneurship: Productive, Unproductive, and Destructive." *Journal of Political Economy* 98 (5): 893–921.

Birch, D. 1979. *The Job Generation Process*. Cambridge, MA: MIT Program on Neighborhood and Regional Change.

Bjorvatn, K., and B. Tungodden. 2010. "Teaching Business in Tanzania: Evaluation Participation and Performance." *Journal of the European Economic Association* 8 (2–3): 561–70.

Block, Z., and S. A. Stumpf. 1992. "Entrepreneurship Education Research: Experience and Challenge." In *The State of the Art of Entrepreneurship*, edited by D. L. Sexton and J. D. Kasarda. PWS-Kent Publishing Company.

Brock, W., and D. Evans. 1989. "Small Business Economics." *Small Business Economics* 1: 7–20.

Brockhaus, R. 2001. "Foreword." In *Entrepreneurship Education: A Global View*, edited by R. Brockhaus, G. Hills, H. Klandt, and H. Welsch. Aldershot, U.K.: Ashgate.

Carree, M., and A. Thurik. 2003. "The Impact of Entrepreneurship on Economic Growth." In *Handbook of Entrepreneurship Research: An Interdisciplinary Survey and Introduction*, edited by Z. Acs and D. Audretsch. Boston, MA: Kluwer Academic Publishers.

Charney, A., and K. E. Libecap. 2000. "The Impact of Entrepreneurship Education: An Evaluation of the Berger Entrepreneurship Program at the University of Arizona, 1985–1999." University of Arizona, Eller College of Business and Public Administration.

Cho, Y., and M. Honorati. 2013. "Entrepreneurship Programs in Developing Countries: A Meta-Regression Analysis." Social Protection and Labor Discussion Paper 1302, World Bank, Washington, DC. http://elibrary.worldbank.org/doi/book/10.1596/1813-9450-6402.

Cloete, G. E., and H. H. Ballard. 2011. "Factors Influencing Academic Resilience of Trainees in Entrepreneurial Development Programmes: A Case from Saldanha Bay Municipal Area in South Africa." *International Journal of Technology Management and Sustainable Development* 10 (3): 217–30.

Curran, J., and J. Stanworth. 1989. "Education and Training for Enterprise: Some Problems of Classification, Evaluation, Policy and Research." *International Small Business Journal* 7 (2): 11–22.

Dana, L. P. 2001. "The Education and Training of Entrepreneurs in Asia." *Education + Training* 43 (8–9).

de Mel, S., D. McKenzie, and C. Woodruff. 2009. "Measuring Microentrerprise Profits: Must We Ask How the Sausage Is Made?" *Journal of Development Economics* 88 (1): 19–31.

Detienne, D. R., and G. N. Chandler. 2004. "Opportunity Identification and Its Role in the Entrepreneurial Classroom: A Pedagogical Approach and Empirical Test." *Academy of Management Learning and Education* 3 (3): 242–57.

Dickson, P. H., G. T. Solomon, and K. M. Weaver. 2008. "Entrepreneurial Selection and Success: Does Education Matter?" *Journal of Small Business and Enterprise Development* 15 (2): 239–58.

EURYDICE. 2012. *Entrepreneurship Education at School in Europe: National Strategies, Curricula, and Learning Outcomes*. Brussels: Education, Audiovisual and Culture Executive Agency, European Commission. http://eacea.ec.europa.eu/education/eurydice/documents/thematic_reports/135EN.pdf.

Farstad, H. 2002. *Integrated Entrepreneurship Education in Botswana, Uganda and Kenya*. Oslo: National Institute of Technology.

Fayolle, A., B. Gailly, and N. Lassas-Clerc. 2006. "Effect and Counter-Effect of Entrepreneurship Education and Social Context on Student's Intentions." *Estudios de Economia Aplicada* 24: 509–23.

Fritsch, M. 2004. "Entrepreneurship, Entry and Performance of New Business Compared in Two Growth Regimes: East and West Germany." *Journal of Evolutionary Economics* 14: 525–42.

Garavan, T. N., and B. O'Cinneide. 1994. "Entrepreneurship Education and Training Programmes: A Review and Evaluation—Part 1." *Journal of European Industrial Training* 18 (8): 3–12.

GEM (Global Entrepreneurship Monitor). 2010a. *A Global Perspective on Entrepreneurship Education and Training*. Global Entrepreneurship Monitor Special Report. Babson Park, MA: Babson College.

———. 2010b. *Global Entrepreneurship Monitor Women's Report*. Babson Park, MA: Babson College.

———. 2012. *Global Entrepreneurship Monitor Global Report*. Babson Park, MA: Babson College.

Gindling, T. H., and D. Newhouse. 2012. "Self-Employment in the Developing World." Policy Research Working Paper 6201, World Bank, Washington, DC.

Glaub, M., and M. Frese. 2011. "A Critical Review of the Effects of Entrepreneurship Training in Developing Countries' Enterprise." *Development and Microfinance* 22 (4): 335–53.

Goppers, K., and M. T. Coung. 2007. "Business Training for Entrepreneurs in Vietnam: An Evaluation of the SIDA-Supported Start and Improve Your Business (SIYB) Project." Swedish International Development Cooperation Agency (SIDA).

Grimm, M., P. Knorringa, and J. Lay. 2012. "Constrained Gazelles: High Potentials in West Africa's Informal Economy." *World Development* 40 (12): 1352–68.

Gundlach, M. J., and S. Zivnuska. 2010. "An Experiential Learning Approach to Teaching Social Entrepreneurship, Triple Bottom Line, and Sustainability." *American Journal of Business Education* 3 (1): 19–28.

Haase, H., and A. Lautenschläger. 2011. "The 'Teachibility Dilemma' of Entrepreneurship." *International Entrepreneurship and Management Journal* 2 (2): 145–62.

Henry, C., F. Hill, and C. Leitch. 2005. "Entrepreneurship Education and Training: Can Entrepreneurship Be Taught?" Part 1. *Education + Training* 47 (2–3).

Hermes, N., and R. Lensink. 2007. "The Empirics of Microfinance: What Do We Know?" *Economic Journal* 117.

Honig, B. 2004. "Entrepreneurship Education: Toward a Model of Contingency-Based Business Planning." *Academy of Management Learning and Education* 3 (3): 258–73.

Hytti, U., P. Stenholm, J. Heinonen, and J. Seikkula-Leino. 2010. "Perceived Learning Outcomes in Entrepreneurship Education: The Impact of Student Motivation and Team Behaviour." *Education + Training* 52 (8–9): 578–606.

Ibrahaim, A. B., and K. Soufani. 2002. "Entrepreneurship Education and Training in Canada: A Critical Assessment." *Education + Training* 44 (8–9): 421–30.

ILO (International Labour Organization). 2011. *Building Business and Entrepreneurship Awareness: An ILO Experience of Integrating Entrepreneurship Education into National Vocational Education Systems*. http://www.ilo.org/wcmsp5/groups/public/---ed_emp/---emp_ent/---ifp_seed/documents/publication/wcms_168356.pdf.

Isaacs, E., K. Visser, C. Friedrich, and P. Brijal. 2007. "Entrepreneurship Education and Training at the Further Education and Training Level in South Africa." *South African Journal of Education* 27: 613–29.

Karlan, D., and M. Valdivia. 2011. "Teaching Entrepreneurship: Impact of Business Training on Microfinance Clients and Institutions." *Review of Economics and Statistics* 93 (2): 510–27.

Kilby, P. 1971. *Entrepreneurship and Economic Development*. New York: Free Press.

Kirzner, I. M. 1973. *Competition and Entrepreneurship*. Chicago, IL: The University of Chicago Press.

Klapper, L., R. Amit, M. F. Guillen, and J. M. Quesada. 2010. "Entrepreneurship and Firm Formation across Countries." In *International Differences in Entrepreneurship*, edited by J. Lerner and A. Schoar. Chicago, IL: The University of Chicago Press.

Klapper, L., A. Lewin, and J. M. Q. Delgado. 2009. *The Impact of the Business Environment on the Business Creation Process*. Washington, DC: World Bank.

Klapper, L., and C. Richmond. 2009. *Patterns of Business Creation, Survival, and Growth: Evidence from a Developing Country*. Development Research Group, World Bank, and Anderson School of Management, University of California, Los Angeles, CA.

Kolvereid, L., and O. Moen. 1997. "Entrepreneurship among Business Graduates: Does a Major in Entrepreneurship Make a Difference?" *Journal of European Industrial Training* 21 (4): 154–60.

Kuratko, D. F. 2003. "Entrepreneurship Education: Emerging Trends and Challenges for the 21st Century." White paper produced for the U.S. Association of Small Business and Entrepreneurship by the Coleman Foundation.

———. 2005. "The Emergence of Entrepreneurship Education: Development, Trends, and Challenges." *Entrepreneurship Theory and Practice* 29 (5): 577–92.

Lautenschläger, A., and H. Haase. 2011. "The Myth of Entrepreneurship Education: Seven Arguments Against Teaching Business Creation at Universities." *Journal of Entrepreneurship Education* 14: 147–61.

Lee, S. M., D. Chang, and S.-B. Lim. 2005. "Impact of Entrepreneurship Education: A Comparative Study of the U.S. and Korea." *International Entrepreneurship and Management Journal* 1: 27–43.

Lee, S. M., S.-B Lim, R. D. Pathak, D. Chang, and W. Li. 2006. "Influences on Students Attitudes toward Entrepreneurship: A Multi-Country Study." *Entrepreneurship Management* 2: 351–66.

Leitch, C. M., and R. T. Harrison. 1999. "A Process Model for Entrepreneurship Education and Development." *International Journal of Entrepreneurial Behaviour & Research* 5 (3): 83.

Levie, J., and E. Autio. 2008. "A Theoretical Grounding and Test of the GEM Model." *Small Business Economics* 31 (3): 235–63.

Levine, R., and Y. Rubinstein. 2013. "Smart and Illicit: Who Becomes an Entrepreneur and Does It Pay?" NBER Working Paper 19276, National Bureau of Economic Research, Cambridge, MA.

Lüthje, C., and N. Franke. 2003. "The 'Making' of an Entrepreneur: Testing a Model of Entrepreneurial Intent among Engineering Students at MIT." *R&D Management* 33 (2): 135–47.

Mahohoma, E., and M. Muyambo. 2008. "The Impact of Junior Achievement in Namibia." Junior Achievement Worldwide and Junior Achievement Namibia. http://www.docstoc.com/docs/51842795/JA-Namibia-Impact-Survey---REPOR.

Martin, B., J. J. McNally, and M. J. Kay. 2013. "Examining the Formation of Human Capital in Entrepreneurship: A Meta-Analysis of Entrepreneurship Education Outcomes." *Journal of Business Venturing* 28 (2).

McKenzie, D., and C. Woodruff. 2012. "What Are We Learning from Business Training and Entrepreneurship Evaluations Around the Developing World?" Policy Research Working Paper 6202, World Bank, Washington, DC.

McKernan, S.-M. 2002. "The Impact of Microcredit Programs on Self-Employment Profit: Do Non-Credit Program Aspects Matter? *The Review of Economics and Statistics* 84 (1): 93–115.

McMullan, W. E., and L. M. Gillin. 2001. "Entrepreneurship Education in the Nineties: Revisited." In *Entrepreneurship Education: A Global View*, edited by R. H. Brockhaus, G. E. Hills, H. Klandt, and H. P. Welsch. Burlington, VT: Ashgate.

Menzies, T. V. 2003. "21st Century Pragmatism: Universities and Entrepreneurship Education and Development." Keynote address presented at the International Council for Small Businesses World Conference, Belfast, June 15–18.

Minniti, M. 2008. "The Role of Government Policy on Entrepreneurial Activity: Productive, Unproductive, or Destructive?" *Entrepreneurship Theory and Practice* 32 (5): 779–90.

Monitor Consulting Group. 2012. "Accelerating Entrepreneurship in Africa: Understanding Africa's Challenges to Creating Opportunity-Driven Entrepreneurship." Monitor Group and the Omidyar Network. http://www.omidyar.com/sites/default/files/file/ON%20Africa%20Report_April%202013_FInal.pdf.

Mwasalwiba, E. S. 2010. "Entrepreneurship Education: A Review of Its Objectives, Teaching Methods, and Impact Indicators." *Education + Training* 52 (1): 20–47.

Nelson, R. E., and S. D. Johnson. 1997. "Entrepreneurship Education as a Strategic Approach to Economic Growth in Kenya." *Journal of Industrial Teacher Education* 35 (1): 7–21.

Nichter, S., and L. Goldmark. 2009. "Small Firm Growth in Developing Countries." *World Development* 37 (9): 1453–64.

North, D. 1990. *Institutions, Institutional Change and Economic Performance*. Cambridge, U.K.: Cambridge University Press.

Oosterbeek, H., M. van Praag, and A. Ijsselstein. 2010. "The Impact of Entrepreneurship Education on Entrepreneurship Skills and Motivation." *European Economic Review* 54: 442–54.

Paulson, A. L., and R. Townsend. 2004. "Entrepreneurship and Financial Constraints in Thailand." *Journal of Corporate Finance* 10: 229–36.

Peña, V., M. Transue, and A. Riggieri. 2010. *A Survey of Entrepreneurship Education Initiatives*. Washington, DC: Institute for Defense Analyses, Science and Technology Policy Institute.

Peterman, N. E., and J. Kennedy. 2003. "Enterprise Education Influencing Students' Perceptions of Entrepreneurship." *Entrepreneurship Theory and Practice* 28 (2): 129–44.

Pittaway, L., and J. Cope. 2007. "Entrepreneurship Education: A Systematic Review of the Evidence." *International Small Business Journal* 25.

Rauch, A., and M. Frese. 2007. "Let's Put the Person Back Into Entrepreneurship Research: A Meta-Analysis on the Relationship between Business Owners' Personality Traits, Business Creation and Success." *European Journal of Work and Organizational Psychology* 16 (4): 353–85.

Reimers, F., P. Dyer, and M. E. Ortega. 2012. "Entrepreneurship Education in the Middle East." https://www.jaworldwide.org/inside-ja/Reports/INJAZ_Al_Arab_Final_Evaluation_Report.pdf.

Rosendahl-Huber, L., R. Sloof, and M. van Praag. 2012. "The Effect of Early Entrepreneurship Education: Evidence from a Randomized Field Experiment." Discussion Paper 6512, Institute for the Study of Labor, Bonn, Germany.

Russell, R., M. Atchisona, and R. Brooks. 2008. "Business Plan Competitions in Tertiary Institutions: Encouraging Entrepreneurship Education." *Journal of Higher Education Policy and Management* 30 (2): 123–38.

Schoof, U. 2006. "Stimulating Youth Entrepreneurship: Barriers and Incentives to Enterprise Start-Ups by Young People." SEED Working Paper 76, International Labor Organization.

Schramm, C., and R. Litan. 2009. "Up from Poverty." *Real Clear Markets*. http://www.realclearmarkets.com/articles/2009/05/up_from_poverty.html.

Schumpeter, J. 1934. *The Theory of Economic Development: An Inquiry into Profits, Capital, Credit, Interest, and the Business Cycle*. 16th ed. New Brunswick, NJ: Transaction Publishers.

Sexton, D. L., and N. B. Bowman. 1984. "Entrepreneurship Education: Suggestions for Increasing Effectiveness." *Journal of Small Business Management* 2: 18–26.

Souitaris, V., S. Zerbinati, and A. Al-Laham. 2007. "Do Entrepreneurship Programmes Raise Entrepreneurial Intentions of Science and Engineering Students." *Journal of Business Venturing* 22: 566–91.

Stevenson, L., and A. Lundström. 2002. *Beyond the Rhetoric: Defining Entrepreneurship Policy and Its Best Practice Components*. Stockholm: Swedish Foundation for Small Business Research.

Teixeira, A. A., and R. P. Forte. 2009. "Unbounding Entrepreneurial Intents of University Students: A Multi-Disciplinary Perspective." FEP Working Paper 322FE, Universidade do Porto, Faculdade de Economia do Porto.

Timmons, J. A., and S. Spinelli. 2004. *New Venture Creation: Entrepreneurship for the 21st Century*. New York: McGraw-Hill.

Todd, P. R., and R. G. Javalgi. 2007. "Internationalization of SMEs in India: Fostering Entrepreneurship by Leveraging Information Technology." *International Journal of Emerging Markets* 2 (2): 166–80.

Unger, J. M., A. Rauch, M. Frese, and N. Rosenbusch. 2011. "Human Capital and Entrepreneurial Success: A Meta-Analytical Review." *Journal of Business Venturing* 26: 341–58.

van der Sluis, J., M. van Praag, and W. Vijverberg. 2005. "Entrepreneurship Selection and Performance: A Meta-Analysis of the Impact of Education in Developing Economies." *The World Bank Economic Review* 19 (2): 225–61.

van Praag, M., and P. H. Versloot. 2007. "What Is the Value of Entrepreneurship? A Review of Recent Research." *Small Business Economics* 29 (4): 351–82.

Vesper, K. H., and W. McMullan. 1998. "Entrepreneurship: Today Courses, Tomorrow Degrees?" *Entrepreneurship Theory and Practice* 29 (4): 7–13.

Volkmann, C. 2009. "Entrepreneurship in Higher Education." In *Educating the Next Wave of Entrepreneurs: Unlocking Entrepreneurial Capabilities to Meet the Global Challenges of the 21st Century*, edited by C. Volkmann, K. E. Wilson, S. Mariotti, D. Rabuzzi, S. Vyakarnam, and A. Sepulveda. Cologny, Switzerland: World Economic Forum.

Volkmann, C., K. E. Wilson, S. Mariotti, D. Rabuzzi, S. Vyakarnam, and A. Sepulveda. 2009. *Educating the Next Wave of Entrepreneurs: Unlocking Entrepreneurial Capabilities to Meet the Global Challenges of the 21st Century*. Cologny, Switzerland: World Economic Forum.

Vyakarnam, S. 2009. "Driving Forces of Entrepreneurship Education." In *Educating the Next Wave of Entrepreneurs: Unlocking Entrepreneurial Capabilities to Meet the Global Challenges of the 21st Century*, edited by C. Volkmann, K. E. Wilson, S. Mariotti, D. Rabuzzi, S. Vyakarnam, and A. Sepulveda. Cologny, Switzerland: World Economic Forum.

Welter, F. 2011. "Contextualizing Entrepreneurship: Conceptual Challenges and Ways Forward." *Entrepreneurship Theory and Practice* 35 (1): 165–84.

Wennekers, S., and R. Thurik. 1999. "Linking Entrepreneurship and Economic Growth." *Small Business Economics* 13: 27–55.

Winslow, E. K., G. T. Wennekers, and A. Tarabishy. 1999. "Empirical Investigation into Entrepreneurship Education in the US: Some Results of the 1997 National Survey of Entrepreneurial Education." Paper presented at the USASBE/SBIDA Annual National Conference, "Sailing the Entrepreneurial Wave into the 21st Century," San Diego, January 14–17.

World Bank. 2010. *Stepping Up Skills: For More Jobs and Higher Productivity*. Washington, DC: World Bank.

———. 2012. *World Development Report 2013: Jobs*. Washington, DC: World Bank.

Wu, J., and N. Pangarkar. 2006. "Rising to the Global Challenge: Strategies for Firms in Emerging Markets." *Long Range Planning* 36: 295–313.

Yaw, D. A. 2007. "Promoting the Informal Sector as a Source of Gainful Employment in Developing Countries: Insights from Ghana." *The International Journal of Human Resource Management* 18 (6).

Zeithaml, C. P., and G. H. Rice. 1987. "Entrepreneurship/Small Business Education in American Universities." *Journal of Small Business Management* 25 (1): 44–51.

CHAPTER 3

Conceptual Framework

Types of EET Programs

Entrepreneurship education and training (EET) programs can be classified under two related but distinct categories: *education programs* and *training programs*. Broadly speaking, both aim to stimulate entrepreneurship, but they are distinguished from one another by their variety of program objectives or outcomes. While differing from program to program, academic entrepreneurship education (EE) programs tend to focus on building knowledge and skills *about* or *for the purpose of* entrepreneurship. Entrepreneurship training (ET) programs, by contrast, tend to focus on building knowledge and skills, explicitly in preparation for starting or operating an enterprise (Volkmann *et al.* 2009; GEM 2010a). While these two categories are conceptually distinct, it should be noted that in practice there are instances where the characteristics of EE and ET overlap or are integrated into a single program.

Advancing the classification of EET, programs can also be distinguished by their target audiences. The academic nature of EE means these programs target two groups in particular: secondary education students and higher education students, the latter including both graduate and undergraduate students enrolled in formal degree-granting programs. By contrast, ET programs target a range of potential and practicing entrepreneurs who are not part of formal, degree-granting programs.

Potential entrepreneurs targeted by ET programs can include, at one end of the range, vulnerable, unemployed, inactive individuals, or necessity-driven potential entrepreneurs, and at the other end of the range, highly skilled, innovation-led, or opportunistic potential entrepreneurs. Likewise, the range of practicing entrepreneurs runs from individuals owning informal, micro- and small enterprises all the way to high-growth potential enterprise owners.

Building on these concepts, this study proposes the following definitions for classifying EET programs according to both program type and target audience (see figure 3.1):

- **EE—for Secondary and Higher Education Students.** This category generally refers to the building of capabilities, skills, and mindsets about or for the purpose of entrepreneurship. The goal is to expand the pool of potential *future* entrepreneurs. Thus, it is generally integrated within formal education institutions at the secondary and higher education levels (including universities, colleges, and vocational schools). In this context, this study examines EE programs targeted at both secondary and higher education students enrolled in formal secondary, undergraduate, and graduate degree-granting programs.

- **ET—for Potential and Practicing Entrepreneurs.** This category generally refers to the building of knowledge and skills in preparation for starting or operating a business. Thus, the goal of ET is to aid potential entrepreneurs to become entrepreneurs as well as help current entrepreneurs become higher performing entrepreneurs. The broad nature of these target audience definitions means that ET programs can target a range of potential and practicing entrepreneurs, regardless of age, level of education, prior experience, or circumstances (e.g., highly skilled and educated, self-employed, underemployed, and informal economy workers).

It should be noted that these constructs do not ignore the reality that secondary education students can indeed be considered "potential entrepreneurs" or that many practicing entrepreneurs may be enrolled in adult education courses at tertiary education institutions. However, these classifications do enable a more focused analysis of the EET landscape for the purpose of providing targeted insights about how programs *generally* can differ depending on where they are being implemented and whom they are targeting.

Figure 3.1 Classifying Entrepreneurship Education and Training Programs

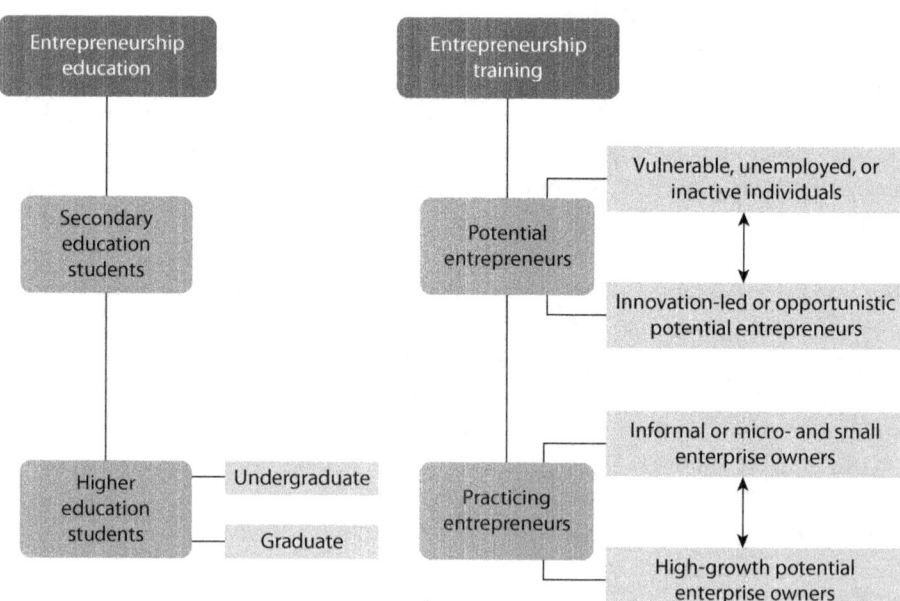

Developing a Conceptual Framework for EET

Determining the outcomes of EET programs is a complex and multidimensional challenge, regardless of whom a program targets (Fayolle, Gailly, and Lassas-Clerc 2006; Pittaway and Cope 2007; Oosterbeek, van Praag, and Ijsselstein 2010). The task is complicated in part because the intended outcomes of EET programs can vary substantially from program to program. Therefore, this study draws upon existing EET research to propose a way of conceptualizing both the results EET programs seek and the factors that can shape those outcomes.

This study puts forth a Conceptual Framework (see figure 3.2) that outlines three dimensions which the research has shown to influence the range of EET outcomes: (a) the context within which programs are implemented, (b) the characteristics of individual participants, and (c) the functional characteristics of the program itself. The Conceptual Framework situates these three dimensions as independent variables in a moderating relationship to the outcomes of EET programs (that is, their outcomes are the dependent variable). The framework additionally suggests that the first two dimensions—program context and participants—can influence the operational characteristics of the program itself (e.g., duration, method of delivery). In sum, a program's outcomes are shaped by both its own programmatic characteristics *and* the contextual and participant-based moderating factors.

Figure 3.2 Conceptual Framework

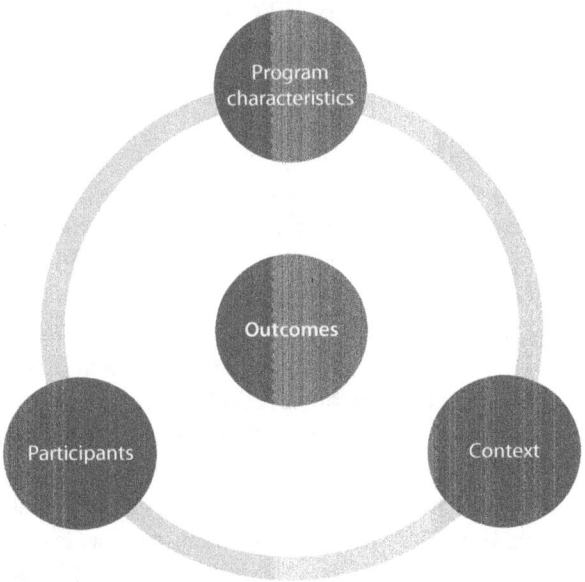

Describing the Framework by Dimension

What follows is a summary of the EET literature supporting this conceptual framework, focusing on the program dimensions that turn entrepreneurial knowledge into a variety of outcomes. This section focuses more on program characteristics than on the other two dimensions, since policymakers and EET practitioners typically have the most leverage over the program design, which is the level that most influences outcomes and most benefits from the experience of good practice. However, this study does recognize that programs "need to be customized ... addressing the specific constraints relevant for [a program's] outcome" (Cho and Honorati 2013, 32). The program design should result from an understanding of the context constraints, participants' needs, institutional framework and capacity, and policy objectives. Policymakers should recognize the lessons learned from other programs and incorporate them into design, implementation, and evaluation, although they should avoid exact replication.

Outcome Domains

While no consensus has been established on a definitive method for measuring EET outcomes (OECD 2009), any study of EET programs must be clear about which outcomes are being measured and how they are being measured. Drawing upon available literature and the evaluations of a range of EET programs, outcomes vary widely. Furthermore, intended outcomes are not limited to the conventional entrepreneurship measures, such as the number of new start-up ventures or their performance. They may also focus on improving skills or changing attitudes, such as encouraging participants to consider entrepreneurship as a career option (Mwasalwiba 2010).

The Conceptual Framework categorizes EET outcomes into a series of four domains: (a) entrepreneurial *mindsets*, (b) entrepreneurial *capabilities*, (c) entrepreneurial *status*, and (d) entrepreneurial *performance* (figure 3.3). Each of these outcome domains is elaborated next.

Entrepreneurial Mindsets

Entrepreneurial mindsets refers to the socio-emotional skills and overall awareness of entrepreneurship associated with entrepreneurial motivation and future success as an entrepreneur. Extensive literature documents a range of socio-emotional skills associated with entrepreneurship, which include self-confidence, leadership, creativity, risk propensity, motivation, resilience, and self-efficacy (Boyd and Vozikis 1994; Luthje and Franke 2003; Rauch and Frese 2007; Cassar and Friedman 2009; Teixeira and Forte 2009; Hytti *et al.* 2010; Cloete and Ballard 2011). Other socio-emotional skills associated with entrepreneurship pertain closely to how individuals interact with others, such as teamwork and social networking. While some entrepreneurial socio-emotional skills are difficult to develop in people, there is evidence that others, such as opportunity recognition, can be taught (Detienne and Chandler 2004; Henry, Hill, and Leitch 2005). Reflecting the importance of socio-emotional skills, a number of programs

Conceptual Framework

reviewed in this study target outcomes related to such skills. As an example, BizWorld Netherlands (Huber, Sloof and van Praag 2012), an EE program, measures participants' improvements in self-efficacy, need for achievement, and risk-taking propensity (see box 3.1).

In addition to socio-emotional skills linked to entrepreneurship, research indicates that entrepreneurial activity is linked to whether participants have a positive perception of entrepreneurship (Souitaris, Zerbinati, and Al-Laham 2007; Martin, McNally, and Kay 2013). Thus, programs seeking to impact entrepreneurial mindset also seek to affect participants' views of the desirability and feasibility of starting a business as well as their intent to do so (Kolvereid and

Figure 3.3 Outcome Domains

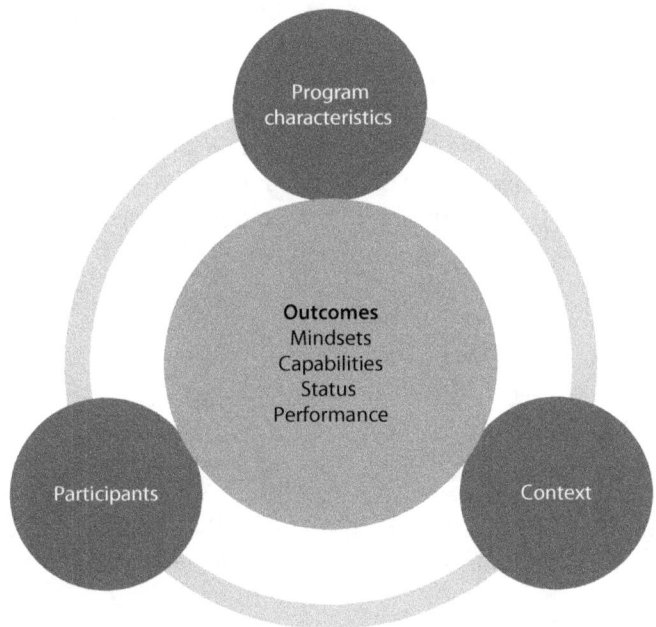

Box 3.1 Building Socio-Emotional Skills: BizWorld (the Netherlands)

BizWorld, launched in the Netherlands in 2004, is an entrepreneurship education (EE) program that takes place in hundreds of Dutch classrooms each year. Companies each sponsor a class of students for an intensive four-day program. In 2011, the BizWorld Netherlands program was evaluated using a randomized field experiment. The evaluation demonstrated that students who completed BizWorld showed much more developed noncognitive skills than the control group—in particular, they showed greater self-efficacy, need for achievement, risk-taking propensity, and analytical skills.

Source: Huber, Sloof, and van Praag 2012.

Moen 1997; Peterman and Kennedy 2003; Fayolle, Gailly, and Lassas-Clerc 2006; Souitaris, Zerbinati, and Al-Laham 2007). Participation in EET has been found to have a positive effect on individuals' overall passion and motivation for entrepreneurship (San Tan and Ng 2006; Richardson and Hynes 2008; Gundlach and Zivnuska 2010) as well as their entrepreneurial intentions (Pruett 2011; Martin, McNally, and Kay 2013).

Entrepreneurial Capabilities
Entrepreneurial capabilities refers to entrepreneurs' competencies, knowledge, and associated technical skills. Some EET programs measure the extent to which programs equip participants with general business knowledge and the basic skills needed for opening and managing a business (Russell, Atchisona, and Brooks 2008; Bjorvatn and Tungodden 2010; Karlan and Valdivia 2011). These progams can target a range of management skills, from accounting and marketing to the ability to manage complex processes, assess risks, and mobilize resources (Curran and Stanworth 1989; Detienne and Chandler 2004; Honig 2004; Summit Consulting 2009). Additionally, some EET programs target specific technical knowledge or skills associated with a particular occupation or sector, such as agriculture. A number of EET program evaluations explicitly cite progress in knowledge and skill acquisition. For example, participants in the FINCA-Peru program demonstrated an increased familiarity with separating money between business and household, reinvesting profits in the business, maintaining records of sales and expenses, and thinking proactively about new markets and opportunities for profits (see box 3.2).

Entrepreneurial Status
Entrepreneurial status refers to the temporal state of a program beneficiary as measured through entrepreneurial activities and beyond (e.g., starting a business, becoming employed, and achieving a higher income). Status outcomes transcend the acquisition of specific mindsets and skills associated with

---

Box 3.2 Improving Entrepreneurial Capabilities: FINCA (Peru)

Founded in 1993, FINCA (Peru) is a microfinance institution that trains low-income entrepreneurs to develop their businesses. FINCA trainings focus on improving clients' capabilities in such areas as how to treat clients, how to use profits, where to sell, how to use special discounts, and how to sell credits. In 2004, a randomized control trial compared participants in FINCA's program to a control group. While the FINCA participants did not have higher profits, they did report significant strides in developing their entrepreneurial skills. Specifically, FINCA participants had a greater familiarity with separating money between business and household, reinvesting profits in the business, maintaining records of sales and expenses, and thinking proactively about new markets and opportunities for profits.

Source: Karlan and Valdivia 2011.

> **Box 3.3 Becoming Entrepreneurs: Student Training for Promoting Entrepreneurship (Uganda)**
>
> Using a randomized control group design, Gielnik *et al.* (2013) found that an EE program targeted at undergraduate students led to an increase in business ownership within a period of 12 months. The program, taught on a weekly basis over a period of 12 weeks, trained students in the last year of their undergraduate studies. The 12-month evaluation study showed a significant impact on new business start-ups, and students in the training group were 50 percent more likely to start a new business than those in the control group.
>
> *Source:* Gielnik et al. 2013.

entrepreneurship—instead focusing on measuring how a participant's individual status has changed or life has improved because of an EET intervention. EET programs have been shown to measure individuals' decisions to seek out new capital and start ventures (Singh and Verma 2010), become employed (Brodmann, Grun, and Premand 2011), and increase income and savings (Cox *et al.* 2012). In many respects, the prevailing purpose of EET programs is to have participants go on to start their own enterprises, and the extent to which programs are yielding these outcomes remains a common area of inquiry. Gielnik *et al.* (2013) conducted a randomized-control experiment to investigate just this question in a Ugandan EET program and found positive effects (see box 3.3).

Entrepreneurial Performance

Entrepreneurial performance refers explicitly to how indicators of a venture's performance have changed as a result of an intervention (e.g., higher profits, increased sales, greater employment of others, higher survival rates). A number of EET studies look at whether participants perform better as entrepreneurs than those who aren't exposed to EET (Volkmann *et al.* 2009; Shane 2010; von Graevenitza, Harhoffa, and Weber 2010). In certain cases, EET program participants show improvement in multiple performance outcomes, including annual sales, number of employees, number of customers, and market expansion (Botha 2006). Additional literature suggests that EET programs also look at performance outcomes related to improved business practices, which in the case of SMEs can include the formalization of an enterprise. Other measured practices include improvement in separating money between business and household, reinvesting profits in a business, maintaining records of sales and expenses, and implementing innovations (Karlan and Valdivia 2011). Understandably, performance outcome indicators are typically associated with ET programs that target practicing entrepreneurs, as is the case with the Interise program (see box 3.4), although measuring these outcomes is not limited to this target group.

Evidence also indicates that many programs measure outcomes in multiple domains. An example of this latter phenomenon is the Women Entrepreneurship Program in South Africa, which measures outcomes under all four categories

Box 3.4 Enhancing Firm Performance: Interise (United States)

Interise is a nonprofit organization that teaches small business owners, principally from underserved populations, to sustain and grow their businesses, create jobs, and strengthen their communities. Participants meet for three hours biweekly for 13 sessions in class sizes of 15–18, and they also form peer mentoring groups to allow for further discussion. Each year, Interise does an extensive evaluation of its program. The 2011 survey indicated that 62 percent of past participants had added jobs to their companies and had given out an average salary of just over $40,000. Furthermore, over half of Interise participants also reported a growing business—with increased revenue and government grants averaging $325,000 per business.

Source: Interise 2011.

(Botha, Nieman, and van Vuuren 2006). Similarly, a global program, Empretec, targets both aspiring and practicing entrepreneurs and measures outcomes under both status and performance (Grossmann 2005). Meanwhile, Start and Improve Your Business (SIYB), which is also in use around the globe, has tracked outcomes under mindsets, capabilities, and performance (Goppers and Coung 2007).

Program Context

The Conceptual Framework accounts for a series of contextual influences shown to impact the likelihood of a program's capacity to generate outcomes (Karimi *et al.* 2010). Studies have looked at the series of economic, political, and social factors that are likely to make individuals more successful at starting new ventures (Pittaway and Cope 2007). As a fundamental example, a market that possesses the unique contextual factors needed to foster entrepreneurship is more likely to have the factors that enable entrepreneurial activity than a market that lacks such contextual factors. Furthermore, EET programs are also likely to face contextual implementation challenges due to their operating locations. The Conceptual Framework recognizes three broad categories of such factors: *economic context, political context,* and *cultural context* (figure 3.4).

The Economic Context

The economic context represents the multiple economic variables that have been found to correlate with entrepreneurship outcomes. "Even potentially skilled entrepreneurs would have difficulty succeeding without access to basic infrastructure and financial resources. In their absence, managerial capacity alone may not be enough" (World Bank 2012c, 115). Contextual economic factors include local economic conditions, such as the investment climate and specific market opportunities. In addition, contextual economic factors can include the local infrastructure, both financial (availability of finance) and physical (access to markets), as well as regulatory and tax structures that relate to the ease and incentives to start a business. McKenzie and Woodruff (2012) suggest

Figure 3.4 Contextual Factors

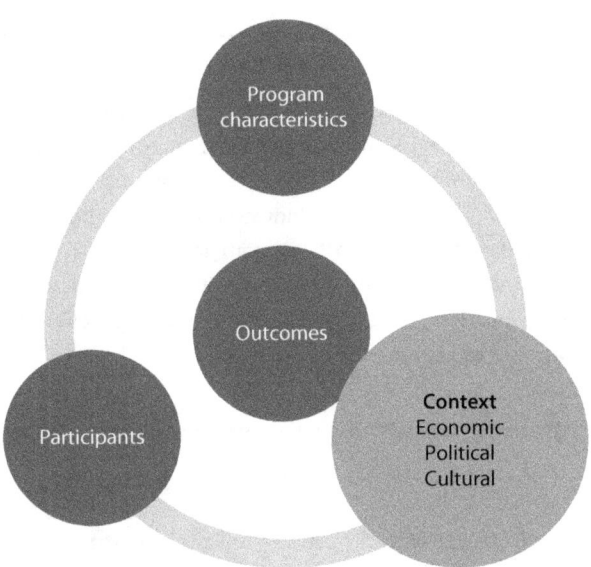

that spillovers (positive or negative) within the economic context from entrepreneurship programs may correlate with entrepreneurship outcomes. The spillovers are mainly driven by competition responses to the activities of trained entrepreneurs. Further illustrating the importance of the relationship between entrepreneurship and economic context, Acs and Szerb (2010) developed the GED Index (The Global Entrepreneurship and Development Index) to measure the quality and quantity of business formation in 71 countries.

The Political Context

The political context refers to both the stability of local society and institutions as well as the leadership and will to promote entrepreneurship through local policies and institutions. While improvement on any economic or human development indicators depends on a particular level of security and local stability, the political context for entrepreneurship can manifest in more explicit and localized ways. Government support for entrepreneurship can take the form of an explicit entrepreneurship promotion framework, with specific policy actions such as government support for fair practices, minimal bureaucratic barriers, and grants and funding opportunities to subsidize programs (Freedom House 2008; Heritage Foundation 2008; World Bank 2012a, 2012b). Additionally, political support can include partnerships with government ministries in the financing and implementation of EET interventions. For example, the SIYB program in Vietnam partners with government through the Ministry of Labor (see box 3.5).

Moreover, the political contexts that influence EET can be found in more localized institutions—like support from community-based organizations, advocates, and the education system—and individuals within schools in which programs are implemented. Pittaway and Cope (2007) highlight the importance

> **Box 3.5 Political Support through Partnership: Start and Improve Your Business (Vietnam)**
>
> The Start and Improve Your Business (SIYB) program in Vietnam trains micro- and small-business owners in basic business management, and helps them—as well as potential entrepreneurs—start up or improve the performance of their businesses. From 1998 to 2004, the Vietnam Chamber of Commerce and Industry (VCCI) and the International Labour Organization (ILO) implemented the SIYB program in Vietnam. Today, however, SIYB is partnering with the Vietnamese government through its Department for Vocational Training (under the Ministry of Labor) to market, select participants for, and deliver the program to over 1 million farmers over the next seven years.
>
> *Source:* Goppers and Coung 2007.

of creating a match between a program and its local institutional context. Several programs underscore the linkages between EET outcomes and instruction-specific program champions, such as teachers, principals, and organizational administrators (Kuratko 2005).

The Cultural Context

Cultural context refers to factors associated with local perceptions of entrepreneurship as well as cultural attitudes toward failure, success, and the traditional roles of certain members of society. These cultural dynamics can either enable or constrain entrepreneurship in a society and, in turn, can moderate EET outcomes. Hofstede (1991) defines cultural values as broad tendencies to prefer specific behavioral patterns over others. Specific cultural dimensions (Rauch, Frese, and Sonnentag 2000; Pinillos and Reyes 2011) and the presence of entrepreneurial values within a society (Davidson and Wiklund 1997) have also been associated with different levels of entrepreneurial activity.

A socially supportive culture relates positively to entrepreneurship (Stephan and Uhlaner 2010). As an example, Russian and Chinese business owners have more entrepreneurs in their families and among childhood friends than otherwise similar individuals, suggesting that social environment also matters (World Bank 2012c). In general, studies have suggested that entrepreneurship is facilitated by cultures that exhibit both collectivism (providing community support) and individualism (valuing individual goals over group loyalty), that are low in uncertainty avoidance (having a risk-taking propensity), and that are low in power-distance (where movement and communication within a hierarchy are allowed). Hayton, George, and Zahra (2002) deduce from this that the greater the cultural distance from this ideal, the lower the levels of entrepreneurship. Since a host of EET programs aim to promote an overall entrepreneurial culture, one may reasonably posit that entrepreneurship promotion must sometimes encounter significant cultural constraints.

Participant Characteristics

Among EET programs' outcomes, a key moderating factor is what individual participants bring with them coming into a program. These individual characteristics are a prominent subject in the EET literature, and certain personality traits have been linked to positive entrepreneurial outcomes (Luthje and Franke 2003; Rauch and Frese 2007). From an operational standpoint, EET programs themselves recognize the role of participant characteristics in moderating outcomes. This would explain why so many EET programs employ a range of selection processes—screening candidates for various characteristics including their educational background, their work experience, and even their personalities (using personality tests to screen for certain character traits). Furthermore, program outcomes can be shaped by dynamics associated with participant behavior, including the nature of participant uptake as well as attrition within a particular program. The Conceptual Framework thus includes five categories of participant characteristics[1] that research indicates can moderate program outcomes: (a) individual profile (both demographic and personality related); (b) education; (c) experience; (d) interest and intentions; and (e) participant behavior. Figure 3.5 illustrates these participant characteristics.

Profile

An individual's profile refers to basic demographic identifiers and factors related to a participant's personality or traits. As is the normal practice in social research, evaluations of EET programs often segment results according to factors such as gender, age, or parental background (Wang and Wong 2004). Evaluations have looked at differences in outcomes across each of these

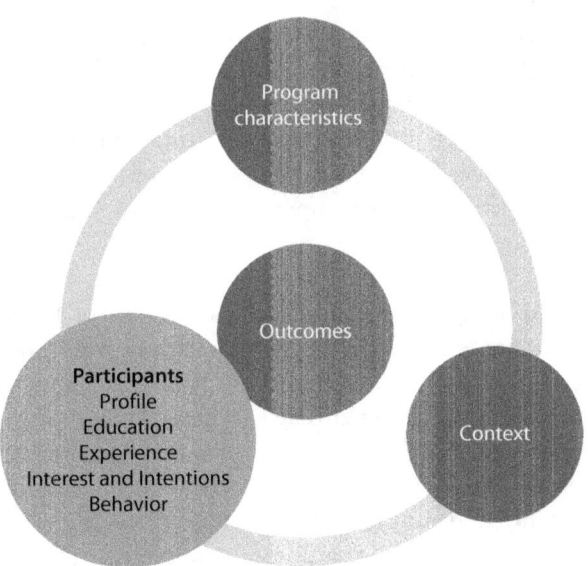

Figure 3.5 Participant Characteristics

Box 3.6 The Gender Effect: National Rural Savings Programme (Pakistan)

Started in 1991 with a focus on reducing poverty and increasing rural development, the National Rural Savings Programme (NRSP) is a microfinance program that works within rural regions of Pakistan to help communities implement a variety of programs that increase productive employment, alleviate poverty, and improve quality of life. NRSP employs a common approach to microfinance lending, which includes a requirement that its members join community organizations.

At the time of its evaluation in 2007, NRSP was tying a series of its microloans to entrepreneurial training sessions that included 46 hours dedicated to business planning, marketing, and financial management. The evaluation found that the inclusion of business training increased participants' business knowledge, enhanced their business practices, and improved several participants' incomes, though this was disproportionately the case among male participants. The evaluation cited remarkably different levels of success between males and females, and noted that this difference could in part be related to Pakistan's segregating its labor markets by gender; to women's exclusion from many occupations reserved for men; and to female wage rates being lower on average. Given the disproportionate effect by gender (favoring men), the evaluation concluded that future interventions will have to be more intensely focused on female participants to realize similar outcomes across men and women.

Source: Gine and Mansuri 2011.

---

categories to discern whether a moderating relationship might exist between components of a participant's profile and the outcomes of an intervention. A prominent example of this is the National Rural Savings Programme (NRSP) in Pakistan. Its evaluation demonstrated disproportionate effects based on gender, favoring males (see box 3.6).

Additionally, certain personality traits have been linked to positive entrepreneurial outcomes (Lüthje and Franke 2003; Rauch and Frese 2007). These personality characteristics are often a reflection of the favorable socio-emotional skills that many EET programs aim to build. As moderating factors, these characteristics, such as self-confidence, risk propensity, resilience, and teamwork, are in effect skills that participants have upon entering a program.

Education

Education refers explicitly to the educational background of a participant, including both level of attainment and basic cognitive skills flowing from formal educational exposure, such as literacy and numeracy. Ruiz and Dams (2012) note that the majority of high-impact women entrepreneurs (those who had a business growth of 20 percent or more over the preceding three years) had an educational attainment level of college or above. Studies point to the role of a participant's educational level in moderating EET outcomes (Oosterbeek, van Praag, and Ijsselstein 2010). Furthermore, the setup of a number of EET programs point to the role of literacy and numeracy skills in influencing outcomes; these cognitive skills are critical for the comprehension and application of entrepreneurship concepts imparted through EET (Kourilsky and Esfandiari 1997) as well as the integration of knowledge into the establishment or strengthening of an enterprise (Peterman and Kennedy 2003; Lans et al. 2008).

Experience

Experience refers to an EET participant's work and employment experience (Oosterbeek, van Praag, and Ijsselstein 2010). Start-up, management, and industry-specific experience have all been shown to moderate the outcomes from EET participant to participant (Unger et al. 2011). Experience brings about a functional level of business knowledge and familiarity with certain markets or opportunities. At the ground level, individuals with some work experience tend to have a better understanding of both the socio-emotional skills as well as technical skills that are requisite for developing and sustaining an enterprise. The experience may come from their own work experience or from other sources, such as from the entrepreneurial experience of family or acquaintances. For example, Ruiz and Dams (2012) find that the majority of women entrepreneurs had relatives with their own business.

Interest and Intentions

Interest and intentions refers to how EET participants' intentions differ, depending on their profiles (Pittaway and Cope 2007) as well as their particular motivations for participating (McClelland 1958; Sengupta and Debnath 1994; Zanakis, Renko, and Bullough, forthcoming). According to the theory of planned behavior (Ajzen 1991), which is extensively cited in the entrepreneurship literature, a person's intentions and relative desire to become an entrepreneur (Peterman and Kennedy 2003) are the most reliable predictor of actions (Krueger, Reilly, and Carsrud 2000; Bullough, Renko, and Myat 2013). A number of programs look at entrepreneurial motivations and intentions through a series of indicators, including self-selection, as was the case with the Entrepreneurship Development Centre (EDC) program in Bosnia and Herzegovina (see box 3.7). Program attendance is also used as a proxy to measure the seriousness of participants' intentions.

Behavior

Individuals' decision to participate and continue participation in a program can influence program outcomes. This includes how participants respond to program offerings or perceive the overall value of a program. Studies point to incentives shaping program outcomes, which in turn influence program uptake, such as when a program ties into financial access or other wrap-around services (World Bank 2012d). Additionally, Botha (2006) finds that the perceived value of other participants can influence the decision of individuals to participate in a program. For example, if a small business owner sees his brother benefiting from participating in a program, he is more likely to participate himself. Furthermore, perceptions of what it means to become an entrepreneur may go beyond monetary incentives. For instance, the women entrepreneurs studied by Ruiz and

> **Box 3.7 Entrepreneurial Intentions: Entrepreneurship Development Center (Bosnia and Herzegovina)**
>
> The Entrepreneurship Development Centre (EDC) ran a comprehensive business training program for existing and potential entrepreneurs who had loans at Partner Microcredit Foundation in 2009. Participants were young adults in Bosnia and Herzegovina who had small businesses or who were developing new enterprises. The randomized control trial took place in 2009, with the evaluation aiming to better understand the effects of business training on emerging entrepreneurs' business success and loan repayment. The evaluation found that while the EDC training program did not influence business survival, it significantly improved business practices, investments, and loan terms for surviving businesses. However, it also noted the important role of uptake in the program, which is only delivered to individuals interested in participating; it is noteworthy too that the program participants had a demonstrable interest in entrepreneurship.
>
> *Source:* Bruhn and Zia 2011.

Dams (2012) listed their top three reasons for becoming entrepreneurs as follows: "independence," "achievement," and "challenge." Interestingly, "money" came in at number six out of nine reasons.

Karlan and Valdivia (2011) shed further light on how participant perceptions can shape program outcomes, specifically on the issue of attrition. They found that rates of program dropout were higher for people with more education and experience, individuals who were also likely to benefit most from the training but were less likely to perceive its value. Supporting this point, they also found stronger training effects among participants who expected less from the training intervention in a baseline survey. These behavioral dynamics influence whether and who elects to participate in a program, as well as how long they participate, which in turn can moderate the ultimate outcomes of the program in question.

Program Characteristics

EET programs may range from full academic courses to short training courses. Program characteristics are an important driver of EET since they are the easiest to manipulate. The entrepreneurship program concept is broader than what can be conveyed by a single course or by the material taught in a classroom alone; instead it comprises a whole portfolio of complementary activities (Souitaris, Zerbinati, and Al-Laham 2007). An appropriate design of this portfolio is important to a program's ultimate outcomes. The portfolio can include the usual components related to classroom activities—such as trainers, curriculum, delivery format, and duration or intensity—as well as wrap-around services like mentoring, networking opportunities, guest speakers, and collaboration with other institutions.

Figure 3.6 Program Characteristics

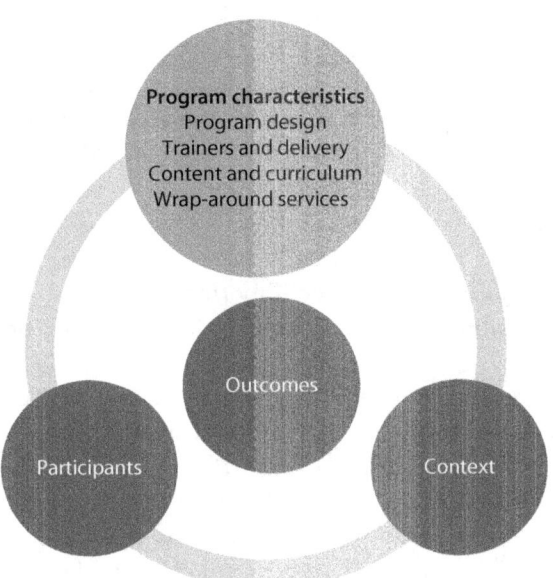

The Conceptual Framework distinguishes among four major categories of program characteristics: (a) program design; (b) trainers and delivery; (c) content and curriculum; and (d) wrap-around services (see figure 3.6). These fundamental categories are included in the framework for two reasons. First, they are grounded in the broad-based discussions found throughout the EET literature. Second, they help meet the need to build a holistic framework for examining common practices across EET programs and informing EET program design or reform.

Program Design

Program design refers to a set of inputs and arrangements that help define a program's goals, scope, financing model, and methods for determining progress. Among the most important components of program design is how a program is financed, in terms of both finance sources and how it costs out its units of service. Design characteristics can also include the extent to which arrangements are made to facilitate collaboration with institutions in the local community (Fuchs, Werner, and Wallau 2008). This includes partnering with area organizations to obtain buy-in from the indigenous community and to recruit participants and trainers.

Trainers and Delivery

Trainers and delivery refers to key program inputs and implementation aspects related to who is delivering the content of the program; that is, whether programs are led by credentialed teachers, professional trainers, or entrepreneurship practitioners, and where these individuals are drawn from (e.g., local schools, international training consultant organizations, or other). Programs can also include a mix of academic and practitioner instructors, with evidence suggesting that a mix—faculty who have the academic and theoretical knowledge combined with practitioners who are experts in the subject area—can provide the best balance of theory and practice for participants (Porter and McKibbin 1988; Pittaway and Cope 2007). For example, the Network for Teaching Entrepreneurship (NFTE) found that participants were more likely to engage in a range of entrepreneurial behaviors—including taking initiative and leading in business, arts, and sports activities—and underscores the importance of training quality instructors and the role of variability in teacher quality in influencing program outcomes (see box 3.8).

These characteristics also include the program setting (e.g., classroom, virtual), the program duration, and the size of the participant class/cohort (Hynes 1996; Shinnar, Pruett, and Toney 2009; GEM 2010a). EET programs that have been evaluated for their impact on entrepreneurship-related outcomes are typically delivered in face-to-face settings. While programs that incorporate experiential learning or virtual learning exist, the prominence of face-to-face delivery is notable.

Content and Curriculum

Content and curriculum often become the focal point of program design efforts because other categories revolve around them. In theory, they have a strong relationship with the outcomes a program aims to deliver. These characteristics include a program's relative thematic content areas (e.g., entrepreneurship awareness, financial literacy, strategic planning). Common areas of focus include

---

Box 3.8 Training the Trainers: Network for Teaching Entrepreneurship (United States)

The Network for Teaching Entrepreneurship (NFTE) program has operated in Boston since 1991, working with 18 public schools there. NFTE targets high schools where at least half of the student body is eligible for free or reduced-price lunch. It focuses on participants' mindsets and capabilities, ultimately aiming to help participants stay in school, recognize business opportunities, and plan for future employment. To deliver the program, NFTE certifies instructors who are already teaching in the schools where their program will take place. Each teacher goes through a four-day training at the beginning of the school year (a so-called "NFTE University") and NFTE provides financial incentives to certified instructors for continuous professional development programs throughout their time teaching the NFTE course. In addition to NFTE-certified instructors, mentors come to class a few times throughout the year to guide their mentees and help students create their business plans, and a handful of guest lectures are delivered during the year by volunteer local business leaders.

Source: Nakkula et al. 2004.

general business skills, socio-emotional skills, and entrepreneurial awareness and business plan development. They also include pedagogy (e.g., whether lecture based or experiential) and teaching techniques.

For example, some programs may link learning with real-world experiences (Porter and McKibbin 1988; Pittaway and Cope 2007). Evidence suggests that delivery is enhanced by including varied teaching techniques, which can range from hands-on experiential exercises to lectures, articles, writing, simulations, and group projects on a variety of integrated subjects. Lastly, these characteristics include how participant learning is evaluated (e.g., tests, business plan presentations) (Henry, Hill, and Leitch 2005; Haase and Lautenschläger 2011; Karlan and Valdivia 2011; Martin, McNally, and Kay 2013). For example, some programs require presentations of plans, proposals, or projects.

Wrap-Around Services

Wrap-around services are aspects of a program that complement the main content and curriculum. These can include arrangements for networking and mentoring as well as opportunities to gain access to financing or other resources (e.g., technical assistance, administrative services, job counseling, incubators, grants) to support participants during or upon the completion of a program (Ibrahaim and Soufani 2002; Volkmann *et al.* 2009). As an example, the Business Plan Thesis Competition program in Tunisia matches participants with entrepreneur coaches during the final stage of its program (see box 3.9).

An evaluation of the Women's Income Generating Support Program (WINGS) in Uganda suggests the potential importance of wrap-around services to EET—indicating that on-going support for young, new entrepreneurs is essential to help them succeed and address the challenges that arise with every nascent business endeavor (Blattman *et al.* 2013). The tier 1 evaluation of the WINGS project also underlines the importance of grants, which the evaluation suggested were "likely the most impactful element of the program" (Blattman *et al.* 2013, 57).

Building upon the structure of the preceding Conceptual Framework, figure 3.7 provides a more granular picture of EET program dimensions, identified through this chapter's summary of research. As a more detailed

---

Box 3.9 Coaching as Follow-Up: Business Plan Thesis Competition (Tunisia)

Introduced by Tunisia's government in the 2009–10 school year, the Business Plan Thesis Competition entrepreneurship program is targeted at undergraduate, engineering graduate, and masters students. The government created the program in the country's 12 public universities to encourage better employment outcomes among college graduates. The program has two parts. First, students are trained in basic entrepreneurship skills around business creation. The second part is more personalized: each student is assigned a coach with an entrepreneurial background who advises him or her on finalizing a business plan.

Source: World Bank 2013.

Figure 3.7 Conceptual Framework: Detailed Structure

Outcome domains	Mindsets		Socio-emotional skills
			Entrepreneurial awareness
	Capabilities		Management skills
			Vocational skills
	Status		Enterprise formation
			Employability
			Income and savings
			Network formation
	Performance		Profits and sales
			Job creation
			Expansion
			Productivity
			Formalization
			Reinvestment
			Implementation of innovation
			Products and services
Program characteristics	Program design	Design	Local partnerships
			Selection process
		Finance	Source of funding
			Unit cost (program and participant)
	Trainers and delivery	Trainers	Teacher/educator
			Practitioner
			Consultant
		Delivery	Face to face
			Online
			Experential
		Class size	10 or less
			11 to 30
			31 to 60
			61 to 100
			More than 100
		Intensity	Daily
			Weekly/bi-weekly
			Monthly
		Duration	One-off
			Less than 2 weeks
			2 weeks to 3 months
			3 to 6 months
			6 months to 1 year
			More than 1 year
	Content and curriculum	Content	Financial literacy/accounting
			Marketing sales
			General business/management
			Vocational
			Leadership and teamwork
			Strategic planning
			Socio-emotional skills
		Curricula	Mixed methods
			Tests/assessments
			Presentations/competitions
	Wrap-around services	Individual	Mentoring and coaching
			Networking
			Job counseling
		Firm	Access to finance
			Technical assistance
Moderating factors	Participants	Profile	Gender
			Age
			Personality and traits
			Family background
		Education	Education level
			Literacy and numeracy
		Experience	Work experience
			Entrepreneurship experience
		Interest and intentions	Interest in entreprenuership
			Intention to start/grow a business
		Behavior	Uptake
			Attrition
	Context	Economic	Conditions
			Infrastructure
		Political	Stability
			Entrepreneurship promotion
		Cultural	Entrepreneurship enabling
			Entrepreneurship constraining

reflection of the Conceptual Framework, this figure will serve as a tool for understanding what shapes EET program outcomes; first, by providing a means for systematically cataloging program-specific information about a global sample of EET programs (contained within the Program Database), and subsequently to structure an analysis of these programs to identify common practices and trends. The findings from this analysis are presented in chapter 4.

Note

1. These participant characteristics apply across all types of programs (Entrepreneurship Education–Higher Education, Entrepreneurship Education–Secondary Education, Entrepreneurship Education–Potential Entrepreneurs, and Entrepreneurship Education–Practicing Entrepreneurs). The distinction relies more on program targeting, although they should not be considered mutually exclusive categories.

Bibliography

Acs, Z. J., and L. Szerb. 2010. *The Global Entrepreneurship and Development. Opening Up Innovation: Strategy, Organization and Technology.* London: Imperial College London Business School.

Ajzen, I. 1991. "The Theory of Planned Behavior." *Organizational Behavior and Human Decision Processes* 5: 179–211.

Bjorvatn, K., and B. Tungodden. 2010. "Teaching Business in Tanzania: Evaluation Participation and Performance." *Journal of the European Economic Association* 8 (2–3): 561–70.

Blattman, C., E. Green, J. Annan, and J. Jamison. 2013. "Building Women's Economic and Social Empowerment through Enterprise: An Experimental Assessment of the Women's Income Generating Support (WINGS) Program in Uganda." Published by enGender Impact, the World Bank's Gender Impact Evaluation Database. http://www.poverty-action.org/sites/default/files/wings_full_policy_report_0.pdf.

Botha, M. 2006. "Measuring the Effectiveness of the Women Entrepreneurship Programme (WEP) as a Training Intervention on Potential or Start-Up and Established Women Entrepreneurs in South Africa." Doctoral Dissertation, Economic and Management Sciences, University of Pretoria, Pretoria, South Africa.

Botha, M., G. H. Nieman, and J. J. van Vuuren. 2006. "Evaluating the Women Entrepreneurship Training Programme." *International Indigenous Journal of Entrepreneurship, Advancement, Strategy and Education* 2: 1–16.

Boyd, N. G., and G. S. Vozikis. 1994. "The Influence of Self-Efficacy on the Development of Entrepreneurial Intentions and Actions." *Entrepreneurship Theory and Practice* 18 (4): 63–77.

Brodmann, S., R. Grun, and P. Premand. 2011. *Can Unemployed Youth Create Their Own Jobs? The Tunisia Business Plan Thesis Competition.* Washington, DC: World Bank.

Bruhn, M., and B. Zia. 2011. "Stimulating Managerial Capital in Emerging Markets: The Impact of Business and Financial Literacy for Young Entrepreneurs." Policy Research Working Paper 5642, Development Research Group, Finance and Private Sector Development Team, World Bank, Washington, DC.

Bullough, A., M. Renko, and T. Myatt. 2013. "Danger Zone Entrepreneurs: The Importance of Resilience and Self-Efficacy for Entrepreneurial Intentions." *Entrepreneurship Theory and Practice*. doi: 10.1111/etap.12006.

Cassar, G., and H. Friedman. 2009. "Does Self-Efficacy Affect Entrepreneurial Investment?" *Strategic Entrepreneurship Journal* 3: 241–60.

Cho, Y., and M. Honorati. 2013. "Entrepreneurship Programs in Developing Countries: A Meta-Regression Analysis." Social Protection and Labor Discussion Paper 1302, World Bank, Washington, DC. http://elibrary.worldbank.org/doi/book/10.1596/1813-9450-6402.

Cloete, G. E., and H. H. Ballard. 2011. "Factors Influencing Academic Resilience of Trainees in Entrepreneurial Development Programmes: A Case from Saldanha Bay Municipal Area in South Africa." *International Journal of Technology Management and Sustainable Development* 10 (3): 217–30.

Cox, P., Koerberle, S. G., Uyanik, T. T., and Chen, N. 2012. *Access to Finance and Capacity Building for Earthquake-Affected Micro and Small Enterprises: Implementation, Completion, and Results Report.* Washington, DC: Multi-Donor Java Reconstruction Fund Grant, International Organization for Migration, World Bank.

Curran, J., and J. Stanworth. 1989. "Education and Training for Enterprise: Some Problems of Classification, Evaluation, Policy and Research." *International Small Business Journal* 7 (2): 11–22.

Davidson, P., and J. Wiklund. 1997. "Values, Beliefs, and Regional Variations in New Firm Formation Rates." *Journal of Economic Psychology* 18 (2–3): 179–99.

Detienne, D. R., and G. N. Chandler. 2004. "Opportunity Identification and Its Role in the Entrepreneurial Classroom: A Pedagogical Approach and Empirical Test." *Academy of Management Learning and Education* 3 (3): 242–57.

Fayolle, A., B. Gailly, and N. Lassas-Clerc. 2006. "Effect and Counter-Effect of Entrepreneurship Education and Social Context on Student's Intentions." *Estudios de Economia Aplicada* 24: 509–23.

Freedom House. 2008. Political Freedom Index. (F. H. Inc., Producer). http://www.freedomhouse.org.

Fuchs, K., A. Werner, and F. Wallau. 2008. "Entrepreneurship Education in Germany and Sweden: What Role Do Different Schools Systems Play?" *Journal of Small Business and Enterprise Development* 15 (2): 365–81.

GEM (Global Entrepreneurship Monitor). 2010a. *A Global Perspective on Entrepreneurship Education and Training.* Global Entrepreneurship Monitor Special Report. Babson Park, MA: Babson College.

———. 2010b. *Global Entrepreneurship Monitor Women's Report.* Babson Park, MA: Babson College.

———. 2012. *Global Entrepreneurship Monitor Global Report.* Babson Park, MA: Babson College.

Gielnik, M., M. Frese, A. Kahara-Kawuki, I. Wassawa Katono, S. Kyejjusa, J. Munene, and T. J. Dlugosch. 2013. "Action and Action-Regulation in Entrepreneurship: Evaluating a Student Training for Promoting Entrepreneurship." *Academy of Management Learning and Education*, October 3. http://amle.aom.org/content/early/2013/10/03/amle.2012.0107.abstract.

Gine, X., and G. Mansuri. 2011. *Money or Ideas? A Field Experiment on Constraints to Entrepreneurship in Rural Pakistan.* Washington, DC: World Bank.

Goppers, K., and M. T. Coung. 2007. *Business Training for Entrepreneurs in Vietnam: An Evaluation of the SIDA—Supported Start and Improve Your Business (SIYB) Project.* Swedish International Development Cooperation Agency (SIDA).

Grossman, M. 2005. *The Impact Challenge: Conducting Impact Assessments for the EMPRETEC Programme: A Background Note.* Oxford, U.K.: Oxford University, Centre on Skills, Knowledge, and Organizational Performance.

Gundlach, M. J., and S. Zivnuska. 2010. "An Experiential Learning Approach to Teaching Social Entrepreneurship, Triple Bottom Line, and Sustainability." *American Journal of Business Education* 3 (1): 19–28.

Haase, H., and A. Lautenschläger. 2011. "The 'Teachibility Dilemma' of Entrepreneurship." *International Entrepreneurship and Management Journal* 2 (2): 145–62.

Hayton, J., G. George, and S. A. Zahra. 2002. "National Culture and Entrepreneurship: A Review of Behavioral Research." *Entrepreneurship Theory and Practice* 26 (4): 33–52.

Henry, C., F. Hill, and C. Leitch. 2005. "Entrepreneurship Education and Training: Can Entrepreneurship Be Taught?" Part 1. *Education + Training* 47 (2–3).

Heritage Foundation. 2008. Index of Economic Freedom. http://www.heritage.org/index.

Hofstede, G. 1991. *Cultures and Organizations: Software of the Mind.* Berkshire, U.K.: McGraw-Hill Book Company Europe.

Honig, B. 2004. "Entrepreneurship Education: Toward a Model of Contingency-Based Business Planning." *Academy of Management Learning and Education* 3 (3): 258–73.

Huber, L., R. Sloof, and M. V. van Praag. 2012. "The Effect of Early Entrepreneurship Education: Evidence from a Randomized Field Experiment." Discussion Paper 6512, Institute for the Study of Labour, Bonn, Germany.

Hynes, B. 1996. "Entrepreneurship Education and Training: Introducing Entrepreneurship Into Non-Business Disciplines." *Journal of European Industrial Training* 20 (8): 10–17.

Hytti, U., P. Stenholm, J. Heinonen, and J. Seikkula-Leino. 2010. "Perceived Learning Outcomes in Entrepreneurship Education: The Impact of Student Motivation and Team Behaviour." *Education + Training* 52 (8–9): 578–606.

Ibrahaim, A. B., and K. Soufani. 2002. "Entrepreneurship Education and Training in Canada: A Critical Assessment." *Education + Training* 44 (8–9): 421–30.

Interise. 2011. *Interise 2011 Report Card: Creating Jobs, Growing Business, Building Communities.* Boston: Interise.

Karimi, S., M. Chizari, H. J. Biemans, and M. Mulder. 2010. "Entrepreneurship Education in Iranian Higher Education: The Current State and Challenges." *European Journal of Scientific Research* 48 (1): 20–35.

Karlan, D., and M. Valdivia. 2011. "Teaching Entrepreneurship: Impact of Business Training on Microfinance Clients and Institutions." *Review of Economics and Statistics* 93 (2): 510–27.

Kolvereid, L., and O. Moen. 1997. "Entrepreneurship among Business Graduates: Does a Major in Entrepreneurship Make a Difference?" *Journal of European Industrial Training* 21 (4): 154–60.

Kourilsky, M. L., and M. Esfandiari. 1997. "Entrepreneurship Education and Lower Socioeconomic Black Youth: An Empirical Investigation." *Urban Review* 29 (3): 205–15.

Krueger, N., M. D. Reilly, A. L. Carsrud. 2000. "Competing Models of Entrepreneurial Intentions." *Journal of Business Venturing* 15 (5–6): 411–32.

Kuratko, D. F. 2005. "The Emergence of Entrepreneurship Education: Development, Trends, and Challenges." *Entrepreneurship Theory and Practice* 29 (5): 577–92.

Lans, T., W. Hulsink, H. Baert, M. Mulder. 2008. "Entrepreneurship Education and Training in a Small Business Context: Insights from Competence-Based Approach." *Journal of Enterprising Culture* 16 (4): 363–83.

Lüthje, C., and N. Franke. 2003. "The 'Making' of an Entrepreneur: Testing a Model of Entrepreneurial Intent among Engineering Students at MIT." *R&D Management* 33 (2): 135–47.

Martin, B., J. J. McNally, and M. J. Kay. 2013. "Examining the Formation of Human Capital in Entrepreneurship: A Meta-Analysis of Entrepreneurship Education Outcomes." *Journal of Business Venturing* 28 (2).

McClelland, D. C. 1958. "Methods of Measuring Human Motivation." In *Motives in Fantasy, Action, and Society*, edited by J. W. Atkinson. Princeton, NJ: D. Van Nostrand Company, Inc.

McKenzie, D., and C. Woodruff. 2012. "What Are We Learning from Business Training and Entrepreneurship Evaluations Around the Developing World?" Policy Research Working Paper 6202, World Bank, Washington, DC.

Mwasalwiba, E. S. 2010. "Entrepreneurship Education: A Review of Its Objectives, Teaching Methods, and Impact Indicators." *Education + Training* 52 (1): 20–47.

Nakkula, M., M. Lutyens, C. Pineda, A. Dray, F. Gaytan, and J. Huguley. 2004. "Initiating, Leading and Feeling in Control of One's Fate: Findings from the 2002–2003 Study of NFTE in Six Boston Public High Schools." Harvard University. http://www.nfte.com/sites/default/files/harvard-nfte_study_02-03_full_report_6-6-04.pdf.

OECD (Organisation for Economic Co-operation and Development). 2009. *Measuring Entrepreneurship: A Collection of Indicators*. Paris: OECD.

Oosterbeek, H., M. van Praag, and A. Ijsselstein. 2010. "The Impact of Entrepreneurship Education on Entrepreneurship Skills and Motivation." *European Economic Review* 54: 442–54.

Peterman, N. E., and J. Kennedy. 2003. "Enterprise Education Influencing Students' Perceptions of Entrepreneurship." *Entrepreneurship Theory and Practice* 28 (2): 129–44.

Pinillos, M. A.-J., and L. Reyes. 2011. "Relationship between Individualist-Collectivist Culture and Entrepreneurial Activity: Evidence From Global Entrepreneurship Monitor Data." *Small Business Economics* 37: 23–37.

Pittaway, L., and J. Cope. 2007. "Entrepreneurship Education: A Systematic Review of the Evidence." *International Small Business Journal* 25.

Porter, L. W., and L. E. McKibbin. 1988. *Management Education and Development: Drift or Thrust into the 21st Century?* Hightown, NJ: McGraw-Hill Book Company.

Pruett, M. 2011. "Entrepreneurship Education: Workshops and Entrepreneurial Intentions." *Journal of Education for Business* 87 (2): 94–101.

Rauch, A., and M. Frese. 2007. "Let's Put the Person Back Into Entrepreneurship Research: A Meta-Analysis on the Relationship between Business Owners' Personality Traits, Business Creation and Success." *European Journal of Work and Organizational Psychology* 16 (4): 353–85.

Rauch, A., M. Frese, and S. Sonnentag. 2000. "Cultural Differences in Planning/Success Relationships: A Comparison of Small Enterprises in Ireland, West Germany, and East Germany." *Journal of Small Business Management* 38: 28–41.

Richardson, I., and B. Hynes. 2008. "Entrepreneurship Education: Towards an Industry Sector Approach." *Education + Training* 50 (3): 188–98.

Ruiz, C., and C. Dams. 2012. "Una Mirada a las Emprendedoras de Alto Impacto en Argentina." A2C Advisors and Multilateral Investment Fund (IDB) and Inter-American Development Bank.

Russell, R., M. Atchisona, and R. Brooks. 2008. "Business Plan Competitions in Tertiary Institutions: Encouraging Entrepreneurship Education." *Journal of Higher Education Policy and Management* 30 (2): 123–38.

San Tan, S., and C. K. Ng. 2006. "A Problem-Based Learning Approach to Entrepreneurship Education." *Education + Training* 48 (6): 416–28.

Sengupta, S. K., and S. K. Debnath. 1994. "Need for Achievement and Entrepreneurial Success: A Study of Entrepreneurs in Two Rural Industries in West Bengal." *Journal of Entrepreneurship* 3 (2): 191–203.

Shane, S. 2010. "Does Entrepreneurship Education Make People Better Entrepreneurs?" *Small Business Trends LLC* (blog), September 9.

Shinnar, R., M. Pruett, and B. Toney. 2009. "Entrepreneurship Education Attitudes across Campus." *Entrepreneurship Education* 84 (3): 151–58.

Singh, S., and H. L. Verma. 2010. "Impact of Entrepreneurship Training on the Development of Entrepreneurs." *Interdisciplinary Journal of Contemporary Research in Business* 1 (10): 61–82.

Souitaris, V., S. Zerbinati, and A. Al-Laham. 2007. "Do Entrepreneurship Programmes Raise Entrepreneurial Intentions of Science and Engineering Students." *Journal of Business Venturing* 22: 566–91.

Stephan, U., and L. M. Uhlaner. 2010. "Performance-Based vs. Socially Supportive Culture: A Cross-National Study of Descriptive Norms and Entrepreneurship." *Journal of International Business Studies* 41: 1347–64.

Summit Consulting. 2009. *Toward Effective Education of Innovative Entrepreneurs in Small Business: Initial Results from a Survey of College Students and Graduates*. Washington, DC: Small Business Administration Office of Advocacy.

Teixeira, A. A., and R. P. Forte. 2009. "Unbounding Entrepreneurial Intents of University Students: A Multi-Disciplinary Perspective." FEP Working Paper 322FE, Universidade do Porto, Faculdade de Economia do Porto.

Unger, J. M., A. Rauch, M. Frese, and N. Rosenbusch. 2011. "Human Capital and Entrepreneurial Success: A Meta-Analytical Review." *Journal of Business Venturing* 26: 341–58.

Volkmann, C., K. E. Wilson, S. Mariotti, D. Rabuzzi, S. Vyakarnam, and A. Sepulveda. 2009. *Educating the Next Wave of Entrepreneurs: Unlocking Entrepreneurial Capabilities to Meet the Global Challenges of the 21st Century*. Geneva: World Economic Forum.

von Graevenitza, G., D. Harhoffa, and R. Weber. 2010. "The Effects of Entrepreneurship Education." *Journal of Economic Behavior and Organization* 76: 90–112.

Wang, C. K., and P. K. Wong. 2004. "Entrepreneurial Interest of University Students in Singapore." *Technovation* 24 (2): 163–72.

World Bank. 2012a. "Doing Business Project." http://www.doingbusiness.org.

———. 2012b. "Enterprise Survey." http://www.enterprisesurveys.org.

———. 2012c. *World Development Report 2013: Jobs*. Washington, DC.

———. 2012d. *Can Skills Training Programs Increase Employment for Young Women? The Case of Liberia*. Adolescent Girls Initiative, Washington, DC.

———. 2013. *Can Entrepreneurship Training Improve Work Opportunities for College Graduates?* Washington, DC.

Zanakis, S., M. Renko, and A. Bullough. Forthcoming. "Where Do New Businesses Come From? Individual-Level Explanations for the Transition to Entrepreneurship." *Journal of Developmental Entrepreneurship* 18 (1).

CHAPTER 4

EET Program Landscape and Analysis

The Conceptual Framework discussed in chapter 3 is based on a review of existing entrepreneurship education and training (EET) research, and thus helps to summarize existing research about EET programs. A secondary purpose of the framework is to enable an analysis of existing EET programs to inform a discussion about what proved to work well, what did not work, and the lessons learned.

As described in the Methodology section in chapter 1, a set of criteria related to the rigor of each program's evaluation generated a sample of programs. While the sample cannot be considered exhaustive, the study identified and analyzed 60 EET programs with evaluations that met the standards of Tier 1 (21 programs), Tier 2 (10 programs), and Tier 3 (29 programs). Of that total, 19 programs were classified as entrepreneurship education (EE), while 41 were classified as entrepreneurship training (ET). This section presents the findings from the Conceptual Framework application—analyzing this sample of EET programs by target group. In particular, findings from the evaluations of Tier 1 and 2 programs inform findings about program outcomes. Tables 4.2, 4.4, 4.7, and 4.10 summarize these findings for each program type. Lastly, where relevant, additional EET literature and available meta-analysis findings informed the study.

Given the heterogeneity of the EET landscape, the analysis is conducted by target group to enable a more focused discussion and breaks down the sample of programs as follows: EE secondary education students, EE higher education students, ET for potential entrepreneurs, and ET for practicing entrepreneurs. Programs falling under the same category were collectively analyzed to produce a set of observations about their common dimensions, which are then organized according to the Conceptual Framework and highlighted in figures 4.1–4.4. These figures feature the distribution of the various outcome domains identified by the evaluations (M = Mindsets, C = Capabilities, S = Entrepreneurial Status, P = Entrepreneurial Performance) and also highlight common program characteristics as well as common moderating influences (individual participant characteristics and contextual factors). Additionally, tables 4.2, 4.4, 4.7, and 4.10 provide more detailed information related to program scope and findings from Tier 1 and 2 evaluations for each program type.

It should be noted that the dimensions discussed here are not intended to be an exhaustive list. The tables in appendixes B through D provide a fuller picture of the many dimensions shared by EET programs examined in this study. Lastly, as already mentioned in the introduction, this book is complemented by a complete master database of the programs that were selected for inclusion in this study. The database provides a fuller and more detailed picture of the individual program characteristics and what characteristics are shared across programs.

Entrepreneurship Education—Secondary Education Students (EESE)

Snapshot

The nine evaluations of entrepreneurship education programs targeted at secondary education students acknowledge both the practical and research constraints to causally linking these programs to students' subsequent success as entrepreneurs. Nevertheless, EESE evaluations do demonstrate that the prevailing focus of these programs is on mindsets and capabilities that research associates with entrepreneurship promotion and success, and moreover that this focus has shown some promising results. The mindsets and capabilities include awareness of entrepreneurship as a concept, basic financial literacy skills, and a range of socio-emotional skills such as self-confidence, locus of control, leadership, creativity, risk propensity, motivation, resilience, and self-efficacy. In addition to measuring knowledge and skill acquisition, EESE evaluations also look at outcomes such as employment and enrollment in post-secondary education, which are examples of positive potential spillovers of equipping young people with desirable skills. This suggests that those who are designing EESE programs view the development of entrepreneurial mindsets and capabilities at a relatively young age to be valuable, whether or not program participation culminates in entrepreneurial activity.

EESE evaluations additionally provide insight into some key program design considerations. Broadly, EESE programs are either designed as an extracurricular activity or are embedded within curricula and thus delivered during normal school hours. Several EESE programs borrow curricula from an international brand or franchise. However, whether or not the program is part of an international brand, delivery is local, highlighting the importance of the role of the teacher. Several evaluations recognize the influence of that role in shaping a program's outcomes, examining both the importance of teacher training and the value of pairing a teacher with an entrepreneur from the community to introduce a real-world dynamic/perspective. Lastly, it must be acknowledged that there is a lack of rigorous EESE evaluations, a weakness partly attributable to the difficulty of measuring these programs' linkages with explicit entrepreneurship outcomes such as enterprise formation or enhanced profits. However, the EESE evaluations undertaken to date do reflect the growing interest in the foundational skills and knowledge associated with entrepreneurship and, equally important, the growing interest in the potential benefits of cultivating these capabilities early on.

Program Landscape

This study identified and examined a total of nine EE programs targeted at secondary education students (see table 4.1, EE-Secondary). Unfortunately, for these nine programs, the only impact evaluation available (Tier 1) targeted children in the final grade of primary school (BizWorld Program), indicating a significant lack of rigorous evaluations on secondary education programs. Four programs had evaluations that satisfied the Tier 2 criteria, and four additional program evaluations met the criteria for Tier 3. See table 4.2 for the list of the programs as well as a summary of the key findings from the evaluations.

The reach of all these programs extends well beyond a single school, and several target either regional or national secondary education systems. Further, several of these programs could be considered international in scope since their evaluations emerged from country-based affiliates of global programs, as in the case of South African Institute for Entrepreneurship (SAIE), Network for Teaching Entrepreneurship (NFTE) in the United States, and Junior Achievement (INJAZ) in the Middle East. While there were no available meta-analyses or systematic rigorous reviews exclusively of EESE programs, a wider body of literature—including the findings of Farstad (2002) from an in-depth analysis of integrated EE in Botswana, Uganda, and Kenya—was also considered to inform the understanding of EESE program dimensions.

Table 4.1 Entrepreneurship Education—Secondary Education Students (EESE) | List of Evaluations

	Program name	Country	Evaluation
BizWorld	BizWorld, Netherlands	Netherlands	Tier 1
EOEAS	Entrepreneurial Orientation and Education in Austrian Secondary Schools Study	Austria	Tier 2
INJAZ	Junior Achievement	Middle East	Tier 2
JACP	Junior Achievement Company Program	Sweden	Tier 2
NFTE	Network for Teaching Entrepreneurship	United States	Tier 2
JAN	Junior Achievement Namibia	Namibia	Tier 3
KAB	Know About Business	Syrian Arab Republic	Tier 3
SAIE	South African Institute for Entrepreneurship/Business venture course	South Africa	Tier 3
YE	Young Enterprise	Denmark	Tier 3

Figure 4.1 Entrepreneurship Education—Secondary Education

Analyzing EESE Programs

Outcomes

Looking at the evaluations of EESE programs, the targeted outcomes were concentrated in the mindset domain. With regard to mindsets, programs sought to enhance a number of socio-emotional skills, including self-efficacy, need for achievement, risk-taking, social orientation, persistence, creativity, and locus of control. In addition to socio-emotional skills, these programs sought to develop students' entrepreneurial awareness by encouraging entrepreneurial thinking and behaviors. On both fronts, program evaluations indicated promising results.

For example, the most rigorously evaluated of all the EESE programs, the BizWorld evaluation, demonstrated moderate positive and significant effects on the development of non-cognitive skills (such as self-efficacy, the need for achievement, risk-taking propensity, persistence, analyzing, creativity, and proactivity) among the students who received the intervention when compared to the control group. The NFTE program, which targets Boston-area secondary students who are low-income and at high-risk of dropping out, also demonstrated positive results in this area. A survey measured the development of students' entrepreneurial attitudes and behavior after participating in the program, using a range of indicators such as taking initiative and taking leadership roles in a range of

Table 4.2 Entrepreneurship Education—Secondary Education Students (EESE) | Key Information

Program name	Program beneficiaries	Evaluation	Sample	Outcomes measured	Key findings
BizWorld | Netherlands Source: Huber, Sloof, and van Praag 2012	Children in the final grades of primary school	Tier 1 | Randomized field experiment	The sample consisted of 85 schools (the universe was 113 schools that had signed up for the program in 2010 and 2011, out of which 75 percent consented to participating in the research)—a total of 118 classes and 2,751 students in the last year of primary school. The response rate was 87.7 percent. Since the program was delivered at this class level, the unit of analysis was the class level rather than the school. Schools and classes were assigned to a treatment or a control group. For both groups, the study applied a pre-test/post-test design to allow an unbiased difference-in-differences estimate of the non-treatment effect.	Direct (short-term) effect of early entrepreneurship education on the development of (a) non-cognitive skills including: self-efficacy, need for achievement, risk taking, social orientation, persistence, motivating, analyzing, proactivity, and creativity; (b) cognitive skills, including entrepreneurship knowledge; and (c) entrepreneurial intentions, including children's intentions to become entrepreneurs.	• The treatment effect was positive and statistically significant for seven of the nine non-cognitive skills tested, namely self-efficacy (0.149***), need for achievement (0.166***), risk-taking propensity (0.114**), persistence (0.105**), analyzing (0.127***), creativity (0.096*), and proactivity (0.144***). Analysis on the heterogeneity of treatment effects showed that the treatment effects remained or increased slightly when controlling for individual, school, and neighborhood characteristics and year of data collection. Also, the size of treatment effects was substantial and comparable to being eligible to one track level in entering high school (i.e., from the baseline of pre-vocational to general secondary education); • The estimated effect on cognitive entrepreneurial skills (entrepreneurship knowledge) was positive although not significant (0.015); and • The estimated effect on entrepreneurial intentions (to own a business) for children was negative and significant (−0.134***). The study acknowledged that the measures used for entrepreneurial intentions were not validated for children and could potentially alter the results.

table continues next page

Table 4.2 Entrepreneurship Education—Secondary Education Students (EESE) | Key Information *(continued)*

Program name	Program beneficiaries	Evaluation	Sample	Outcomes measured	Key findings
EOEAS | Entrepreneurial Orientation and Education in Austrian Secondary Schools Study | Austria *Source:* Frank et al. 2005	General and vocational secondary education students (focusing on business, technical careers, trades and commerce)	Tier 2 | Quasi-experimental design	The sample included six general secondary schools, four commercial academies, three secondary technical schools, and one secondary school for technical and business professionals. In addition, a sample of Austrian participants in an international junior entrepreneur contest ("junior") was selected. Among the 15 schools, a total of 875 students and 36 contest participants were surveyed in 2001. Survey participants were 15–18 years old.	Personality (achievement, motivation, locus of control, innovative orientation); resources (attention to business and economics, knowledge of business and economics, experience in leadership and organization, network and activities inside and outside school); start-up inclination (start-up probability); environment (entrepreneurs in the student's surroundings, use of technology, supportive upbringing); and process (entrepreneurship orientation of the school, independence/criticism as values in instruction, entrepreneurship-oriented instruction methods, and team-oriented methods).	• Self-employment was the least preferred option in all school types; • Commercial academy and secondary technical schools graduates were more likely to start a career after graduation; • Commercial academy students had more opportunities to gain practical experience and demonstrated the strongest entrepreneurship orientation, though these conditions did not lead to higher start-up inclinations or a pronounced entrepreneurial orientation; and • Education processes seemed to fulfill an important function in the development of entrepreneurial orientation. Schools could influence this effect by reinforcing business and economics knowledge. However, the development of start-up inclinations seemed to be more closely linked to social influences in the microsocial environment. For example, the most important predictors of start-up inclinations included: entrepreneurs in the surroundings (0.31***); innovative orientation (0.27***); experience in leadership and organization (0.19***); and team-oriented instruction methods (0.11***).

table continues next page

Table 4.2 Entrepreneurship Education—Secondary Education Students (EESE) | Key Information *(continued)*

Program name	Program beneficiaries	Evaluation	Sample	Outcomes measured	Key findings
NFTE	Network for Teaching Entrepreneurship	United States *Source:* Nakkula et al. 2004	High school students (currently in 18 high schools) in Boston. The program targets high schools where at least half of the student body is eligible for free or reduced-price lunch	Tier 2	Quasi-experimental design	The sample included a total of 17 classrooms, 13 teachers, and 268 students, out of which 158 students received the NFTE program (treatment) and 110 students were selected in the comparison classes (control)	Entrepreneurship thinking; entrepreneurial behavior (EB) through an entrepreneurial activities checklist (49 activities organized around different domains and dimensions); locus of control. Applied new scales to measure healthy or positive development (using the values-in-action scale that gauges originality, curiosity, industriousness, and hopefulness).	• Entrepreneurial behavior increased for NFTE students compared to the control group. The EB score for NFTE students registered a significant increase of 7.5 percent ($p<0.01$). The changes in the two groups were large and significant for the starter dimension and business domain; • In contrast, the EB score for comparison students did not register significant changes, although in some domains the trend declined; • Although the results for locus of control were not significant, the scores followed the hypothesized pattern. While NFTE students began with marginally lower locus of control scores than the comparison group, they increased their score by about 3 percent after the intervention, outscoring the control group. Similarly, immigrant students participating in the program improved in their locus of control by about 4.5 percent, while the score of similar students in the comparison group declined by approximately 2.5 percent; • Locus of control findings were strongest for students taught by one particular teacher in one of the schools with a strong track record of effective teaching (i.e., had received recognition); • Results on students' connectedness were generally negative;

table continues next page

Table 4.2 Entrepreneurship Education—Secondary Education Students (EESE) | Key Information *(continued)*

Program name	Program beneficiaries	Evaluation	Sample	Outcomes measured	Key findings
					• Results from the values-in-action scales (originality, curiosity, industriousness, and hopefulness) were not found to be significant. Despite this, NFTE students scored marginally higher than the comparison group in the pretest; meanwhile, the gap narrowed at post-test with the comparison group increasing their score and the NFTE students decreasing the score; • Overall, NFTE students trained by top-notch teachers showed a higher degree of general student-teacher connectedness, unlike the comparison group; and • Similar to the findings from the first phase, relative to the comparison group, NFTE students expressed increasingly strong interest in occupations requiring advanced training or formal education, including college.

table continues next page

Table 4.2 Entrepreneurship Education—Secondary Education Students (EESE) | Key Information *(continued)*

Program name	Program beneficiaries	Evaluation	Sample	Outcomes measured	Key findings
INJAZ	Junior Achievement	Morocco, Lebanon, Jordan, Saudi Arabia, United Arab Emirates, and Egypt, Arab Rep. *Source:* Reimers, Dyer, and Ortega 2012[a]	Students in upper secondary that participated in the INJAZ company program	Tier 2	Quasi-experimental design	The pool of students came from a small number of cities in the six countries. Its total size was 1,454 students, of whom 617 were interviewed for the baseline of the comparison group and 837 for the treatment group. Students were not randomly assigned to either group, and due to limitations in implementation, researchers could only match pre- and postsurveys in limited cases. (The baseline questionnaire was collected in December 2010 and January 2011, and the follow-up survey was collected in July and November 2011.)	Student knowledge, skills and attitudes, and behavioral intentions about entrepreneurship.	• Participants in the Junior Achievement programs had very high levels of access to entrepreneurs in their lives. Around 80 percent had siblings who were entrepreneurs, and 30–74 percent indicated that their parents or neighbors were entrepreneurs; • They had medium levels of knowledge of basic entrepreneurial concepts; • They had high and positive aspirations, views of self and others, self-efficacy and interest in business creation; and • They had favorable attitudes toward entrepreneurship and business.
JACP	Junior Achievement Company Program	Sweden *Source:* Elert, Andersson, and Wennberg 2013	Upper secondary-level students in Swedish schools	Tier 2	Quasi-experimental design using Propensity Score Matching (PSM)	The pool of individuals for the treated was around 166,606 individuals. The sample size was 224,838 individuals, of whom 10,103 comprised the treatment group (individuals who participated in the JACP between 1994 and 1996) and 214,735 comparable non-participant individuals	Probability of starting a business, entrepreneurial income, and firm survival.	• Participation increased the likelihood of starting a new business by at least 20 percent ($p<0.1$) when compared to the non-participants of JACP; • JACP participation had a positive effect of expected income in the range of 7 percent ($p<0.05$) to 18 percent ($p<0.01$); and • There was no significant effect on firm survival due to JACP participation.

a. A summary of this paper is available at http://www.nfte.com/sites/default/files/harvard-nfte_study_02-03_full_report_6-6-04.pdf. Full text is available upon request.

activities including business, art, and sports. The evaluation found a relatively large and statistically significant increase in entrepreneurial behavior among NFTE students compared to the control group. Further, NFTE students increased their scores on locus of control by about 3 percent after the intervention—outscoring the control group—but the increase was not statistically significant. Finally, the findings from the evaluations of other EESE programs, including EOEAS, SAIE, and INJAZ, also indicate progress in cultivating entrepreneurial mindsets. The evaluation of EOEAS in Austria assessed the extent to which entrepreneurial thinking was promoted in vocational and general secondary education; it found that targeted instruction in start-up and entrepreneurial knowledge supports the development of a positive attitude toward entrepreneurship as a goal in life.

With regard to the other outcome domains, several programs seek to enhance the entrepreneurial capabilities of students, including expanding knowledge of business, economics, financial literacy, and other work-related life skills. The evaluations of the programs themselves, however, are sparse in reporting impacts in this area. The BizWorld evaluation described a positive, but insignificant, effect on enhancing students' cognitive entrepreneurial skills. Furthermore, while a review of integrated EE in Botswana, Uganda, and Kenya (Farstad 2002) found that failure rates on post-intervention examinations were low, suggesting some level of knowledge and skill transfer, its examination lacked any additional verification of actual skill acquisition.

In terms of the entrepreneurial status outcomes, some EESE programs look to enhance students' intentions to become an entrepreneur as well as their probability of actually starting a business. The evaluation for BizWorld found a moderately large and significant negative effect on entrepreneurial intentions (opening a business). Only one program evaluation (JACP) referenced the firm performance outcome domain, reporting no significant effect of the program on firm survival. The JAN program evaluation examined how students provided benefit to enterprises run by their parents, alluding to students being better able to help parents with particular business practices such as bookkeeping. Of interest, Fairlie and Robb (2004) found that skills learned from experience working in a family member's enterprise to be associated with later business success.

Taken as a whole, the evaluations of EESE programs are consistent in suggesting that these programs can achieve positive changes in outcomes associated primarily with foundational entrepreneurial mindsets and the range of socio-economic skills that literature associates with entrepreneurship. Skills such as self-confidence, locus of control, leadership, creativity, risk propensity, motivation, resilience, and self-efficacy are particularly common. By contrast, EESE programs are clearly only able to target entrepreneurial capabilities, indicating more heterogeneous results among cognitive entrepreneurial skills. The EESE program evaluations support the potential role of secondary schools as environments for the promotion and acquisition of foundational entrepreneurial mindsets and some entrepreneurial capabilities. Such findings are consistent with other research that positions EESE programs as a means for ensuring young people possess knowledge, capabilities, and attitudes associated with entrepreneurship (Isaacs et al. 2007). These skills serve as the foundation for a more focused managerial and business education and training at a later point in time (ILO 2011).

Program Characteristics

EESE program characteristics are influenced by already being within secondary schools. As such, from a design standpoint, many of these programs demonstrate a degree of functional collaboration with schools themselves or with the broader education system through program integration into standard curricula. The ILO (2011) describes how EESE programs can represent "pilot" programs, in which different content and teaching methods are tested within particular schools or within current areas of study, like the JAN program, whose evaluation covers the pilot program across several Namibian schools.

Furthermore, an EESE program can also be part of a broader or more national rollout, in which the program is being adopted into curricula on a mass scale. Farstad (2002) outlines examples of this in Botswana, Uganda, and Kenya, with integration being the most thorough in Kenya, where EE has been a compulsory aspect of all levels of Technical Vocational Education and Training (TVET) since the 1990s. The KAB program in the Syrian Arab Republic has also been integrated into the curricula of vocational secondary schools. Lastly, INJAZ represents yet another program design approach, one in which the program is an extracurricular activity although it is still implemented in partnership with the relevant education authorities.

While the EESE programs examined by this study represent a mix of all program design approaches, many share association with global "brands" in EE—such as BizWorld, Junior Achievement, the National Foundation for Teaching Entrepreneurship, and Know about Business (program of the International Labour Organization). Thus, from a program design standpoint, EESE programs can represent an intriguing blend of the global (international nongovernmental organizations [NGOs]) and the local (individual schools).

The duration of EESE programs can range from five days (BizWorld) to a whole school year (NFTE). The intensity of the program within this duration can range as well. Farstad (2002), looking at curricula-integrated programs in Botswana, Uganda, and Kenya, found that allocated time never exceeded an average of two hours a week. The SAIE program evaluation examined results according to the duration of the intervention, finding stronger performance improvements after a two-year period in comparison to a one-year period, and indicated that entrepreneurial skill acquisition takes place over a longer period of time than anticipated.

EESE programs' content and curricula understandably correspond with the general focus on the promotion of entrepreneurial mindsets and capabilities in the outcome dimension. Of note is the focus on various socio-emotional skills, such as leadership, creativity, and teamwork, as well as on entrepreneurship awareness. The NFTE program includes the concepts of competitive advantage, ownership, opportunity recognition, marketing, finance, and product development—which all tie back to core math and literacy skills.

Concerning how this content should be delivered, the ILO (2011, 4) suggests a "learning-by-doing" approach, stressing the importance of activities that expose students to concrete entrepreneurial practices. This can include simulations (mock businesses), competitions, and teamwork. The EOEAS program evaluation found team-oriented instruction methods to be among the most important predictors of students' post-program entrepreneurial inclinations. The learning-by-doing approach appears to echo the recommendations of Volkmann (2009), who highlights the value of business plan development and competitions, which are components of NFTE and INJAZ. However, Farstad (2002) warns of the danger of over-relying on such methods for learning entrepreneurship concepts, describing how students tend to focus on copying the business plans of other students to ensure good grades.

EESE program evaluations and research also identify instructors as exposing students to concrete entrepreneurial practices. BizWorld includes a local businessperson as a volunteer instructor, and JACP curricula are implemented by community volunteers. Local businesspeople serve as volunteer mentors to students in the NFTE program, although that curriculum is largely implemented by specially trained, existing teachers. The NFTE program emphasizes the role of teachers in shaping the outcomes of the program, finding that effects are strongest for students taught by a teacher with a strong record of effective teaching.

Volkmann (2009) focuses on the need for teachers trained in the specific pedagogies and content of EESE programs. Bolstad (2006) describes a specific initiative designed to further the teaching of EE, the Northland Enterprising Teachers initiative in New Zealand, which targets teachers in subjects across the curriculum (not only those with economics or finance backgrounds) to reinforce the broad applicability of entrepreneurial skills. Farstad (2002) finds that whereas in Kenya, EE has been a part of all teachers' training since 1993, in Botswana, Uganda, and Kenya, most teachers of entrepreneurship are from business management or economics backgrounds.

Finally, looking at the evaluated programs, very little information is available on their costs. The exceptions are the BizWorld and KAB programs. BizWorld is financed through a public-private partnership, with companies sponsoring a class of students. BizWorld costs a business US$1,300 to sponsor a classroom at a school, which includes providing a businessperson who serves as a volunteer instructor. KAB is free for students, but it costs US$15,000 to hire a trainer to teach instructors the KAB curriculum in each school. Farstad (2002) also encountered challenges in establishing the costs related to EE in part due to (a) the reluctance to disclose financial information and (b) the fact that much of EESE program cost is often indiscernible from the broader operational cost of secondary education institutions. Overall, the costs of EESE programs would be expected to fluctuate with the relative costs of classroom time for other subjects, the extent to which specialized teaching materials are needed, and whether certain learning activities are implemented (e.g., competitions, field trips). For this study, no information on the financial analysis of EESE programs was found.

Moderating Factors

Evaluations of EESE programs cite a range of factors—related to both individual participants and program context—that potentially moderate outcomes. At the participant level, some program evaluations indicate that outcomes are influenced by students' expressed interest in entrepreneurship, by their parental background (e.g., parents' level of education, immigrant status), and by their own self-concept. The EOEAS evaluation suggests that the development of start-up inclinations was more closely linked to *social influences*, with relatively large and positive effects. Social influences are features such as entrepreneurs in the surroundings, innovative orientation, experience in leadership and organizations, and team-oriented instruction. Furthermore, INJAZ students, who elected to take part in extracurricular programs, tended to have high levels of access to entrepreneurs in their lives through family members or neighbors.

Importantly, when considering EESE program outcomes, evaluations acknowledge the practical constraints to interventions influencing secondary education students becoming self-employed or launching entrepreneurial ventures. As program participants, secondary students may have several years before entering the workforce. Farstad (2002) echoes this insight, underscoring how students' age, maturity level, and lack of life experience or productive and marketable skills all complicate their ability to become self-employed, and that many students may opt for more education after an intervention. This finding is reflected in the NFTE evaluation, where participants expressed an increasingly strong interest in occupations requiring advanced training or formal education, including college. Volkmann (2009) further indicates that many students are considered minors by law and in turn face legal constraints to establishing an enterprise or corporate entity. For those who do pursue self-employment, Farstad (2002) finds a higher frequency among TVET students, suggesting a number of possible explanations; these include TVET students' higher ages, their lower access to white-collar career paths, and the fact that TVET equips students with productive knowledge and skills.

Program evaluations also cite various economic, cultural, and institutional contextual factors as moderating factors. The SAIE program evaluation indicated that extraneous factors (the socioeconomic profile of students) were a powerful influence on student performance, even more influential than teaching materials. Farstad (2002) finds that students in rural areas tend to enter self-employment more frequently than their urban counterparts, suggesting an influence of the socioeconomic dynamics of rural communities. Farstad's study also touches on the capital constraints that students face and a culture of skepticism that surrounds self-employment in Botswana, Uganda, and Kenya. On the question of whether contextual factors can influence mindset and skills acquisition, program evaluations cite the socioeconomic level of community and school as well as the relative quality of instruction, which are issues not uncommon to broader discussions of contextual influences on student learning in education research.

Entrepreneurship Education—Higher Education Students (EEHE)

Snapshot

This study included 10 entrepreneurship education programs targeted at higher education students, including two impact evaluations. Notably, both impact evaluations provide compelling evidence of the capacity of EEHE programs to foster growth in mindsets and capabilities, although they produce mixed results around entrepreneurial status and whether or not students go on to become entrepreneurs by launching their own enterprise. These results could be considered promising, since most evaluations of EEHE programs were largely concerned with measuring the extent to which students were enhancing capabilities (knowledge and skills) in the first place as predictors of potential entrepreneurial activity and success.

Evaluations also indicated that an encouraging tactic for transmitting these specific capabilities is simulation activities, such as setting up mock enterprises or business plan competitions. While in the higher education context, programs are subject to a high level of self-selection (few programs are integrated across a mandatory curriculum within post-secondary institutions), nevertheless most programs appear designed to provide enrichment and opportunity to any student with an initial interest in entrepreneurship. Enrichment often includes wrap-around services such as coaching and mentorship. On the whole, with program characteristics ranging from a focus on strategic business planning to personalized coaching, EEHE programs are primarily concerned with cultivating innovation-driven entrepreneurs and high-growth enterprises. The ability of their evaluations to demonstrate links between the programs and these outcomes remains, however, tenuous at this point.

Program Landscape

This study identified and examined a total of 10 EE programs targeted at higher education students (EEHE) (see table 4.3). Of these 10 programs, impact evaluations were available for two that met the Tier 1 criteria (impact evaluations with an experimental design), one program had an evaluation that satisfied the Tier 2 criteria, and seven programs met the criteria for Tier 3 (see table 4.4 for a list of

Table 4.3 Entrepreneurship Education—Higher Education Students (EEHE) | List of Evaluations

	Program name	Country	Evaluation
BPTC	Business Plan Thesis Competition	Tunisia	Tier 1
STEP	Student Training for Promoting Entrepreneurship	Uganda	Tier 1
UTES	University Training for Entrepreneurs	Sweden	Tier 2
APSB	Auchi Polytechnic School of Business	Nigeria	Tier 3
BEP	McGuire Entrepreneurship Program (formerly Berger)	United States	Tier 3
Bødo	Bødo Graduate School of Business	Norway	Tier 3
CCOE	College Carve-Out Education	China	Tier 3
FEE	Finland Entrepreneurial Education	Finland	Tier 3
GE	*Grande École*	France	Tier 3
MIT	The Making of an Entrepreneur	United States	Tier 3

Figure 4.2 Entrepreneurship Education—Higher Education

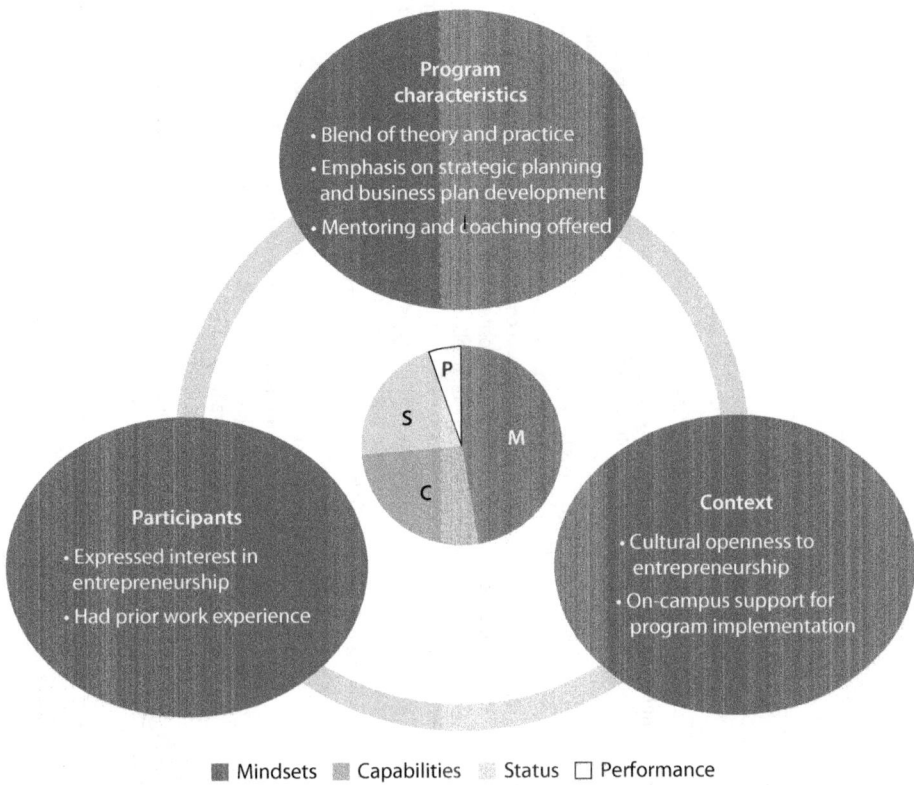

these programs as well as a summary of the key findings from the evaluations). In terms of geographic distribution, 4 of the 10 programs are found in Western Europe, 2 in the United States, 3 in Africa, and 1 in East Asia. The scope of these programs is most discernible by the number of higher education campuses where they are delivered. Only three are delivered at more than two campuses, and three others are isolated, each at a single campus. Seven of these programs are delivered exclusively to undergraduate students, two are delivered to undergraduate and graduate students, and only one specifically targets graduate students.

In addition to the aforementioned sample of EEHE program evaluations, this portion of the analysis draws upon broader research, including a recent meta-analysis conducted by Martin, McNally, and Kay (2013)—a quantitative review of EET literature based upon 42 independent samples (N = 16,657). This study is particularly relevant to EEHE, since the authors delineate between academic-focused EET (EEHE) interventions and training-focused EET interventions.

Analyzing EEHE Programs

Outcomes

The EEHE programs included in this study target outcome domains largely related to entrepreneurial mindsets and capabilities and to a lesser extent

Table 4.4 Entrepreneurship Education—Higher Education (EEHE) | Key Information

Program name	Program beneficiaries	Evaluation	Sample	Outcomes measured	Key findings
STEP | Student Training for Promoting Entrepreneurship | Uganda Source: Gielnik et al., 2013	Undergraduate students in their final semester	Tier 1 | Randomized controlled field experiment	Students at Makerere University and Uganda Christian University. Among the 651 applications received, 200 were selected to receive the training right away (treatment group) and 200 were placed in a waiting group (control group) that received the training after completion of the study. The data were collected using a pretest/posttest design at three points in time (T1, T2, and T3)	Entrepreneurial self-efficacy, action knowledge, action planning, entrepreneurial goals, entrepreneurial action, business opportunity identification, and business ownership	• Action knowledge was a central factor promoting the initiation and maintenance of entrepreneurial activity. Compared to the control group, the training increased the likelihood of starting a business by 50 percent, and compared to the initial status in the training group, the training increased the likelihood of starting a business by 219 percent; • The training had a positive and significant effect on (a) entrepreneurial self-efficacy ($F = 10.44$, $p<0.01$, interaction effect = 0.03 and group effect after training 0.44); (b) action knowledge ($F = 17.65$, $p<0.01$, interaction effect = 0.05 and group effect after training 0.61); (c) action planning ($F = 5.53$, $p<0.05$, interaction effect = 0.02 and group effect after training 0.47), and business opportunity identification ($F = 7.70$, $p<0.01$, interaction effect = 0.02 and group effect after training 0.42). The effect of training on entrepreneurial goals was marginally supported ($F = 2.88$, $p<0.10$, interaction effect = 0.01 and group effect after training 0.31); and • Entrepreneurial action at T2 had a significant effect on entrepreneurial action at T3 ($\beta = 0.26$; $p<0.01$) and action knowledge had a significant and positive effect on entrepreneurial action ($\beta = 0.13$; $p<0.05$). The coefficient on entrepreneurial self-efficacy on entrepreneurial action was not significant.

table continues next page

Table 4.4 Entrepreneurship Education—Higher Education (EEHE) | Key information *(continued)*

Program name	Program beneficiaries	Evaluation	Sample	Outcomes measured	Key findings
BPTC	Business Plan Thesis Competition	Tunisia *Source:* Premand et al. 2012	Undergraduate students enrolled in Tunisian universities	Tier 1	Impact evaluation using a randomized assignment	For the academic year of 2009–10, 1,702 students (about 9 percent of all eligible students nationwide) participated in the entrepreneurship track—some students applied in pairs, so a total of 1,506 projects were registered. The evaluation assigned 757 projects to the treatment group and 742 to the control group. Information was collected at the beginning of the 5-month program (February 2009) and 9 to 12 months after graduation from the program (April–June 2011)	Self-employment, employment status, employment characteristics, business skills, preference and behavioral skills, attitudes toward the future, and access to credit	• Approximately one year after graduation, graduates of the entrepreneurship track had a higher probability of being self-employed. Although the effects were small in absolute terms (ranging from 1 to 4 percentage points), given the low prevalence of self-employment in the control group, the small absolute effects imply that beneficiaries were on average 46–87 percent more likely to be self-employed compared to the control group; • There was no evidence that the program significantly affected overall employment as captured by the likelihood of being employed in the last seven days. In fact, estimates were negative and pointed to a reduction in the probability of holding wage employment; and although not significant, the decrease was of the same magnitude as the increase in self-employment, suggesting the possibility of substitution effect from wage employment to self-employment; • The program did not promote higher-quality jobs among participants. There were no significant program impacts on employment in the formal sector, firm size, hours of work, or earnings; • The intervention produced strong impacts on participants' self-reported business skills and networking proxies. About 77 percent of program graduates reported knowing how to produce a business plan, compared to 45 percent in the control group; • Intervention led to measurable, significant, and robust changes in several domains of the "Big Five," including a decrease in agreeableness (0.23–0.25 sd compared to control group) and an increase in extraversion (albeit a less robust finding compared to the previous trait). There was no evidence to indicate that the entrepreneurship training positively affected conscientiousness and emotional stability, and other entrepreneurial traits such as tenacity or power motivation remained unchanged; and • Participants were found to be more likely to be confident in obtaining credit and to have applied for credit (conditional on having a business idea), but they were not more likely to know how to apply for credit or to have obtained credit.

table continues next page

Table 4.4 Entrepreneurship Education—Higher Education (EEHE) | Key information *(continued)*

Program name	Program beneficiaries	Evaluation	Sample	Outcomes measured	Key findings
UTES | University Training for Entrepreneurs | Sweden *Source:* Johannisson, Landström, and Rosenberg 1998	Business undergraduate and engineering graduate students at two Swedish universities	Tier 2 | Development and application of three tests	Between 1994 and 1995, tests were administered to 265 business students at Vaxjo and Halmstad universities, 110 engineering students at Halmstad University, and 213 business owner-managers of small firms (less than 20 employees)—the latter group was subdivided into traditional and single-venture owner-managers and genuine or multiple-venture owner-managers. The locus-of-control test was not applied to the owner-managers.	Entrepreneurial action capability (EAC), locus of control, and an entrepreneurial value index	• Contrary to expectations, no significant differences in entrepreneurial action capability (EAC) were found between single owner-managers and multiple owner-managers; • Results on the EAC and entrepreneurial value index were highest for business students participating in entrepreneurship programs (7.11 and 3.28, respectively), followed by engineering students (6.51 and 2.47, respectively) and lastly owner-managers (6.03 and 2.29, respectively); the differences between business students and owner-managers were significant at $p<0.01$, and between engineering students and owner-managers significant at $p<0.10$; • Business students enrolled in entrepreneurship programs showed higher entrepreneurial action capability compared to business students from conventional programs (significant at $p<0.01$). However, business students in conventional programs scored higher on the entrepreneurial value index and locus of control, suggesting that showing entrepreneurial value did not necessarily lead to orientation in entrepreneurial action (locus of control was significant at $p<0.01$); • Contrary to expectations, there was no evidence that students in entrepreneurial programs with an engineering orientation had higher scores on entrepreneurial action capability compared to students enrolled in parallel business programs (significant at $p<0.01$); and • Academic training had an impact on students' entrepreneurial action capability; however, the short-term effects were stronger than the long-range effects.

table continues next page

Table 4.4 Entrepreneurship Education—Higher Education (EEHE) | Key information *(continued)*

Program name	Program beneficiaries	Evaluation	Sample	Outcomes measured	Key findings
BEP	McGuire Entrepreneurship Program (formerly Berger)	United States *Source:* Charney and Libecap 2000	Business undergraduate and graduate students at the University of Arizona	Tier 3	Tracer Survey	A total of 2,024 surveys were mailed to graduates from the non-entrepreneurship business school graduates and 460 were mailed to entrepreneurship graduates, all of whom had graduated from the university between 1985 and 1998. The final response rate was 511 for the non-entrepreneurship business graduates and 105 for the entrepreneurship graduates. Response rates were generally uniform across levels of degrees and types of programs, but the response rate was extremely low at 21 percent.	Formation of new ventures, likelihood of self-employment, sales growth rate of emerging firms, accumulation of graduates' assets, and technology transfer from the university to the private sector	• Entrepreneurship education increased the probability of an individual being involved in a new business venture by 25 percent over non-entrepreneurship graduates. Entrepreneurship students were 11 percent more likely than non-entrepreneurship students to own their own businesses after graduation; • Entrepreneurship education contributed to the growth of firms, especially smaller emerging firms. On average, smaller emerging firms that were owned by or employed entrepreneurship graduates had greater than five times the sales and employment growth than those that employed non-entrepreneurship graduates; • Entrepreneurship graduates received an average annual income that was 27 percent higher compared to the average annual income of non-entrepreneurship graduates; • Entrepreneurship education increased a business school graduate's probability of being associated with a high-tech firm by nearly 13 percent and of developing new technological products by almost 9 percent; and • Entrepreneurship education enhanced the transfer of technology from the university to the private sector, and promoted technology-based firms and products. Among self-employed entrepreneurship graduates, nearly 23 percent owned a high-technology firm, compared to less than 15 percent of non-entrepreneurship graduates who owned a firm.

table continues next page

Table 4.4 Entrepreneurship Education—Higher Education (EEHE) | Key information *(continued)*

Program name	Program beneficiaries	Evaluation	Sample	Outcomes measured	Key findings
Bødo | Bødo Graduate School of Business | Norway *Source:* Kolvereid and Moen 1997	Business school students entering their fifth year	Tier 3 | Tracer Survey	Graduate students in business at Bødo Graduate School of Business (15–30 students per year)	Entrepreneurial behavior and entrepreneurial intention	• Entrepreneurship was found to be a function of factors that can be altered through education; • Having a major in entrepreneurship was positively associated with new firm formation (a major in entrepreneurship was the only variable that was significantly related to new firm formation [r = 0.20, p<0.001]); and • Having a major in entrepreneurship was positively associated with entrepreneurial intentions (r = 0.26, p<0.001).
CCOE | College Carve-Out Education | China *Source:* Zhang et al. 2012	Undergraduates in China	Tier 3 | Structure equation model using survey data from current students	A total of 300 questionnaires were distributed and 214 were completed, of which 200 were valid (response rate of 93 percent)	Carve-out education, business knowledge, entrepreneurial abilities, psychological quality, and entrepreneurial intention	• The evaluation found a positive and significant correlation between (a) college carve-out education and business knowledge (estimate 0.513***), entrepreneurial ability (0.641***), and psychological quality (0.385***); (b) business knowledge and intention (0.243***); (c) entrepreneurial ability and intention (0.201***); and (d) psychological quality and intention (0.276***); and • The evaluation did not find a significant correlation between education (0.077) and intention or knowledge and ability (0.006).

table continues next page

Table 4.4 Entrepreneurship Education—Higher Education (EEHE) | Key information *(continued)*

Program name	Program beneficiaries	Evaluation	Sample	Outcomes measured	Key findings
GE	*Grande École*	France Source: Klaper 2004	Undergraduate and master's students in France	Tier 3	Surveys of undergraduate and graduate students	From December 2002 to February 2003, two groups of young people were surveyed about their attitudes toward entrepreneurship and entrepreneurs, as well as their desired career choices. The sample consisted of a group of undergraduates between ages 19 and 22 who were either about to enter the program (first-year students) or had just completed the program (second-year students). The intention was to identify differences between first- and second-year students. The survey was sent to 280 first-year students, of whom 82 responded, and 276 second year students, of whom 60 students responded.	Students' perspectives on entrepreneurs and entrepreneurship, students' attitudes toward entrepreneurship, and the influence of entrepreneurs as family members on the career choices of students	• There was an upward shift in students' attitudes toward entrepreneurship as a career choice between first- and second-year students. While only 26.5 percent of first-year students surveyed saw themselves as potential entrepreneurs, the percentage for second-year students surveyed was 50. Similarly, while 30.9 percent of first-year students could envisage setting up their own business, among second-year students, this rose to 53 percent; • About 81 percent of first-year students surveyed mentioned wanting to work in a large organization upon completion of their studies, compared to 60 percent for second-year students; and • The proportion of students who mentioned wanting to work in a small or medium enterprise dropped from 54 percent for first-year students to 31.7 percent for second-year students.

Box 4.1 Examining the Formation of Human Capital in Entrepreneurship

A study by Martin, McNally, and Kay (2013) reviewed the literature on EET, specifically human capital and educational activities outcomes. The authors included 42 studies that met several criteria: (a) the predictor variable had to be in either entrepreneurial education or training, (b) criterion variables had to be related to either human capital assets or entrepreneurship outcomes, and (c) the reported data could be included in a meta-analysis (with r values or data to transform into r values). The results suggested that there was a positive and significant relationship between EET and entrepreneurship-related human capital assets ($r_w = 0.217$) and performance ($r_w = 0.159$). The moderator analyses suggested a stronger relationship between EET and outcomes resulting from academic-focused EET ($r_w = 0.238$), similar to EEHE programs, than from training-focused EET ($r_w = 0.151$), similar to ET program types. The implications of these results are that positive returns were achieved on investments in developing EET programs, and the inclusion of more conceptual material would benefit students in training-focused EET to achieve entrepreneurial success.

Source: Martin, McNally, and Kay 2013.

---

entrepreneurial status and performance. Reflecting this pattern, the findings from the evaluations of EEHE programs are heavily concentrated in the mindsets and capabilities domains. This concentration in outcomes is consistent with the profile of the target group for EEHE programs: students in tertiary education institutions who are typically preparing to enter the world of work and, thus, entrepreneurship.

The meta-analysis of Martin, McNally, and Kay (2013) (see box 4.1) does find a relationship between entrepreneurship outcomes and academic-focused EET interventions. In fact, that relationship is stronger for the academic-focused EET interventions, which are likely to resemble EEHE programs ($r_w = 0.238$), than for training-focused EET interventions ($r_w = 0.151$), which are more likely to resemble ET program types. This finding focuses on the potential role of EEHE programs in engendering outcomes that are related not only to mindsets and capabilities, but also to entrepreneurial status (e.g., enterprise start-up) as well as performance (e.g., enterprise survivability). A discussion of whether the included EEHE program evaluations support these findings follows.

Particular attention is paid to the two Tier 1 EEHE impact evaluations available—the STEP program in Uganda and the BPTC program in Tunisia. Both evaluations provide compelling results for the capacity of EEHE programs to foster positive effects in mindsets and capabilities, but produce mixed results around entrepreneurial status. The STEP program evaluation indicated that, thanks to an action-based training method implemented over a 12-month period, the program increased the likelihood of treated students starting a business, compared to the control group. In particular, the evaluation underlined the central importance of action-regulatory mechanisms in entrepreneurship and showed how action-oriented ET[1] provided the necessary skills and knowledge to start a business and pursue the career option of an entrepreneur.

The evaluation of the BPTC program examined participants' aspirations for the future, personality traits, and behavioral skills, all as related to entrepreneurship. The intervention produced strong impacts on participants' self-reported business skills and networking proxies. About 77 percent of program graduates reported knowing how to produce a business plan, compared to 45 percent in the control group. The intervention also led to changes in several domains of the "Big Five" socio-emotional skills, including a large decrease in agreeableness and a moderate increase in extraversion, when compared to a control group. There was, however, no evidence that the ET positively affected conscientiousness and emotional stability, while other entrepreneurial traits such as tenacity and power motivation remained unchanged.

The BPTC evaluation also examined effects through a number of entrepreneurial-status outcomes, like self-employment and wages. In contrast to the results on mindsets and capabilities, the intervention made it only slightly more probable that students would become self-employed than members of the control group. The evaluation indicated a small but positive increase in the probability of being self-employed for graduates of the entrepreneurship track after one year of graduation. There was, however, no evidence that the program significantly affected overall employment as captured by the likelihood of being employed in the last seven days. In fact, estimates were negative and pointed to a reduction in the probability of holding wage employment; and although this reduction was not significant, the decrease was of the same magnitude as the increase in self-employment, suggesting the possibility of a substitution effect from wage employment to self-employment.

The evaluations of the other EEHE programs also appear to reflect promising results in the mindsets and capabilities domains. For example, program evaluations for the CCOE program in China and the GE program in France focus on the entrepreneurial intentions of participants. To gauge these intentions, the CCOE evaluation examined a number of proxies, including business knowledge, abilities, and psychological qualities. It found a positive and significant correlation between (a) college carve-out education and business knowledge, entrepreneurial ability, and psychological quality; (b) business knowledge and intention; (c) entrepreneurial ability and intention; and (d) psychological quality and intention. The evaluation of the GE program indicated that the positive perception of entrepreneurship doubled from the first year to the second year of the program. However, the number of students that wanted to work in a small or medium enterprise (SME) dropped in the same period. Lastly, the evaluation of the Bødo program in Norway, which targets business students, found a positive correlation between education in entrepreneurship and entrepreneurial behavior, both for actual behavior and for behavioral intentions.

On the whole, the evaluations of EEHE programs provide less robust insight on which programs influence indicators in the entrepreneurial status and performance domains. Notable exceptions are the evaluations of the Bødo program in

Norway and the BEP program in the United States. The Bødo evaluation indicated that having a major in entrepreneurship was positively associated with new firm formation, thus finding a positive correlation between education in entrepreneurship and subsequent EB. Furthermore, the BEP evaluation described how participants were three times more likely to be involved in the creation of a new business venture than non-entrepreneurship-track business students. It also indicated that EEHE may benefit firms and individuals beyond the realm of self-employment and entrepreneurship in the traditional sense, suggesting that the program corresponded with higher salaries and asset growth for its graduates as compared with traditional business school graduates.

Lastly, the BEP evaluation was the only EEHE program to explicitly examine outcomes relevant to firm performance. Its findings suggest that existing companies that either hired or were owned by its entrepreneurship graduates demonstrated higher sales and growth in employment. The evaluation also claims BEP played a role in fostering innovations in existing businesses by enhancing the transfer of technology from the university to the private sector. It is important, however, to note the limitations of the BEP evaluation, as well as the applicability of its findings on the whole, given that the program targets a limited number of selected participants (about 80) per year, who through self-selection are highly motivated to work in entrepreneurship.

Program Characteristics

While the EEHE program design is influenced by the context in which these programs are delivered—within tertiary education institutions—the programs still exhibit heterogeneity. In some cases, they are implemented across a number of tertiary education institutions at a national level. Examples of this include the BPTC program, a new entrepreneurship curriculum being implemented by the Tunisian government, and the APSB program, which is an effort by the Nigerian government to introduce EE into tertiary institutions. By contrast, individual institutions are implementing a number of program initiatives and course offerings. In either case, the duration and intensity of programs appears to typically follow the norms of other higher education courses and programs of study (e.g., courses last several weeks or a full semester) and, importantly, programs are typically delivered by faculty members. Notable exceptions include the short-course (6–12 hours) GE program option, as well the STEP program, where students do not receive credit or grades for participation.

The literature suggests that entrepreneurship is a multidisciplinary field drawing upon a number of disciplines including psychology, economics, and business administration (Baron 2007). Across EEHE programs, other common areas of curricular focus are general business education, entrepreneurship awareness, marketing, and accounting. A number of the evaluated programs place emphasis on the knowledge and skills required to develop a business plan as well as contribute to the strategic development of an enterprise. To facilitate this learning, several EEHE programs use business plan competitions and enterprise simulations. Emblematic of this approach, the BPTC program allows students to substitute a thesis requirement by developing a business plan. Plan completion culminates in a competition, where the winner receives start-up capital. The BEP has a year-long focus on developing a new venture, which also culminates in a year-end competition. Further, STEP uses an action-oriented approach to shape positive outcomes—students form small teams and use US$100 in start-up capital to launch an actual business. This helps students apply lessons directly to facilitate learning.

Common EEHE wrap-around services include mentoring and coaching, typically from entrepreneurs, as is the case with the BEP and BPTC programs. These types of wrap-around services focus on exposing students to innovation-driven entrepreneurs, suggesting that several EEHE programs are looking to cultivate high-growth potential entrepreneurs and enterprises.

Even in the case of EEHE, the information on program costs is limited, with only three of the evaluated programs providing such data. Two of these programs are in the United States (BEP and MIT) and one in Norway (Bødo, BPTC). Tuition rates vary for the BEP program, depending on the track of the course taken and where the students are from (e.g., in-state tuition is cheaper than that charged to out-of-state students, so tuitions range from US$5,000 to US$15,825); while the university's cost to deliver the total program is approximately US$900,000 annually. Similarly, in the case of the MIT program, the cost is US$41,770 for a master's engineering student's annual tuition. By contrast, the Bødo program is offered at no cost to students, because public higher education in Norway is free. The wide range of costs reflects different program structures and content, as well as varying education policies among countries.

Moderating Factors

The profiles of EEHE students—and thus their general human capital assets—are similar across programs when compared to other EET program types, given that EEHE students are at the tertiary level. EEHE program evaluations nevertheless indicate that individual characteristics can have a moderating effect on program outcomes. For example, the CCOE program evaluation in China found that the role of a student's profile, such as his or her prior work experience, was a key moderating factor; while several programs (Bødø, BPTC) cited the role of students' predisposition and interest in entrepreneurship, which drew them to the program in the first place. The MIT evaluation indicated that the interest in entrepreneurship itself may be influenced by students' particular personality traits, indicating that students with a high risk-taking propensity and those with an internal locus of control were more likely to be interested in entrepreneurship.

Self-selection and selectivity are at the center of participant behavior dynamics for EEHE programs. The self-selection issue is this: it is possible that entrepreneurship programs' participants would have chosen to become entrepreneurs even if the programs did not exist. This dynamic would benefit the targeting of a program, but would negatively affect the program evaluation. For example, the BEP consists of students who are personally motivated to apply for the entrepreneurship major. Students also opt into the entrepreneurship track with the BPTC program. Additionally, selectivity is assumed to be a barrier to entry to these programs for some students. In the case of STEP, the program includes an application process (student must elect to apply), and if accepted, a student must pay a US$10 deposit (refunded at the end of the program), which further underscores the program's effort to select dedicated participants.

Evaluations of EEHE programs place little emphasis on contextual factors' moderating role. The main exceptions to this are (a) the GE program in France, which emphasizes the culture of French society itself and the GE culture of inhibiting students' desire to start or work for SMEs; and (b) programs implemented at multiple campuses, where evaluations recognize how differences among institutions and on-campus support for entrepreneurship promotion can all play a role in outcomes (BPTC, CCOE). Other notable exceptions include the evaluations of BEP, reflecting the strength of the U.S. economy and the entrepreneurial ecosystem in the 1990s, and of BPTC, which suggests that the Arab Spring and Tunisian revolution have helped foster a cultural excitement and interest in entrepreneurship. The STEP evaluation also cited the highly entrepreneurial Ugandan context as potentially playing an enabling role in students' decisions to become entrepreneurs.

Entrepreneurship Training—Potential Entrepreneurs (ETPo)

Snapshot

Of the 16 evaluations examining ETPo programs, 7 are classified as impact evaluations. ETPo evaluations tend to examine the impact of ET on specific, often vulnerable groups of participants, including women, unemployed youth, and welfare recipients. In targeting these groups, evaluations pay particular attention to the extent to which these programs are able to impact their economic well-being. This is measured not only by how many go on to launch an enterprise but—arguably of more importance for vulnerable groups—by the extent to which they are able to generate income. On both fronts, evaluations provide mixed evidence, but there are promising indications that training can contribute to growth in entrepreneurial activity (start-ups), income, and employability. However, they offer little evidence to prove the training's impact on new enterprises' longer-term viability or eventual growth or whether the income gains were sustained over time. Further, there is no evidence from the evaluations suggesting that training fostered the creation of high-revenue or high-employment enterprises.

Several notable ETPo programs were embedded within broader support programs that included wrap-around services, such as grants, conditional cash transfers, and follow-up sessions with trainers to provide further technical assistance in implementing new business practices. These ETPo programs appear comparatively "high-touch," offering a range of complementary services and focused attention from trainers. This may help to explain some of the more promising, immediate results. This also aligns with how these programs target vulnerable populations, people for whom short-term income and employment alternatives may be limited beyond the entrepreneurial paths that the ETPo programs themselves offer. Several evaluations also examined the effects on various socio-emotional skills and on participants' psychological and social well-being, such as participants' self-confidence and teamwork. In general, ETPo program evaluations tend to focus more than other types of EET do on improving the immediate well-being of vulnerable populations. This suggests that in these particular contexts, EET is viewed as a means to the end of immediate poverty alleviation, rather than as a means to the end of fostering entrepreneurs and entrepreneurship.

The Program Landscape

This study identified and examined a total of 16 ET programs targeted at potential entrepreneurs (listed in table 4.5). Of these 16 programs, impact evaluations were available for 7 that met the criteria for Tier 1 (impact evaluations with an experimental design), the evaluation of 1 additional program satisfied the criteria for Tier 2, and 8 program evaluations met the criteria for Tier 3 (see table 4.7 for a list of the programs as well as a summary of the key findings). In terms of geographic distribution, there were four programs delivered in Latin America, three in South Asia, four in the United States, three in Sub-Saharan Africa, one in Western Europe, and one in East Asia. The scope of ET programs targeted at potential entrepreneurs is large, with 10 of the

Table 4.5 Program List: Entrepreneurship Training—Potential Entrepreneurs (ETPo) | List of Evaluations

	Program name	Country	Evaluation
AAC	*Atención a Crisis*	Nicaragua	Tier 1
EPAG	Economic Empowerment of Adolescent Girls and Young Women	Liberia	Tier 1
GATE	Growing America Through Entrepreneurship Project	United States	Tier 1
JE	*Juventud y Empleo*	Dominican Republic	Tier 1
JEA	*Jóvenes en Acción*	Colombia	Tier 1
WINGS	Women's Income Generating Support Program	Uganda	Tier 1
YOP	Youth Opportunities Program	Uganda	Tier 1
MEP	*Micro-emprendimientos Productivos*	Argentina	Tier 2
ACTiVATE	Achieving the Commercialization of Technology in Ventures through Applied Training for Entrepreneurs	United States	Tier 3
BACIP	Building and Construction Improvement Program	Pakistan	Tier 3
DCEI	Dade County Entrepreneurial Institute	United States	Tier 3
ENBDP	Entrepreneurship and New Business Development Programme	Sweden	Tier 3
SEWA	SEWA Bank	India	Tier 3
SIYB	Start and Improve Your Business Program	Vietnam	Tier 3
WEMTOP	Women's Enterprise Management Training Outreach Program	India	Tier 3
WSBP+MBDP	Training Women for Success	United States	Tier 3

Figure 4.3 Entrepreneurship Training—Potential Entrepreneurs

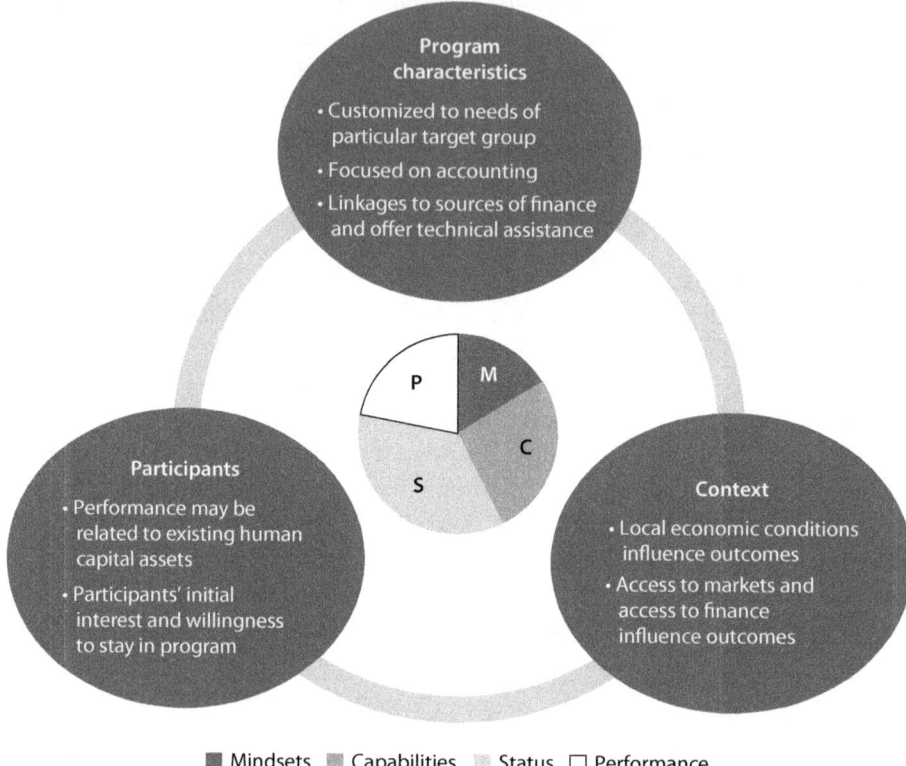

14 programs serving over 1,000 beneficiaries and several serving upwards of 10,000 beneficiaries.

In addition to the program evaluations, the analysis of ETPo programs is informed by insights from relevant literature, including available meta-analyses and systematic reviews. These include Martin, McNally, and Kay (2013); Cho and Honorati (2013), which includes 37 impact evaluations of entrepreneurship programs and 1,116 estimates for six different types of outcomes[2]; Glaub and Frese (2011), a critical review of 30 studies that evaluated 10 different entrepreneurship programs in developing countries; and McKenzie and Woodruff (2012), a critical review of business training program evaluations in developing countries.

Analyzing ETPo Programs

Outcome Domains

Evaluated ETPo program objectives include income diversification, economic assistance, and the reduction of unemployment. In line with these objectives, a number of the ETPo programs are designed to target vulnerable groups, including women, unemployed youth, and welfare recipients. The targeted outcomes of evaluated ETPo programs are primarily concentrated in the entrepreneurial status domain and, to a lesser extent, in the domains of entrepreneurial performance, capabilities, and mindsets. With regard to entrepreneurial status, several of the evaluations demonstrate mixed though sometimes promising results around the capacity of these programs to improve employment, income, and savings for beneficiaries.

An evaluation of the AAC program in Nicaragua, which provides beneficiaries with a cash transfer, training, and a productive investment grant, suggested that there were (significant) increases in self-employment, household consumption, and income two years after the end of the intervention. The evaluation of the GATE program in the United States, however, suggested that the effects on business ownership and employment were positive and significant in the short-run when compared to a control group, although they were mainly driven by a significant likelihood of business start-ups[3] rather than no effect on the likelihood of a business exiting.[4] Nevertheless, these positive effects vanished over the medium and long term. Additionally, the GATE evaluation did not find any evidence of training programs having effects on other business performance and labor market outcomes, such as household income and work satisfaction. Conversely, the evaluation of the EPAG program in Liberia evidenced gains in weekly income and savings among trainees compared to a control group. The evaluation of the WINGS program in Uganda, which targeted poor and capital- and credit-constrained women, also found significant impacts on income, consumption, and savings.

Evaluations of ETPo programs also examined impacts on earnings and employment beyond self-employment. For example, the evaluation of the JEA program in Colombia reported that the training moderately increased wage and salary earnings in the formal sector and had a small positive effect on the probability of having a formal sector job. Interestingly, the JEA program indicated that while training increased wage and salary earnings in the formal sector, the same effect was not realized in the informal sector. The evaluation of the MEP program in Argentina, which aimed to promote self-employment among welfare recipients, indicated that program participants substituted away from other jobs and realized no significant gains in short-run income. The JE program in the Dominican Republic evaluation also described disappointing results, finding no impact on the employment rate of participants.

In McKenzie and Woodruff's (2012) review of ET programs in developing countries (see box 4.2), the authors indicate that some of the stronger effects relate to helping potential owners launch new businesses more quickly. This study, however, finds that at least among the more rigorously evaluated ETPo programs, few evaluations look explicitly at rates of new business start-ups. Instead, as appears to have been the approach with the McKenzie and Woodruff review, proxies for business start-up, such as self-employment and increased business income, are more common in these evaluations. This could be because many of the more rigorously evaluated programs tend to target vulnerable groups and in turn place a focus on enhancing the individual's status in terms of income and

Box 4.2 What Are We Learning from Business Training and Entrepreneurship Evaluations around the Developing World?

A paper by McKenzie and Woodruff (2012) looks at what can be learned from evaluations of business training programs to draw out lessons for policy and the next generation of research. The authors review evaluations focusing on enterprise management for practitioner entrepreneurs. They review 20 studies that include randomized experiments, regression discontinuity designs, and experiments on individualized consulting services. The results evidenced considerable heterogeneity across interventions in terms of content and participants, which made it difficult to compare the impact measures from different evaluations. Also, evaluations suffered from low statistical power, short time horizons, and attrition, which limited their internal and external validity.

The paper suggests that evaluations of business training found stronger evidence of helping potential owners to launch new business more quickly, and that practitioners tended to put in practice what they learned in training. The paper presents several recommendations for future work. These deal with: (a) increasing the size and homogeneity of firms in both treatment and control groups, (b) seeking better outcome measurements that overcome problems with the profit-and-revenue challenges encountered in many evaluations, as well as the limited time horizon, (c) evaluation designs that take into account spillover effects, (d) testing of different types of interventions, and (e) understanding market failures and building relevant solutions.

Source: McKenzie and Woodruff 2012.

---

employment, as opposed to enterprise creation. It could also be an issue of defining what constitutes a formal enterprise or an entrepreneur versus the self-employed.

In comparison to the findings on the status outcomes domain, findings across other ETPo domains are comparatively weak and sparse. In firm performance, the WINGS program evaluation recorded an increase in imports from major trading centers, and the ACTiVATE program reported positive job creation results (Tier 3 evaluation). The most promising firm performance result was enhancing business practices, with several program evaluations indicating improved record keeping (SIYB), formal registration (YOP), access to new loans (SEWA), and a more strategic orientation of the business (ENBDP). Nonetheless, there is no evidence from the evaluated programs that training fostered the creation of high-revenue or high-employment firms in the long run.

In terms of the capability outcomes domain, several ETPo program evaluations described gains in general business knowledge and skills, as well as in business plan development, enhanced understanding of the market and marketing (SIYB, WSBP), and enhanced vocational skills (BACIP). The YOP program evaluation found that after four years, members of the treatment group were 65 percent more likely to practice a skilled trade. Lastly, program evaluations also gave attention to the effects on various socio-emotional skills and entrepreneurial awareness. Several program evaluation cited increases in participants' self-confidence and teamwork (WEMTOP, WSBP). Of interest, the WINGS program evaluation examined a range of social indicators and registered mixed results; for example, finding little effect on the psychological and social well-being of participants. The YOP program evaluation found weak evidence of a social impact two years following the training. The focus on such indicators also suggests that many ETPo program evaluations cover interventions aimed at improving the immediate, material well-being of vulnerable populations.

Program Characteristics

The characteristics of ETPo programs reflect the diversity of individuals these programs target and outcomes they pursue. Many of these programs are designed to meet the specific needs of particular vulnerable groups in specific contexts. In some cases, the training is embedded within a broader support program that may include a number of services in addition to training. These include grants, conditional cash transfers, and intensive follow-ups. For example, the safety net program AAC in Nicaragua was a one-year pilot program designed to support agricultural households in mitigating the risks associated with climate change. The program included cash transfers and either a vocational training scholarship or a productive investment grant. However, AAC offered little information on the characteristics of the training program itself (other than that it offered a training scholarship).

The WINGS program in Uganda, an experiment in which vulnerable women in a conflict-prone region participated in a five-day training and then received a start-up grant and regular follow-up visits from trained community workers, has a comprehensive evaluation. EPAG in Liberia targets young women and is training focused, with six months of classroom-based training on entrepreneurship, job, and life skills, followed by six months of job placement and support. Finally, the BACIP program in Pakistan targets unemployed young adults, integrating ET with specific vocational skills training in the housing or sales sectors. Despite the heterogeneity of these programs, they are relatively expansive in scale, covering between 500 and 1,500 participants, often across a number of communities. They can be time-limited, however, closing after a few years.

Not all ETPo programs are time-limited, one-off projects. Some that frequently serve at-risk populations are ongoing. These tend to be stand-alone training programs, serving comparatively smaller numbers of beneficiaries. Two examples in the United States are ACTiVATE, a year-long program meeting once a week in cohorts of 30 aspiring women entrepreneurs that is delivered within a local higher education institution, and the DCEI program in the United States, consisting of three five-week courses implemented by local higher education institutions and targeted at minority communities. The ENBDP program in Sweden and the WSBP/MBDP program in the United States also serve as examples of smaller-scale, ongoing, stand-alone programs, both of which operate in a business-incubator model of workspace and technical assistance. Interestingly, although these four programs are more focused on training than the larger scale, more comprehensive programs described above, the available evaluations of them are less rigorous.

Additionally, several ETPo programs appear to represent targeted initiatives to expand specific populations' access to formal technical training (in partnership with public and private providers) to promote entrepreneurship. In the SIYB program in Vietnam, the ILO's *Start and Improve Your Business* curriculum was implemented in partnership with the General Department of Vocational Training to deliver training to one million farmers across Vietnam over seven years. Three additional programs have relationships with training institutions in Latin America. Examples include the JEA program in Colombia, which targets young people from low socioeconomic backgrounds in large cities across the country with training institutions offering classroom trainings and internships; the JE program in the Dominican Republic, which targets young people from disadvantaged backgrounds without a secondary education, contracting with local training institutions; and the MEP program, which serves welfare recipients in Argentina, relying on local universities, technical institutions, and NGOs to deliver technical assistance.

Across this varied field of ETPo programs, the content ranges from business knowledge to entrepreneurial skills to financial literacy and accounting to marketing, sales, general management skills to vocational and life skills. Most ETPo programs appear to include some wrap-around services. According to available ETPo evaluations, the training components that combine grants with activities such as internships and mentoring services have higher impacts than simple training programs. In particular, the ETPo evaluations show that grants are a key component of some of these programs (e.g., AAC and WINGS).

ETPo programs have more cost data available compared to other program types. Out of the 16 programs, 10 programs present some data on their costs (see table 4.6). The available costs, however, are heterogeneous and not comparable, for three reasons: (a) they reflect the heterogeneity of content that the programs provide, with training of different lengths and varying wrap-around services; (b) they refer to different years and countries; and (c) in some cases they reflect the costs of the overall program, while in others they reflect the costs of only some activities.

Additionally, five financial analyses were conducted as part of the evaluations to assess the programs' sustainability. The cost-benefit analyses for the JEA and JE programs indicate that the net benefits more than justified the programs' existence and possibly their expansion. For the EPAG program, the results had a relatively high per-participant cost, but despite the high initial investment, the expected returns of one of the trainings offered (the business skills training) were compelling. It will likely take two years for business skill training participants to increase their earnings in an amount equal to the original investment; while participants in the other training (the job skills training) will take as long as eight years. Conversely, in the case of the WINGS program in Uganda the impacts of

Table 4.6 Available Information on Costs | ETPo Programs

Program name	Country/region	Costs of implementation	Cost recovery
AAC	*Atención a Crisis*	Nicaragua	All beneficiaries received a basic transfer of US$145. Participants with children received an additional US$90 per household and US$25 per child. One-third of the beneficiaries also received a scholarship to attend a vocational training course. Another one-third of the beneficiaries also received a US$200 grant each for productive investments.	—
ACTiVATE	Achieving the Commercialization of Technology in Ventures through Applied Training for Entrepreneurs	United States	The annual cost to run the program is estimated at US$200,000, or about US$8,000 per participant.	Tuition is estimated at US$3,000 (as of 2010).
DCEI	Dade County Entrepreneurial Institute	United States	—	—
ENBDP	Entrepreneurship and New Business Development Program	Sweden	The cost to run the program for 10–12 participants was US$66 (but does not include the costs of running the incubator or conducting seed capital activities).	—
EPAG	Economic Empowerment of Adolescent Girls and Young Women	Liberia	A total of US$1,221 per student was allocated for business skills training and US$1,678 per student for job skills training.	—
GATE	Growing America Through Entrepreneurship Project	United States	Course costs fluctuated between US$850 and US$1,300 per participant.	—
JEA	*Jóvenes en Acción*	Colombia	Cost was about US$750 per participant.	—
WEMTOP	Women's Enterprise Management Training Outreach Program	India	Initially the cost per enterprise support team was US$1,485 and over time, the cost was reduced to US$341.	—
WINGS	Women's Income Generating Support Program	Uganda	About US$922 per person	—
WSBP+MBDP	Training Women for Success	United States	—	Tuition is estimated at US$2,500

Note: — = not available.

the intervention struggled to pass the cost-benefit analysis. Finally, in the case of the MEP program in Argentina, the evaluation indicated that the program did not reach average significant income gains in the short-run, so the program is not cost-effective in the short-run.

Moderating Factors
ETPo programs have fewer moderating factors. The majority of these programs make note of participants' characteristics upon entry, including their gender, educational background, and previous exposure to self-employment. With regard to contextual moderating factors, the program outcomes are cited as being

Table 4.7 Entrepreneurship Training—Potential Entrepreneurs (ETPo) | Key Information

Program name	Program beneficiaries	Evaluation	Sample	Outcomes measured	Key findings
AAC | Atención a Crisis | Nicaragua Source: Macours, Premand, and Vakis 2012	Agricultural households that faced increased exposure to weather shocks linked to changes in rainfall and temperature patterns. The program was targeted primarily toward women.	Tier 1 | Randomized control trial	The sample included 3,002 eligible households in the treatment communities (56) and a random sample of 1,019 eligible households in the control communities (50). Eligible households were assigned to one of three packages: (a) the basic conditional cash transfer (CCT) (US$145 plus US$90 per household for households that had children ages 7–15 attending primary school plus an additional US$25 per child); (b) the basic conditional cash transfer plus a scholarship for a vocational training (training focused on diversification outside subsistence farming and labor market and business skills training workshops); and (c) the basic CCT plus the productive investment grant (US$200 to encourage starting nonagricultural activities)	Consumption, income, and income diversification; participation and returns in nonagricultural activities.	• Two years after the end of the intervention, both the productive investment grant and the training helped to protect against the negative impact of shocks and reduce the variability of consumption and income, while the basic CCT package did not offer protection against the negative effect of shocks; • The productive investment grant and training showed positive and significant results in increasing consumption (12 percent and 9 percent, respectively) as shock intensity increased by one standard deviation (s.d.). The effect on consumption of only the training package showed a strong positive and significant impact. Conversely, there was no significant impact found on consumption for only the vocational training package; • In terms of household participation and returns to nonagricultural activities, results showed that the households that received the productive investment grant package were 13 percentage points more likely to engage in nonagricultural self-employment, although no significant impact was found on nonagricultural wage employment. The magnitude of the impact on returns is large, amounting to a 15–20 percent annual return on the initial investment of US$200. For households that received the training package the increases shown were not significant.

table continues next page

Table 4.7 Entrepreneurship Training—Potential Entrepreneurs (ETPo) | Key Information *(continued)*

Program name	Program beneficiaries	Evaluation	Sample	Outcomes measured	Key findings
EPAG	Economic Empowerment of Adolescent Girls and Young Women	Liberia *Source:* World Bank 2012.	About 2,500 beneficiaries in nine communities in Monrovia and Kakata City	Tier 1	Randomized pipeline research design	Approximately 2,500 young women were accepted to participate in the program. The evaluation randomized participants into two types of treatment groups: (a) training package on business development and life skills; and (b) training package on job, entrepreneurship, and life skills. There was also a control group. Impact was defined as the change in outcomes between the time the program started and six months after the classroom training ended, as compared to a statistically similar control group (the second-round trainees).	Employment, behaviors, empowerment and agency, and family welfare.	• The program was well received—the retention rate was 95 percent and attendance averaged 90 percent; • The program increased employment among trainees by 50 percent compared to those in the control group; • Positive employment outcomes were driven primarily by the business development skills trainees, whose monthly income increased by US$75 per month; • The program increased girls' savings compared to the control group. At midline, the treatment group had a total of US$44 more in savings compared to the control group; and • There were no significant changes to borrowing or lending among beneficiaries.

table continues next page

Table 4.7 Entrepreneurship Training—Potential Entrepreneurs (ETPo) | Key Information *(continued)*

Program name	Program beneficiaries	Evaluation	Sample	Outcomes measured	Key findings
GATE | Growing America Through Entrepreneurship Project | United States	Potential entrepreneurs within seven sites in three states.	Tier 1 | Randomized control trial	The sample consisted of 4,197 individuals seeking training, who had to attend an orientation meeting that made them eligible. They all had to fill a baseline application form. The applications were reviewed and randomly assigned (2,094 to treatment and 2,103 to control). Attrition was not large, but it was larger for the control group than for the treatment.	The outcomes measured were related to business ownership, business performance and size, and labor market (employment, household income, and work satisfaction). Additionally, the measurement looked at heterogeneous treatment effects over various rationales for providing training subsidies (credit constraints, human and managerial capital constraints, labor market discrimination, and unemployment insurance frictions).	• Training significantly increased short-run business ownership and employment, but these effects vanished over the long term.
JE | *Juventud y Empleo* | Dominican Republic Source: Ibarraran, Rosas, and Soares 2006	Young people between ages 16 and 29 from disadvantaged backgrounds who did not have secondary education.	Tier 1 | Experimental design	The sample had 786 individuals in the treatment group and 563 in the control group. About 93 percent of the individuals who started the training completed it, and of those, 84 percent started an internship. Baseline data was collected in May–July 2005 and a follow-up interview was carried out, on average about 13 months after the completion of the program.	Employment search time, unemployment, employability, income, and duration of employment	• There was no impact found on the employment rate of participants. Employment rate postintervention was 57 percent for the treatment group and 56 percent for the controls; • Although there were caveats in the estimation, the treatment group had higher monthly labor earnings—about 17 percent higher than the control group (about 10 percent on average). The earnings effects were larger for the youngest age group, for residents of Santo Domingo, and for those with some secondary education; • There were no large or systematic effects on hours worked per week in the overall sample or by subgroups; and • There was no evidence of a large or systematic quality effect in terms of training institutions.

table continues next page

Table 4.7 Entrepreneurship Training—Potential Entrepreneurs (ETPo) | Key Information *(continued)*

Program name	Program beneficiaries	Evaluation	Sample	Outcomes measured	Key findings
JEA | *Jóvenes en Acción* | Colombia Source: Attanasio, Kugler, and Meghir 2009	Young people between the ages of 18 and 25 in the two lowest socioeconomic strata of the population, living in the seven largest cities (Barranquilla, Bogota, Bucaramanga, Cali, Cartagena, Manizales, and Medellin) were eligible for the program	Tier 1 | Randomized control trial	The total sample consisted of 3,300 individuals broken down into a treatment group (1,650) and a control group (1,650). Anticipating a level of attrition of 24 percent for program participants and 40 percent for non-program participants, the samples were increased to 2,040 for the treatment and 2,310 for the control group. Baseline data was collected in 2005 and a follow-up individual interview was carried out between August and October 2006. Telephone updates were done four months after the completion of the program and the individual interviews were carried out between 9 and 11 months after the telephone update.	Employment, earning effects, formal sector employment	• Individuals who were offered the training did better in the labor market. Compared to those not offered training, they were more likely to be employed, showed a 6.8 percent increase in paid employment, and had about 12 percent higher wage and salary earnings. • Women offered training were more likely to have paid employment and to be employed in the formal sector and earn higher overall and formal wages (results for men were estimated imprecisely); • Training increased the probability of having a formal sector job by 0.053 and a written contract by 0.066; • Training increased wage and salary earnings in the formal sector but not in the informal sector; • A cost-benefit analysis using an average monthly increase in earnings of 25,500 Colombian pesos for men and 30,000 Colombian pesos for women and a discount rate of 5 percent over a 40 year period yielded a net gain of US$2,344 for men and US$2,749 for women. Using a 5 percent discount rate and depreciation in earnings of 10 percent annually, the results were still positive for men US$906 and women US$1,066.

table continues next page

Table 4.7 Entrepreneurship Training—Potential Entrepreneurs (ETPo) | Key Information *(continued)*

Program name	Program beneficiaries	Evaluation	Sample	Outcomes measured	Key findings
WINGS | Women's Income Generating Support Program | Uganda Source: Blattman et al. 2013	1,800 beneficiaries (86 percent poor women) in 120 villages across two districts in Northern Uganda	Tier 1 | Randomized control experiment with mixed-methods data collection	The sample consisted of 1,800 (mostly) poor women ages 14–30 from 120 villages (15 beneficiaries per village). The evaluation built a waitlist control group, whereby 900 of the beneficiaries were randomized in the program in phase 1 (mid 2009) and another 900 in phase 2 (early 2011). For phase 1, the program evaluation placed the randomized participants into three groups: one received the WINGS program, another group received the core package plus the cross-cutting design package (support for business networks), and the last group acted as the waitlisted control group.	Earnings, earning opportunities, distribution of poverty impacts, savings, characteristics of individual success, health (sick days, hunger, health status, index of depression and anxiety), empowerment (indexes of economic decision making, gender attitudes, interpersonal violence, independence household support), and social capital (groups and networks, trust, social cohesion, collective action)	• A year after the intervention, monthly cash earnings doubled from 16,500 to 31,300 Uganda Shillings 31,300 (US$ 6.60–12.52), cash savings tripled, and short-term expenditure on goods and services, and durable assets increased 30–50 percent relative to the control group (the average treatment effect is 16,200 Uganda shillings per month and the median treatment effect is 9,700 Uganda shillings per month); • The treatment had the greatest impact on the people with the lowest initial levels of capital and access to credit; • Among those who responded to treatment with more economic success (rather than average levels of economic success), the study found that women had lower success and individuals with higher levels of access to credit at baseline saw fewer gains; • There was no large positive effect of skills/ education, patience, or good health on response to treatment; • There were few health and social effects (positive or negative) of the intervention on beneficiaries; • There was little effect on psychological or social well-being from the observed reduction in poverty; • There was no effect found on women's independence, status in the community, or freedom from intimate-partner violence;

table continues next page

Table 4.7 Entrepreneurship Training—Potential Entrepreneurs (ETPo) | Key Information *(continued)*

Program name	Program beneficiaries	Evaluation	Sample	Outcomes measured	Key findings
					• Involving male partners and training the couples brought more positive results on the couples' interactions and on women's physical and mental health, but not on women's empowerment;
					• There were large spillovers in the small village economies, including more women becoming traders, an increase in imports from major trading centers, and a fall in the consumer price index;
					• Close supervision and advising by the NGO led to slight increases in economic success;
					• The rate of return calculated for the WINGS full package plus administration (using an increase in income of 6,200 Uganda shillings per month for 15 years) was −33 percent when applying a discount rate of 15 percent for 15 years, +36 percent when applying a 3 percent discount rate for 15 years. Although the return of the intervention using the average income effect was positive at a lower discount rate, it was not possible to determine whether the inputs that went into the program were the most appropriate or optimal combination, versus their individual contribution to the outcome.

table continues next page

Table 4.7 Entrepreneurship Training—Potential Entrepreneurs (ETPo) | Key Information *(continued)*

Program name	Program beneficiaries	Evaluation	Sample	Outcomes measured	Key findings
YOP	Youth Opportunities Program	Uganda *Source:* Blattman, Fiala, and Martinez, Forthcoming	Poor and underemployed youth ages 16–35 in Uganda's north	Tier 1	Randomized control trial	From the pool of 535 groups, 265 were randomly assigned to the intervention (treatment) and the remaining 279 to the control. The treatment and control youth were surveyed three times—at baseline and two and four years post-intervention	Investment, occupational choice/levels, social issues and income	• The treatment group invested most of the grant in skills and business assets, and after four years, they were 65 percent more likely to practice the skilled trade; • Earnings were 49 percent greater than the control group and 41 percent greater after four years; • The treatment group was more likely to engage in business practices such as keeping records, registering, and paying taxes; • There was a shift in occupational choice toward skilled work, where the treatment group was around 38 percent higher than the control, and it was larger for women; • Labor supply increased in response to the increase in capital for both men and women; • Earnings were larger for the treatment group and for both genders, but there was a catch-up by the control group after four years, primarily among men; • The wealth index was 0.2 standard deviation greater for the treated than for the control; and • There was limited and weak evidence of a positive social impact after two years and none after four.

table continues next page

Table 4.7 Entrepreneurship Training—Potential Entrepreneurs (ETPo) | Key Information *(continued)*

Program name	Program beneficiaries	Evaluation	Sample	Outcomes measured	Key findings
MEP	*Micro-emprendimientos Productivos*	Argentina *Source:* Almeida and Galasso 2007	All beneficiaries of *Jefes*, a large-scale workfare program in Argentina	Tier 2	Quasi-experimental design	The sample covered 553 beneficiaries of whom 309 were program participants (301 households and a total of 1,340 individuals) and 244 non-participants (244 households and a total of 1,116 individuals). The attrition rate was 14 percent, and the final sample was 476 beneficiaries, of whom 279 were program participants and 197 were non-participants	Labor participation, hours of work, individual and household income	• Program participants substituted away from other jobs and significantly increased their total weekly hours worked; however, this did not happen for other household members; • There was no evidence of a significant increase in individual income or total household income; • Effects were differentiated across gender, where women were more likely to combine self-employment with other jobs; and • Income effects were targeted to a subset of younger and more educated beneficiaries, and for those for whom the self-employment was related to an ongoing activity.

influenced by factors relating to local economic conditions and infrastructure, including access to finance and access to markets.

Looking across ETPo program evaluations, however, participant characteristics do at times appear to moderate outcomes. For example, the evaluation of the JEA program demonstrated heterogeneity in impacts, with male teens in particular being the group that most benefited from the program. The WINGS evaluation indicated that the training had the greatest impact on the people with the lowest initial levels of capital and access to credit. The JE program evaluation (the Dominican Republic) found that earning effects were larger for the youngest age group, for residents of Santo Domingo, and for those with some secondary education. The evaluation for the MEP program in Argentina, which overall did not demonstrate significant positive results in regard to income, described how subsets of participants did have evident gains—in particular, younger and more educated participants and those with self-employment experience saw improvements in income. Finally, the GATE program examined different rationales on the provision of training subsidies. The evidence suggested no lasting effect on the provision of training in terms of credit constraints, human and managerial constraints, and labor market discrimination. However, there was a positive and significant effect on business ownership for the unemployed, but this effect was only short term.

McKenzie and Woodruff (2012) discuss the issue of program uptake by the participants in ET programs, raising a set of issues particularly pertinent to the larger scale, comprehensive ETPo programs described earlier in this section. The authors describe how often, despite training being offered for free, uptake was rarely close to universal. Across the studies they examined, they estimate the average uptake rate to have been 65 percent. In light of these challenges, programs may offer incentives for uptake as well as completion. For example, the EPAG program offered a small stipend and a bonus for completion. While not necessarily a function of these incentives, EPAG's retention rate was 95 percent and attendance averaged 90 percent over the course of the program. The JE program experienced similar promising results—with approximately 93 percent of the individuals who started the training completing it. That said, the evaluation of the JE program's outcomes was less promising, indicating that uptake and completion were unlikely to be deterministic unto themselves.

Entrepreneurship Training—Practicing Entrepreneurs (ETPr)

Snapshot
The most robust body of evidence within this study examines programs targeting practicing entrepreneurs, including 11 impact evaluations with an experimental design and four meta-analyses. Evaluations looking at ETPr programs are additionally set apart by being best positioned to provide the most direct insight on how training can impact the performance of an enterprise—specifically how training

programs can help an enterprise survive and grow. Despite a comparatively larger body of available evidence, results across ETPr evaluations are mixed about the effect of training on firm performance, whether that is measured by firm expansion, profits, or survivability. ETPr evaluation findings are more supportive of the capacity of these programs to enhance participants' business knowledge and skills as well as the practices entrepreneurs implement in their businesses.

While the evaluations do not draw a conclusive line connecting enhanced knowledge, skills, and practices (on the one hand) and the overall performance of an enterprise (on the other), two meta-analyses profiled in this study that do address this issue demonstrate promising linkages. Thus, while the results of the ETPr evaluations indicate that training by itself is unlikely to sufficiently transform an enterprise in the short run to be captured by these evaluations, training programs do appear to have the potential to strengthen existing entrepreneurs' knowledge, skills, and business practices, which may accrue benefits to entrepreneurs and their enterprises over time. Additionally, the evaluations do find notable, positive, and significant impacts on enhancing entrepreneurs' access to loans, although this may say more about who often sponsors this type of training—commercial banks and micro-finance institutions, for example—than it says about the quality and content of the training itself. Given the population these programs are targeting, their value depends on how useful they are to the individual entrepreneur who is investing precious time and resources to participate.

The Program Landscape

This study identified and examined a total of 25 ET programs targeted at practicing entrepreneurs. Of these programs (see table 4.8), 11 impact evaluations met the Tier 1 criteria (impact evaluations with an experimental design), while an additional 4 evaluations satisfied the Tier 2 criteria, and 10 met the Tier 3 criteria (see table 4.10 for a list of these programs as well as a summary of the key findings). Geographically, two regions are dominant: nearly half of these programs (11 of them) are delivered in Sub-Saharan Africa and an additional 7 are in Latin America. Their scope varies considerably, ranging from a program in South Africa targeting an exclusive group of four to six high-growth-potential entrepreneurs a year, to a program in Kenya training 35,000 SME proprietors in the informal sector over the course of eight years. In the ETPr category, several programs are directly linked to or targeted at existing clients of microfinance or commercial financial institutions. Finally, it should be noted that three of these programs target practicing entrepreneurs along with potential entrepreneurs.

In addition to the program evaluations, the ETPr program analysis is informed by insights from relevant literature, including available meta-analyses and systematic review. These include Martin, McNally, and Kay (2013); Cho and Honorati (2013), which includes 37 impact evaluations of entrepreneurship programs and 1,116 estimates for six different types of outcomes[5]; Glaub and Frese (2011), a critical review of 30 studies that evaluated

Table 4.8 Entrepreneurship Training—Practicing Entrepreneurs (ETPr)

	Program name	Country	Evaluation
Tier 1 Programs			
EDC	Entrepreneurship Development Centre	Bosnia and Herzegovina	Tier 1
FINCA	Foundation for International Community Assistance Entrepreneurship Program	Peru	Tier 1
GNAG	Ghana National Association of Garages	Ghana	Tier 1
MiDA-FBO	Millennium Development Authority—Farm-Based Organization	Ghana	Tier 1
NRSP	National Rural Support Program	Pakistan	Tier 1
PBS	Production and Business Services	El Salvador	Tier 1
PRIDE	PRIDE Microfinance	Tanzania	Tier 1
ROT	Rules of Thumb	Dominican Republic	Tier 1
SIYB-SL	Start and Improve Your Business (ILO)	Sri Lanka	Tier 1
ULTP	Urban Land Titling Program	Peru	Tier 1
WEP	Women Entrepreneurship Program	South Africa	Tier 1
Tier 2 Programs			
DDFET	Dutch Dairy Farming Entrepreneurship Training	Netherlands	Tier 2
END	Endeavor	South Africa	Tier 2
FTDAP	Farmer Training and Development Assistance Program	Honduras	Tier 2
TECH	TechnoServe	Central America	Tier 2
Tier 3 Programs			
10KW	10,000 Women India		Tier 3
CEM	Certificate in Entrepreneurial Management	Nigeria	Tier 3
CREA	*Capitación y Reclutamiento Empresarial Americana*	Mexico	Tier 3
DFCU	Development Finance Company of Uganda	Uganda	Tier 3
ELP	Executive Leadership Program	Northern Ireland	Tier 3
GOWE	Growth-Oriented Women Entrepreneurs	Kenya	Tier 3
INT	Interise	United States	Tier 3
MSETTP	Micro and Small Enterprise Training and Technology Project	Kenya	Tier 3
PAVCOPA	Agricultural Trading and Processing Promotion Pilot Project	Mali	Tier 3
WETVBI	Women's Virtual Business Incubator	Tanzania	Tier 3

10 different entrepreneurship programs in developing countries; Unger *et al.* (2011) a meta-analysis of the effects of human capital on entrepreneurial success covering 70 studies from an overall sample size of 24,733; and McKenzie and Woodruff (2012), a critical review of evaluations of business training programs in developing countries.

Figure 4.4 Entrepreneurship Training—Practicing Entrepreneurs

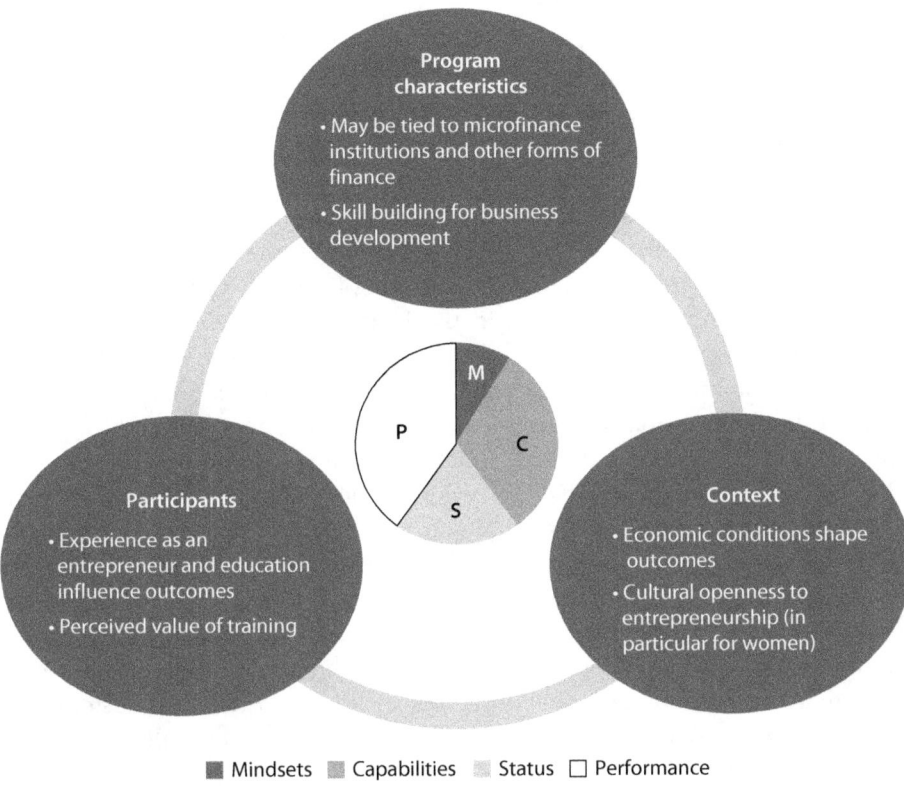

Analyzing ETPr Programs

Outcome Domains

The most common stated objectives of ETPr programs relate to the firm performance outcome domain, which corresponds to the immediate needs of the target audience, practicing entrepreneurs. Common targeted performance objectives include increases in profits, employees, and productivity; business expansion in markets, financing, and investment; and the implementation of better business practices and innovations. Despite being the most targeted program objective, ETPr program evaluations indicated mixed results around firm performance.

In terms of firm profits or revenues, evaluations found limited effects. For example, the evaluation of the FINCA program in Peru did not demonstrate higher profits or revenues; however, difference-in-difference specifications did find a positive but small impact on enterprise revenues. The FINCA program also led to a 4 percentage point increase in the client retention rate, which corresponded with increased net revenue for FINCA trainees' firms. The more promising results on this indicator were from the ROT program in the Dominican Republic, where a subset of beneficiary entrepreneurs treated with "rules-of-thumb" training registered a substantial increase in revenues (US$31) during bad weeks, at a significant level of 5 percent, and an increase in savings of about

6 percent. The END (Endeavor) program in South Africa also indicated positive effects on the sales growth of the beneficiary firms; however, the highly selective program included a sample size of only 19 treated and 33 control, non-selected applicants (who received no training at all).

Among program evaluations indicating improvement in sales, enterprise growth shows mixed results. For example, the SIYB-SL (Sri Lanka) program evaluation indicated that trainees' enterprises were more profitable. However, training alone did not necessarily lead the businesses to grow. Additionally, the ULTP program in Peru did not find statistically significant effects on sales increases or employment gains. More promising firm growth findings emerged from the INT program evaluation in the United States, which demonstrated gains in firm revenue as well as full-time employment, and from the TECH program, also in the United States, whose evaluation suggested that the intervention led to an expansion of the businesses in the treatment group through job creation, and increases in wage and benefits as well as revenue.

Echoing these mixed results, the review of business training programs conducted by McKenzie and Woodruff (2012) indicates that few studies found significant impacts on profits or sales, although they did find modest effects on practicing entrepreneurs' decision to implement better business practices. It was also on this front that the landscape of ETPr program evaluations found the most promising effects. The ROT program evaluation suggested a small but significant increase in the likelihood of individuals reporting the separation of business and personal cash accounts, keeping accounting records, and formally calculating revenues. The NRSP program in Pakistan also indicated improvements in business practices, including recording sales on paper and separating household and business accounts. The SIYB-SL training led to improvements as well, albeit small in magnitude, in improved business practices for existing firms, and the ULTP program in Peru showed moderately sized and statistically significant positive average effects on improved business practices.

In a few cases, however, better business practices did appear to lead to more profitable enterprises in the long run. The FINCA program showed positive changes in keeping records and the use of profits for business growth; however, no effect was found on profits and revenues. The evaluation of the EDC program in Bosnia and Herzegovina demonstrated significant improvements in business practices and investments, but results were not statistically significant for broader business performance indicators. The Cho and Honorati (2013) meta-analysis produces similar findings, demonstrating that improved business practices within an enterprise do not necessarily coincide with improved business performance (business income).

With regard to lending, the microfinance institution program evaluations, such as FINCA and EDC, did not report significant changes on beneficiaries' loan sizes. The evaluation of the MiDA-FBO program in Ghana did demonstrate an increase in participants' use of formal sources for loans. Moreover, there was a significant impact on loan restructuring and a significant increase in client retention rate, generating a portfolio of better quality and increased net revenues for the financial institution. Similar results were found for the NRSP program in Pakistan, where the opportunity to access larger loans had little effect on the beneficiary entrepreneurs.

ETPr programs target entrepreneurial status as a common outcome domain, reflected in training programs that aim to help existing enterprises survive as well as enhance the personal income and savings of training participants. A handful of program evaluations noted mixed results around entrepreneurial status. For example, the evaluation for the GNAG program in Ghana found that to raise the probability of enterprise survival by 8 or 9 percentage points, while the evaluation of the EDC program in Bosnia and Herzegovina found that it did not appear to influence business survival. These mixed findings align with McKenzie and Woodruff (2012), who find only relatively modest impacts of training on survivorship among existing firms. The results are more promising in connection with personal household savings. The evaluation of the ROT program in the Dominican Republic found economically large increases in savings, and the evaluation of the ULTP program in Peru detailed increased participation in savings for both family and personal purposes.

In the capabilities domain, some of the rigorously evaluated ETPr programs indicate positive outcomes. These programs include PRIDE in Tanzania, a program targeting small-scale microcredit entrepreneurs, whose evaluation found gains in business knowledge as measured by multiple-choice tests given to participants; and the WEP program in South Africa, which demonstrated statistically significant gains across several skill areas, including business knowledge and business skills. The evaluation of the NRSP program in Pakistan described gains in business knowledge, and the EDC program evaluation indicated positive gains in both business and financial knowledge at the time of follow-up to the training, although the treatment effect was not statistically significant.

Several meta-analyses give more weight to the promise of ETPr programs to enhance trainees' entrepreneurial capabilities (knowledge and skills) by shedding light on how these capabilities may ultimately contribute to better entrepreneurial performance. A meta-analysis by Unger *et al.* (2011) (see box 4.3) estimates the effects of human capital on entrepreneurial success, demonstrating a significant but small relationship between human capital and success ($r_c = 0.098$). The relationship is stronger for outcomes of human capital investments (knowledge and skills) than for capital investments (such as education and experience) and stronger for human capital related to entrepreneurial tasks than for human capital that is not related to entrepreneurial tasks. Martin, McNally, and Kay (2013) find a significant relationship between EET and entrepreneurship-related human capital assets ($r_c = 0.217$) and entrepreneurship outcomes ($r_c = 0.159$). Both meta-analyses cite methodological issues, however, and a third meta-analysis by Cho and Honorati (2013) indicates that while programs can improve knowledge, this does not necessarily lead to related gains in performance and status outcomes.

Lastly, a handful of ETPr evaluations indicated an interest in strengthening the entrepreneurial mindsets of practicing entrepreneurs, in particular, focusing on

Box 4.3 Human Capital and Entrepreneurial Success

A paper by Unger *et al.* (2011) reviews the literature and estimates the magnitude of the relationship between human capital and entrepreneurial success. The paper aims to test whether different conceptualizations of human capital relate to business success, and proposes that human capital is most important for success if it is based on current task-related knowledge. The analysis is based on 70 studies that defined entrepreneurship as business ownership and active management, and that reported a correlation between an indicator of human capital and entrepreneurial success or statistics to estimate it. The evidence suggested an overall positive relationship between human capital and entrepreneurial success ($r_c = 0.098$). Furthermore, there was evidence of moderating variables, such as task-relatedness, country contexts, age of business, and success measurements, suggesting that the relationship is more closely correlated with the outcomes of human capital investments than with human capital investments themselves.

Source: Unger et al. 2011.

---

self-confidence (10KW, WEP) as well as broader life skills. Program evaluations' measurements of these mindset outcomes, however, were relatively sparse. The notable exception to this is the WEP program in South Africa, which demonstrated statistically significant gains in the entrepreneurial characteristics and entrepreneurial orientation of participants, including confidence building and the enhanced use of role models. Perhaps as a proxy for strengthening the socio-emotional skills and entrepreneurial awareness of participants, the INT program in the United States found gains in the community involvement of participants. The ULTP program in Peru, which included modules on personal development, indicated that participants were more likely to participate in business associations after the training.

Furthermore, the meta-analysis by Glaub and Frese (2011) (see box 4.4), which indicates that ET seems to positively affect entrepreneurial performance, brings attention to training programs that focus on enhancing certain entrepreneurial mindsets—namely the psychological factors impacting business growth, such as entrepreneurial motivation to stand out from competitors, to be innovative, and to expand. While citing a number of methodological challenges, Glaub and Frese (2011) find that training programs that focus on these psychological factors tend to be more successful than business management training for practicing entrepreneurs (see box 4.4).

Program Characteristics

As is the case with other EET program types, there is considerable heterogeneity across the characteristics of ETPr programs. One trend of note is that several ETPr programs appear to be linked to a particular microfinance institution or commercial bank (e.g., PRIDE, ROT, NRSP, FINCA, EDC, DFCU). Further, a number of evaluations describe programs with a particular sector or target group

Box 4.4 Effects of Entrepreneurship Training in Developing Countries

A paper by Glaub and Frese (2011) looks at the methodology used in different evaluations of entrepreneurship training (ET) programs to assess whether they promote entrepreneurship. It aims to determine how different content (such as psychological factors and business management skills) contributes to entrepreneurial success. Using independent consultants, the paper reviews and rates 30 studies that evaluated 10 different ET interventions. The studies were both published and unpublished and met three criteria: (a) they were conducted in developing countries; (b) they were published in English; and (c) they reported quantitative data. No pure case studies were included. The studies were evaluated by sample size and quality, evaluation design and measures, and data analyses. The results suggest that the majority of studies (80 percent) rated low on the methodology used, so their results were not conclusive and not supported. Notwithstanding, interventions appeared to have positive effects on knowledge, behavior, and business success across all studies. Lastly, the studies found that training in psychological factors influenced business growth, whereas business management skills positively affected start-ups, even though these two are different facets of entrepreneurial success.

Source: Glaub and Frese 2011.

---

focus, including agriculture (DDFET, FTDAP), construction (NRSP), garage mechanics and metal workers in industrial clusters (GNAG), and *Jua Kali* informal sector workers (MSETTP). A number of programs also focus exclusively on women entrepreneurs (10KW, CREA, DFCU, GOWE, SIYB, ULTP, WEP, WETVBI).

The scale and duration of ETPr programs ranges considerably as well, from the MSETTP program in Kenya serving the proprietors of nearly 35,000 MSEs, to the DFCU program in Uganda serving 50 women per cohort, to the highly selective END programs in South Africa serving four to six beneficiaries per cohort. The duration and intensity can vary from less than 10 days (SIYB, NRSP) to approximately one month (CREA, ROT) to several months (FINCA, ULTP). In terms of delivery, there is notable integration with formal education institutions across a number of programs. The CREA and CEM programs (in Mexico and Nigeria) are led by university faculty, while GNAG and MSETTP (in Ghana and Kenya) are delivered in partnership with vocational training institutions, the latter a voucher program for trainees to procure services from both public and private training providers. The END program is led by both an academic faculty member and entrepreneurs from the surrounding community. The meta-analysis by Cho and Honorati (2013) also indicates that involving the private sector in the delivery of programs is associated with improved program effects.

Out of the 25 programs, 10 have made information about their costs publicly available (see table 4.9). Similar to the programs for potential entrepreneurs, the range of costs is heterogeneous, since the programs vary, providing different content across different years and countries. In some cases, the cost reflects

Table 4.9 Available Information on Costs | ETPr Programs

Program name	Country/region	Costs of implementation	Cost recovery
CREA | *Capacitación y Reclutamiento Empresarial Americana*	Mexico	—	There was no tuition or enrollment fee required.
EDC | Entrepreneurship Development Center	Bosnia and Herzegovina	—	There was no tuition or enrollment fee required. Participants were provided a stipend of US$35 for the cost of their time and receive transportation to and from the program location.
GNAG | Ghana National Association of Garages	Ghana	About US$40,000 to set up and run the program and subsequently about US$740 per participant.	—
GOWE | Growth-Oriented Women Entrepreneurs	Kenya	US$13 million allotted for funding the project.	—
INT | Interise	United States	—	Local partners set their own tuition rates, ranging from US$500–US$2,000 per participant.
MSETTP | Micro and Small Enterprise Training and Technology Project	Kenya	About US$7.5 million to reach 35,000 MSEs with training	—
PBS | Production and Business Services	El Salvador	The average cost per participant ranged from around US$1,600 in the forestry value chain to over US$3,200 in the dairy value chain. Overall, the average cost per participant for all the value chains was US$2,995.	—
PRIDE	Tanzania	—	There is no tuition or enrollment fee required.
ROT | Rules of Thumb	Dominican Republic	About US$17 per participant	—
TECH | TechnoServe	Central America	The implementation cost to run the initial program was US$343,420.	Participants paid an application fee of US$15. No information available regarding tuition requirements.

Note: — = not available.

the cost of the overall program, while in other cases, it reflects only the costs of some activities. No financial analyses of programs were found in the Tier 1 and 2 evaluations.

While there is considerable variation in the common areas of content (financial literacy and accounting, marketing and sales, management skills, and strategic planning), a few available meta-analyses describe the differential effects of content types on program outcomes. Glaub and Frese (2011) point to the more positive effects for programs that focus on the aforementioned psychological factors of entrepreneurship. Cho and Honorati (2013) indicate that general business training tends to work better than financial training. Overall, this attention to program content places weight on considerations about the extent to which

Table 4.10 Entrepreneurship Training—Practicing Entrepreneurs (ETPr) | Key Information

Program name	Program beneficiaries	Evaluation	Sample	Outcomes measured	Key findings
EDC | Entrepreneurship Development Center | Bosnia and Herzegovina Source: Bruhn and Zia 2011	18–25-year-old clients of Partner Microcredit Foundation around Tuzla, Bosnia and Herzegovina	Tier 1 | Randomized control trial	The sample size had 445 active business loan clients between ages 18 and 35 who were interested in the training after an initial phone screening. The evaluation design suffered some changes over time. By the end, the treatment group had 117 individuals (39 percent of whom were invited to the training) and 148 in the control group.	Business creation and survival, business performance, business growth, business practices and investments, and loan behavior	• The training program did not influence the business survival; it did improve the business practices, investments, and loan terms for businesses; • The training improved business and financial knowledge on average (after the training, the total score of the exit test had increased from a baseline of 2.6–2.9). At follow-up, the average treatment effect of the training on business and financial knowledge was positive, but not statistically significant; • The strongest effects of the training were on improvements in business practices and investments: the treatment group was 17 percent more likely to implement new production processes than the control group, and 11 percent more likely to inject new investment into the business; • The training increased business profits by 54 percent for entrepreneurs with above-median financial literacy at baseline, although the results were not statistically significant at conventional levels; and • No impact was found on loan amounts, but there were significant impacts on loan restructuring. The treatment group was 3.4 percent more likely than the control group to refinance its loans. This effect was large, indicating that the treatment almost doubled the likelihood of refinancing loans.

table continues next page

Table 4.10 **Entrepreneurship Training—Practicing Entrepreneurs (ETPr) | Key Information** *(continued)*

Program name	Program beneficiaries	Evaluation	Sample	Outcomes measured	Key findings
FINCA	FINCA Entrepreneurship Program	Peru Source: Karlan and Valdivia 2011	Clients of FINCA microfinance institution (approx. total of 16,000 clients in Lima and two Andean provinces)	Tier 1	Randomized control trial	The sample was the preexisting lending groups of FINCA clients. On average, they were organized in groups of 20 women randomly assigned to control and treatment groups, stratified by credit officer. There were 139 groups assigned to treatment and 101 to control.	Business outcomes, business processes and knowledge, household outcomes, and microfinance institutional outcomes	• Basic business training to preexisting clients did not lead to higher profits or revenues on average. However, difference-in-difference specifications found a positive but small impact on enterprise revenues; • Positive changes in four business skills and practices outcomes were significant at 95 percent (keeping records, an index of business knowledge, the use of profits for business growth, and implementation of innovations in the business); • No training impact was found on household decision making; • The training led to a 4 percentage point increase in the client retention rate—generating an increased net revenue for FINCA; • The training had no effect on loan size or accumulated savings; and • Sometimes the stronger training effects were found for those clients who expressed less interest in the training in the baseline survey.
GNAG	Ghana National Association of Garages	Ghana Source: Mano et al. 2011	Approx. 1,000 metalwork entrepreneurs in the Suame Magazine, located in the city of Kumasi, Ghana	Tier 1	Randomized control trial	The pool of entrepreneurs was 167 metalwork entrepreneurs randomly selected from the GNAG member list. However, due to attrition and to implementation problems, the final sample was 113 entrepreneurs. The treatment group had 47 entrepreneurs, while the control had 66.	Adoption of practices and financial outcomes	• The training had a strong impact on the adoption of the recommended practices, although the firms experienced decreased profitability due to new competition; • After the training, the percentage of firms in the treatment group keeping records increased by 36 percentage points, whereas the increase was 6 percentage points in the control group; • Similarly, the percentage of firms in the treatment group analyzing business records increased by 34 percentage points, while the increase was about 3 percentage points in the control group; • However, these effects were not homogeneous, because between a third and half of participants did not adopt these practices;

table continues next page

Table 4.10 Entrepreneurship Training—Practicing Entrepreneurs (ETPr) | Key Information *(continued)*

Program name	Program beneficiaries	Evaluation	Sample	Outcomes measured	Key findings
MiDA-FBO | Millennium Development Authority—Farm-Based Organization Training | Ghana *Source:* Institute of Statistical, Social and Economic Research, 2012	Farm-based organizations (FBOs) in 30 districts in the Northern Agricultural Zone, the Central African Basin Zone, and the Southern Horticultural Belt	Tier 1 | Randomized phase-in approach	Approximately 1,200 FBOs were ex ante designed to be interviewed as part of the evaluation. There was an attrition rate of 10 percent.	Loans accessed and estimates on behavior (cultivated land size, chemical use and value, labor hours, and seed use)	• The decrease in the sales and gross profits after the training was somewhat smaller for the treatment group than for the control group, respectively, −12.9 percentage points compared to −19.6 for the sales, and −2.8 percentage points compared to −6.9 for the gross profits. Also, the effects of the training on the gross profits were much more significant than the effects of the training on sales revenues; and • Participation in the training program increased the probability of survival by 8 or 9 percentage points. • There was no evidence of intervention impact on crop yields and crop incomes overall, but there were significant zonal differences with crop incomes; • Training positively impacted the loan amounts that households received; • Training increased farmers' use of more formal sources for loans; and • The intervention led to an increase in the use of improved seeds and fertilizers by farmers, but that was mainly driven by the starter pack that participants received.
NRSP | National Rural Support Program | Pakistan *Source:* Gine and Mansuri 2011	Over 300 groups of borrowers at five branches of a microfinance institution in three districts of rural Pakistan	Tier 1 | Randomized control trial	The experiment offered training to the randomly selected half of 747 groups of borrowers from five different branches of three different districts (treatment group), while the other half did not receive training (control group).	Business knowledge, creation, and performance	• Business training led to increased business knowledge (estimate value of 0.058, with significance at the 10 percent level); • No effect of business training was found on business creation either with or without access to the larger loan (estimate value of −0.006); • Offer of business training led to improvements in business practices, such as recording the sales on paper and separating business from household accounts; • Female community organization members who had lower levels of business knowledge at baseline increased business knowledge by about 87 percent (p-value 0.12), but unlike the men, they were unable to put into practice their newly acquired knowledge;

table continues next page

Table 4.10 Entrepreneurship Training—Practicing Entrepreneurs (ETPr) | Key Information *(continued)*

Program name	Program beneficiaries	Evaluation	Sample	Outcomes measured	Key findings
PBS | Production and Business Services | El Salvador *Source:* Blair et al. 2012	Over 13,500 participants in El Salvador's Northern Zone over approximately four years	Tier 1 | Randomized rollout design	The sample size was 1,736 of which 518, 593, and 625 individuals were distributed in dairy, horticulture, and handicrafts chains, respectively	Producer level and household level	• Business training led to a reduction in business failure by 6.1 percent among male business owners, compared to the control group, but there was no effect among business women (p-value of 0.98); and • Access to the larger loan, in contrast, had little effect on anyone. • The offer of PBS had a positive and statistically significant effect on employment in the handicrafts chain, but not in the dairy or horticulture chains; • Among all artisans in the treatment group, PBS assistance resulted in 0.13 additional jobs (Intention to Treat Effect—ITT); • Among artisans who participated in the intervention, PBS assistance resulted in 0.19 additional jobs (Treatment on the Treated Effect—TOT). This difference was equivalent to nearly 50 days of full-time employment per year; • Only in the dairy value chain did the offer of PBS have a significant positive impact, around US$1,850, on dairy producers' productive income (ITT), with a p-value of 0.01. At over US$3,000, this impact was even larger among individuals who participated in PBS assistance; • Across all three value chains, there was no significant impact of PBS on producers' investments and costs detected using ITT and TOT approaches; and • No statistically significant impact of PBS on net household income was found in any value chain; • No impact of PBS on household consumption was found in any value chain.
PRIDE | PRIDE Microfinance | Tanzania *Source:* Bjorvatn and Tungodden 2010	The more than 300 clients of PRIDE microfinance in Dar es Salaam, Tanzania	Tier 1 | Randomized control trial	A randomly selected subset was drawn from the pool of clients who were offered training. The sample size is 126 from the treated group and 126 from the control group. There was an attrition	Participation and performance (the latter measured as entrepreneur business skills)	• The mean attendance for the sub-sample of the treated participants was 15.9 out of 21 sessions (76 percent), indicating that the training was perceived as beneficial for the businesses; • More schooled, more skilled (in terms of math), and more experienced (in terms of age) entrepreneurs had higher attendance than those who scored lower on these dimensions. The values of attendance were, respectively, 1.70 (significant at 10 percent), 1.62 (significant at 10 percent), and 2.26 (significant at 5 percent);

table continues next page

Table 4.10 Entrepreneurship Training—Practicing Entrepreneurs (ETPr) | Key Information *(continued)*

Program name	Program beneficiaries	Evaluation	Sample	Outcomes measured	Key findings
			rate of 15 percent for the treatment and 13 percent for the control, but it did not affect the randomization. The final sample was 107 for the treatment and 104 for the control.		• On average, the treatment group had a 9 percent higher score on the business knowledge test than the control group; and • The effect of training appeared to be highest for entrepreneurs who participated frequently in the course, and who initially did not have a lot of formal education but who did have strong cognitive skills.
ROT | Rules of Thumb | Dominican Republic *Source:* Drexler, Fischer, and Schoar 2010	1,200 clients of ADOPEM, a microfinance institution in Santo Domingo, Dominican Republic	Tier 1 | Randomized control trial	Because of baseline survey errors, the sample was reduced to 1,193. The distribution across the treatment groups was as follows: 402 assigned to accounting courses, 404 to ROT courses, and 387 to the control group.	Business practices and performance	• The impact of financial literacy training varied by its delivery method: the training program based on simple rules of thumb led to significant improvements in the way SMEs managed their finances relative to groups not offered training or offered the standard accounting training; • ROT training increased by 6–12 percent the reported likelihood of separating business and personal cash and accounts, keeping accounting records, and calculating revenues formally, in comparison with the control group, which did not receive training. The estimates were significant at the 5 percent level. No statistically significant effects were found on the business practices of those assigned to the accounting treatment; • Individuals assigned to the ROT treatment reported a substantial increase (about US$31) in revenues during bad weeks. This value was significant at the 5 percent level. No discernible effects of the accounting program were found on revenues; • Economically large increases in savings (6 percent) were found for the participants in the ROT trainings and were significant at the 10 percent level. No effect on savings was found for the group that received the basic accounting training; and

table continues next page

Table 4.10 Entrepreneurship Training—Practicing Entrepreneurs (ETPr) | Key Information *(continued)*

Program name	Program beneficiaries	Evaluation	Sample	Outcomes measured	Key findings
					• Follow-up visits did not affect the outcomes for clients in the rule-of-thumb-based training. In contrast, the follow-up visits to the participants in the basic accounting training showed a significant increase in savings levels of about 10 percent and an increase in the probability of implementing the accounting practices taught in class. But no improvements on real outcomes of the businesses, such as sales, were found. This suggested that effectiveness might be a matter of delivery method or the likelihood of implementing techniques conditional on understanding them.
SIYB-SL | ILO's Start and Improve Your Business training program | Sri Lanka *Source:* de Mel, McKenzie, and Woodruff 2012	Women who operate subsistence enterprises and have been out of the labor force but are interested in starting a business	Tier 1 | Randomized control trial	Samples of the two groups of 628 women were randomly allocated into three smaller groups: (a) training only: 200 individuals invited to training; (b) training-plus grant: 200 individuals invited to training, who received a grant of 15,000 Rs (US$130) conditional on finishing training; and (c) control group of 228 individuals.	Business practices and business outcomes for both sets of groups (business owners and potential business owners)	• Training alone did not appear to be enough to get subsistence businesses run by women to grow, although results were more encouraging for using business training to help women out of the labor force as well as for improving profits and management of these businesses; • Training led to improvements in business practices for existing firms, although the magnitude was relatively small; • Training (with or without grants) had no impact on the survival of existing firms; • Training along with grants had no significant impact on the profits or sales of existing firms; • Training sped up the creation of new businesses; and • Businesses started by trained entrepreneurs were more profitable up to two years later, with profits and sales that were up to 40 percent higher.
ULTP | Urban Land Titling Program | Peru *Source:* Valdivia 2011	Micro-entrepreneurs who were beneficiaries of a titling program in Lima	Tier 1 | Randomized control trial	1,983 eligible women were placed in two treatment groups and one control group. The distribution of women was as follows: 709 in the Treatment 1 (T1) group, which received only the general training (GT)	The outcomes were in terms of business practices	• Treatment induced women to make important adjustments to their business practices, although they differed across the type of treatment; • Positive differences in business sales were found among the treated micro-entrepreneurs, but they were not statistically different from zero. The sales increases came mainly from those for whom the treatment included GT+TA. In a normal month, those treated with GT+TA sold 19 percent more than their control counterparts;

table continues next page

Table 4.10 Entrepreneurship Training—Practicing Entrepreneurs (ETPr) | Key Information *(continued)*

Program name	Program beneficiaries	Evaluation	Sample	Outcomes measured	Key findings
			component; 709 in the Treatment 2 (T2) group, which received the general training component first, and then the technical assistance (TA) component; with the remaining 565 assigned to the control group. There was an attrition rate of 18 percent in the treatment group and 21 percent in the control group.		• No significant employment effect was found due to the training, so the sales increases imply a productivity gain for the GT+TA treatment group; • GT+TA trained women were 5.7 percentage points more likely to participate in business-related associations; • GT treated women were more likely to close their old businesses (3.5 percentage points) once they realized that they were not profitable, while those who received GT+TA were more prone to plan and implement innovations in their current business (about 3.5 percentage points); • Business results effects accrued among the businesses run by single women (0.34 s.d.), with a more entrepreneurial attitude index (0.36 s.d.), in households with titled dwellings (0.09 s.d.), and where the woman's business was relatively more important for the household's budget (0.25 s.d.), and for larger businesses (0.11 s.d.); • The aggregate standardized index for business practices showed statistically significant positive average effects of the training (0.037 s.d.), in particular, for those who received full treatment (0.049 s.d.); and • Increased participation in savings/borrowing for family or personal purposes was found.
WEP | Women Entrepreneurship Program | South Africa *Source:* Botha, Nieman, and van Vuuren 2006	Women who want to start their own business or have one and seek to improve their entrepreneurial and management skills.	Tier 1 | Randomized control trial	New and established women entrepreneurs in South Africa. The evaluation had a treatment group of 116 women and a control group of 64 women.	Skills and knowledge on running a business, increase in number of employees, turnover, productivity, and profit	• There were statistically significant gains in the four skills transfer factors (entrepreneurial characteristics, entrepreneurial orientation, business knowledge, entrepreneurial and business skills) between treatment and control group; • There were statistically significant (at a 5 percent level) differences in effectiveness between treatment and control group in relation of business improvement factors; • There was improvement in the number of employees and the number of customers for the treatment group (statistically significant), whereas this was not the case for the control group;

table continues next page

Table 4.10 Entrepreneurship Training—Practicing Entrepreneurs (ETPr) | Key Information *(continued)*

Program name	Program beneficiaries	Evaluation	Sample	Outcomes measured	Key findings
					• However, in business performance indicators (annual sales/turnover, value of capital assets, number of employees, number of customers per month, success of the businesses, probability of the businesses, satisfaction of the customers, and break-even point), both groups presented improvements before and after (mainly due to improvement in external factors of the economy). But they were statistically significant for the treatment group in 5 out of 6 indicators, while only 2 out of 6 indicators were statistically significant for the control group; • 98.12 percent of the treatment group were satisfied with WEP and indicated that they would recommend it to a friend or a colleague; and • 96.94 percent of the experimental group stated that WEP had helped them grow their businesses and 97.96 percent indicated that WEP had some effect on their businesses six months after the training.
DDFET | Dutch Dairy Farmers Entrepreneurship Training | Netherlands *Source:* Bergevoet et al. 2005	Fewer than 100 dairy farmer beneficiaries per cohort in Netherlands	Tier 2 | Case–control study	Two groups of full-time Dutch dairy farmers were selected to participate in the study. One group (N = 75) participated in the training program, the second group (N = 180) served as a control group. The sample size was 164, of which 50 comprised the treatment group and 114 the control group.	Farm and farmer characteristics and entrepreneurial competencies	• On average, all participants benefited from the program, irrespective of farmer, farm characteristics, or the level of competencies at the start of the program; • It was possible to improve entrepreneurial competencies of dairy farmers through similar training programs; and • Strategic competencies of dairy farmers had a positive relationship with farm size; supporting the general idea that when farms become larger, it becomes more important for farmers to be able to set, implement, and evaluate a strategy.

table continues next page

Table 4.10 Entrepreneurship Training—Practicing Entrepreneurs (ETPr) | Key Information *(continued)*

Program name	Program beneficiaries	Evaluation	Sample	Outcomes measured	Key findings
END	Endeavor	South Africa Source: IFC Monitor 2006	The target is mostly small and medium enterprises that are particularly conducive to innovation in South Africa	Tier 2	Quasi-experimental design	Sample size included a treatment group of 19 selected enterprises (EEs)—those who received the whole range of Endeavor's services—and a control group of 33 non-selected (non-EEs) applicants	The effect of being chosen as a program participant on firms; total sales, export sales, number of employees, and income	• The program had positive effects on sales growth; • On average, sales for EEs increased by approximately US$193,000–290,000 more than non-EEs; • The effect on the percentage of export sales was not statistically significant; and • EEs' most used services were the mentoring, training course, and networking opportunities, but not all the services were used, showing that achieving all program objectives required some additional effort.
FTDAP	Farmer Training and Development Assistance Program	Honduras Source: NORC 2012	7,500 smallholder farmers in 16 departments of Honduras	Tier 2	Quasi-experimental design	Two rounds of surveys yielded 7,262 completed interview questionnaires, of which 4,526 were from the baseline surveys conducted, and 2,736 were from the follow-up survey	Increased cultivation of horticultural crops, household income, and employment	• FTDAP had a positive impact on activities related to horticultural crops, but a broader positive impact on household income and expenditures was not detected; • The results also showed that net income change from other crops was on average 11,360 lempiras (US$601) higher for program participants than for nonparticipants; • All of the income/expense components for other (horticultural) crops had positive effects; • There was no effect on the proportion of farmers growing horticultural crops; and • There was an effect on income, net income, expenditures, and labor expenditures for other crops.
TECH	TechnoServe	Central America Source: Klinger and Schündeln 2007	Individuals or existing small and medium-scale enterprises in Central America who were interested in setting up a new business or expanding business services	Tier 2	Quasi-experimental (regression discontinuity)	The sample size was 655 applications in the three countries, where 377 received at least some training and 278 were rejected applicants who did not receive any training	Business start-ups or business expansions	• The evidence suggested that receiving business training significantly increased the probability of business start-ups and expanded existing business; • The training program led to an effect of a higher probability—9 to 11 percentage points—of opening a business (for individuals without a business before the start of the program) in the treatment group and a 23–26 percentage point higher probability of expanding a business (for individuals with an existing business before the program) in the treatment group; • Winning the competition led to economically significant changes in the probability of starting or expanding a business, suggesting the presence of financial constraints; and • Financial constraints were more important for women who wished to start or expand a business than for men.

115

content aligns with the (heterogeneous) needs of ETPr participants. To this point, the rigorous evolution of the ROT program in the Dominican Republic demonstrated that training based on simple "rules of thumb"—or the simplification of financial decision making without explaining the motivation—led to significant improvements in the way SMEs managed their finances relative to groups not offered training or standard accounting training.

Additionally, program evaluations suggested positive results for both training with a technical assistance component and training that was more specifically tailored to the needs of the targeted entrepreneurs. This is consistent with the literature, where ample debate surrounds the optimal method and content for introducing training for practicing entrepreneurs. For example, the program evaluation of ULTP in Peru found that beneficiary micro entrepreneurs receiving general training and technical assistance reported a statistically relevant increase in sales compared to the control group and to those beneficiaries who had been treated only with the general training. Furthering the point about catering to the target audiences, END, INT, and DDFET (in South Africa, the United States, and the Netherlands, respectively) principally aimed to serve proprietors of high-growth potential enterprises, and from a content standpoint they understandably appeared to focus on the development of strategic management and growth plans.

Lastly, over half of these program evaluations indicated that the program offered some kind of wrap-around service linked to accessing finance or financial assistance, which proved to be important during program implementation. Such wrap-around services are to be expected with ETPr programs linked to banking institutions. The evaluation of the TechnoServe program in Central America noted that the program conducted a competition where participants could win a financial prize. This led to economically significant changes in the probability of starting or expanding a business. Additionally, several programs included wrap-around services like networking and mentoring (DFCU, END, GOWE, INT, WETVBI)—interestingly, they were found across programs serving both necessity-driven as well as high-growth-potential practicing entrepreneurs.

Moderating Factors

In the relatively more targeted programs at the ETPr level, there is an implicit appreciation of the potential for individual and contextual factors to influence entrepreneurial outcomes. Nonetheless, the field of ETPr programs shows a number of moderating influences. At the level of the participant, ETPr program evaluations highlighted participant profiles, including gender, level of literacy and education, and past experiences as entrepreneurs. In the NRSP program in Pakistan, women participants experienced differentiated results from men. While both genders increased their baseline business knowledge, female participants were unable to put their newly acquired knowledge into practice, and while NRSP training was associated with a reduction in business failure among male business owners compared to the control group, there was no statistically significant effect among women. The ULTP program in Peru found that businesses accrued more profits when they were run by participants who were single women, by participants who had a higher entrepreneurial attitude index, and when the business was relatively more important to the participants' households' budgets.

In addition to the participant profile, ETPr programs appear to acknowledge the role of participant behaviors around program uptake and attrition in shaping program outcomes. In some cases, programs offered incentives for participation and retention, such as access to finance (SIYB, NRSP, ROT, GOWE), transportation and stipends (EDC), as well as starter packs of fertilizer, seeds, and other resources (MiDA-FBO). Other programs (END) deployed a highly selective vetting process to attract suitable participants and combat attrition.

The importance of uptake, attendance, and attrition is illustrated in the program evaluation of PRIDE in Tanzania, which found the mean attendance for the subsample of treated participants to be 15.9 out of 21 sessions (76 percent) and indicated that more schooled, more skilled (in terms of math), and more experienced (in terms of age) entrepreneurs had higher attendance than those who scored lower on those dimensions. The evaluation suggested that the effect of training appeared to be highest for entrepreneurs who participated frequently in the course, who initially did not have a lot of formal education but did have strong cognitive skills. Interestingly, the evaluation of FINCA in Peru indicated that the effects of the training were higher for participants who expressed less interest in the training in the baseline survey. This related to ETPr addressing market and information failures and individuals accurately gauging the potential value of EET programs as a whole. These points are particularly relevant considering that the opportunity cost of attending ET programs is higher for practicing entrepreneurs than it is for the target groups of the other EET programs. This underscores the implications of preparing ETPr interventions that stimulate participation and reduce attrition, since no-shows and drop-outs could be the ones with the highest learning potential.

In terms of context, ETPr programs cited the broader economic environment as both an opportunity (WEP) and a constraint, specifically the investment climate, financial infrastructure, and access to markets. These also flowed from geographic-related moderators, such as rural location and proximity to training (EDC, MSETTP). Additionally, cultural moderators, such as attitudes toward gender (NRSP), were also identified as influencing outcomes. These moderators explained the variability in outcomes across participants and suggest the importance of tailoring programming to address such cultural factors. The role of contextual moderators was surprisingly underemphasized, perhaps again related to the targeted nature of these programs (which may mean a greater appreciation for and effort to combat the influence of external contextual factors on program outcomes).

Notes

1. An action-oriented entrepreneurship training is based on the propositions of action regulation theory (Frese and Zapf 1994). Such trainings feature the following components: teaching the training content in the form of action principles, learning-by-doing,

providing positive as well as negative action feedback, and matching training tasks and real-world tasks to increase transfer. The training thus goes beyond other trainings that focus mainly on learning-by-doing.

2. Includes entrepreneurship training programs as well as programs providing microfinance—only insights from training programs were considered.
3. Based on individuals who did not own a business at baseline.
4. Based on individuals who had a business at baseline.
5. Includes an entrepreneurship training program as well as programs providing microfinance, although only insights from training programs were considered.

Bibliography

Almeida, R., and E. Galasso. 2007. "Jump-Starting Self-Employment? Evidence among Welfare Participants in Argentina." Policy Research Working Paper 4270, Development Research Group, World Bank, Washington, DC.

Attanasio, O., A. Kugler, and C. Meghir. 2009. "Subsidizing Vocational Training for Disadvantaged Youth in Developing Countries: Evidence from a Randomized Trial." Discussion Paper 4251, Institute for the Study of Labor, Bonn, Germany.

Baron, R. A. 2007. "Behavioural and Cognitive Factors in Entrepreneurship: Entrepreneurs as the Active Element in New Venture Creation." *Strategic Entrepreneurship Journal* 1: 167–82.

Bergevoet, R. H., G. W. Giesen, C. M. van Woerkum, and R. B. Huirne. 2005. "Improving Entrepreneurship in Farming: The Impact of a Training Programme in Dutch Dairy Farming." Presentation at the 15th Congress of the International Farm Management Association, "Developing Entrepreneurship Abilities to Feed the World in a Sustainable Way," Campinas, Brazil, August 14–19. http://www.ifmaonline.org/pdf/congress/05Bergevoet%20et%20al.pdf.

Bjorvatn, K., and B. Tungodden. 2010. "Teaching Business in Tanzania: Evaluation Participation and Performance." *Journal of the European Economic Association* 8 (2–3): 561–70.

Blair, R., L. Campuzano, L. Moreno, and S. Morgan. 2012. *Impact Evaluation Findings After One Year of the Productive Business Services Activity of the Productive Development Project, El Salvador*. Washington, DC: Mathematica Policy Research. http://www.mathematica-mpr.com/publications/PDFs/international/el_salvador_impact.pdf.

Blattman, C., N. Fiala, and S. Martinez. Forthcoming. "Generating Skilled Self-Employment in Developing Countries: Experimental Evidence from Uganda." *Quarterly Journal of Economics*. http://papers.ssrn.com/sol3/papers.cfm?abstract_id=2268552.

Blattman, C., E. Green, J. Annan, and J. Jamison. 2013. "Building Women's Economic and Social Empowerment through Enterprise: An Experimental Assessment of the Women's Income Generating Support (WINGS) Program in Uganda." enGender Impact, Gender Impact Evaluation Database, World Bank. http://www.poverty-action.org/sites/default/files/wings_full_policy_report_0.pdf.

Bolstad, R. 2006. "Evaluation of the Northland Enterprising Teachers (NET) Initiative." New Zealand Council for Educational Research. http://www.nzcer.org.nz/pdfs/15059.pdf.

Botha, M., G. H. Nieman, and J. J. van Vuuren. 2006. "Evaluating the Women Entrepreneurship Training Programme." *International Indigenous Journal of Entrepreneurship, Advancement, Strategy and Education* 2: 1–16.

Bruhn, M., and B. Zia. 2011. "Stimulating Managerial Capital in Emerging Markets: The Impact of Business and Financial Literacy for Young Entrepreneurs." Policy Research Working Paper 5642, Development Research Group, Finance and Private Sector Development Team, World Bank, Washington, DC.

Charney, A., and K. E. Libecap. 2000. "The Impact of Entrepreneurship Education: An Evaluation of the Berger Entrepreneurship Program at the University of Arizona, 1985–1999." Eller College of Business and Public Administration, University of Arizona.

Cho, Y., and M. Honorati. 2013. "Entrepreneurship Programs in Developing Countries: A Meta-Regression Analysis." Social Protection and Labor Discussion Paper 1302, World Bank, Washington, DC. http://elibrary.worldbank.org/doi/book/10.1596/1813-9450-6402.

de Mel, S., D. McKenzie, and C. Woodruff. 2012. "Business Training and Female Enterprise Start-up, Growth and Dynamics." Policy Research Working Paper 6145, World Bank, Washington, DC.

Drexler, A., G. Fischer, and A. Schoar. 2010. "Keeping it Simple: Financial Literacy and Rules of Thumb." Discussion Paper 7994, Centre for Economic Policy Research, London.

Elert, N., F. Andersson, and K. Wennberg. 2013. "The Impact of Entrepreneurship Education in High-School on Subsequent Entrepreneurial Performance: A Longitudinal Study." The Ratio Institute, Sweden.

Fairlie, R., and A. Robb. 2004. "Families, Human Capital, and Small Business: Evidence from the Characteristics of Business Owners Survey." Working Paper ysm435, Yale School of Management, Yale University, New Haven, CT.

Farstad, H. 2002. *Integrated Entrepreneurship Education in Botswana, Uganda and Kenya.* Oslo: National Institute of Technology.

Frank, H., C. Karunka, M. Lueger, and J. Mugler. 2005. "Entrepreneurial Orientation and Education in Austrian Secondary Schools." *Journal of Small Business and Enterprise Development* 12 (2): 259–73.

Freedom House. 2008. Political Freedom Index. (F. H. Inc., Producer). http://www.freedomhouse.org.

Frese, M., and D. Zapf. 1994. "Actions as the Core of Work Psychology: A German Approach." In *Handbook of Industrial and Organizational Psychology*, 2nd ed., vol. 4, edited by H. C. Triandis, M. D. Dunnete, and J. M. Hough. Palo Alto, CA: Consulting Psychology Press.

Fritsch, M. 2004. "Entrepreneurship, Entry and Performance of New Business Compared in Two Growth Regimes: East and West Germany." *Journal of Evolutionary Economics* 14: 525–42.

Gielnik, M., M. Frese, A. Kahara-Kawuki, I. Wassawa Katono, S. Kyejjusa, J. Munene, and T. J. Dlugosch. 2013. "Action and Action-Regulation in Entrepreneurship: Evaluating a Student Training for Promoting Entrepreneurship." *Academy of Management Learning and Education*, October 3. http://amle.aom.org/content/early/2013/10/03/amle.2012.0107.abstract.

Gine, X., and G. Mansuri. 2011. *Money or Ideas? A Field Experiment on Constraints to Entrepreneurship in Rural Pakistan.* Washington, DC: World Bank.

Glaub, M., and M. Frese. 2011. "A Critical Review of the Effects of Entrepreneurship Training in Developing Countries' Enterprise." *Development and Microfinance* 22 (4): 335–53.

Huber, L., R. Sloof, and M. V. van Praag. 2012. "The Effect of Early Entrepreneurship Education: Evidence from a Randomized Field Experiment." Discussion Paper 6512, Institute for the Study of Labour, Bonn, Germany.

Ibarraran, P., D. Rosas, and Y. Soares. 2006. *Impact Evaluation of a Youth Job Training Program in the Dominican Republic*. Washington, DC: Inter-American Development Bank. http://www.iadb.org/en/publications/publications-detail,7101.html?id=18088.

IFC Monitor. 2006. "Do Programs Supporting High Growth Entrepreneurs Work? Evaluating the Endeavor-South Africa Project." Monitor 45322, Endeavor Global, International Finance Corporation, and World Bank Group, Washington, DC.

ILO (International Labour Organization). 2011. *Building Business and Entrepreneurship Awareness: An ILO Experience of Integrating Entrepreneurship Education into National Vocational Education Systems*. http://www.ilo.org/wcmsp5/groups/public/---ed_emp/---emp_ent/---ifp_seed/documents/publication/wcms_168356.pdf.

Isaacs, E., K. Visser, C. Friedrich, and P. Brijal. 2007. "Entrepreneurship Education and Training at the Further Education and Training Level in South Africa." *South African Journal of Education* 27: 613–29.

ISSER. 2012. *An Impact Evaluation of the MIDA-FBO Training*. Institute of Statistical, Social and Economic Research, University of Ghana, Millennium Development Authority (MiDA), and Millennium Challenge Corporation (MCC).

Johannisson, B., H. Landström, and J. Rosenberg. 1998. "University Training for Entrepreneurship—An Action Frame of Reference." *European Journal of Engineering Education* 23 (4): 477–96.

Karlan, D., and M. Valdivia. 2011. "Teaching Entrepreneurship: Impact of Business Training on Microfinance Clients and Institutions." *Review of Economics and Statistics* 93 (2): 510–27.

Klaper, R. 2004. "Government Goals and Entrepreneurship Education—An Investigation at a Grande Ecole in France." *Education + Training* 46 (3): 127–37.

Klinger, B., and M. Schündlen. 2007. "Can Entrepreneurial Activity be Taught? Quasi-Experimental Evidence from Central America." Working Paper 153, Center for International Development at Harvard University, Cambridge, MA.

Kolvereid, L., and O. Moen. 1997. "Entrepreneurship among Business Graduates: Does a Major in Entrepreneurship Make a Difference?" *Journal of European Industrial Training* 21 (4): 154–60.

Macours, K., P. Premand, and R. Vakis. 2012. "Transfers, Diversification and Household Risk Strategies: Experimental Evidence with Lessons for Climate Change Adaptation." Policy Research Working Paper 6053, World Bank, Washington, DC.

Mann, P. H. 1990. "Non-Traditional Business Education for Black Entrepreneurs: Observations from a Successful Program." *Journal of Small Business Management* 28 (2): 30–36.

Mano, Y., A. Iddrisu, Y. Yoshino, and S. Tetsushi. 2011. "How Can Micro and Small Enterprises in Sub-Saharan Africa Become More Productive? The Impacts of Experimental Basic Managerial Training." Policy Research Working Paper 5755, World Bank, Washington, DC.

Martin, B., J. J. McNally, and M. J. Kay. 2013. "Examining the Formation of Human Capital in Entrepreneurship: A Meta-Analysis of Entrepreneurship Education Outcomes." *Journal of Business Venturing* 28 (2).

McKenzie, D., and C. Woodruff. 2012. "What Are We Learning from Business Training and Entrepreneurship Evaluations Around the Developing World?" Policy Research Working Paper 6202, World Bank, Washington, DC.

Nakkula, M., M. Lutyens, C. Pineda, A. Dray, F. Gaytan, and J. Huguley. 2004. "Initiating, Leading and Feeling in Control of One's Fate: Findings from the 2002–2003 Study of NFTE in Six Boston Public High Schools." Harvard University. http://www.nfte.com/sites/default/files/harvard-nfte_study_02-03_full_report_6-6-04.pdf.

NORC. 2012. *Impact Evaluation of the Farmer Training and Development Activity in Honduras: Final Report.* Chicago, IL: University of Chicago. http://www.oecd.org/countries/honduras/report-100512-evaluation-hon-farmer-training-and-development.pdf.

Premand, P., S. Brodman, R. Almeida, R. Grun, M. Barouni. 2012. "Entrepreneurship Training and Self-Employment among University Graduates: Evidence from a Randomized Trial in Tunisia." Policy Research Working Paper 6285, World Bank, Washington, DC.

Reimers, F., P. Dyer, and M. E. Ortega. 2012. "Entrepreneurship Education in the Middle East." Summary findings. https://www.jaworldwide.org/inside-ja/Reports/INJAZ_Al_Arab_Final_Evaluation_Report.pdf.

Unger, J. M., A. Rauch, M. Frese, and N. Rosenbusch. 2011. "Human Capital and Entrepreneurial Success: A Meta-Analytical Review." *Journal of Business Venturing* 26: 341–58.

Valdivia, M. 2011. "Training or Technical Assistance? A Field Experiment to Learn What Works to Increase Managerial Capital for Female Micro-Entrepreneurs." Working Paper 2011/02, Banco de desarrollo de América Latina (CAF), Lima. http://siteresources.worldbank.org/INTGENDER/Resources/336003-1303333954789/final_report_bustraining_BM_march31.pdf.

Volkmann, C. 2009. "Entrepreneurship in Higher Education." In *Educating the Next Wave of Entrepreneurs: Unlocking Entrepreneurial Capabilities to Meet the Global Challenges of the 21st Century*, edited by C. Volkmann, K. E. Wilson, S. Mariotti, D. Rabuzzi, S. Vyakarnam, and A. Sepulveda. Geneva, Switzerland: World Economic Forum.

World Bank. 2012. *Can Skills Training Programs Increase Employment for Young Women? The Case of Liberia.* Washington, DC: Adolescent Girls Initiative, World Bank.

Zhang, G., P. Cheng, L. Fan, and Z. Chu. 2012. "An Empirical Study on Impact of College Carve-Out Education on Entrepreneur Intention." Social Science Research Network (SSRN). http://ssrn.com/abstract=2034168.

CHAPTER 5

Implications for Program Design and Implementation

This study examined the range of entrepreneurship education and training (EET) interventions and has sought to address four key questions about the global landscape of EET programs, namely: *(a) Who do EET programs target? (b) What outcomes do EET programs aim to achieve? (c) What dimensions shape these outcomes?* and *(d) At what cost are outcomes achieved?* Building off the analysis of a body of research as well as the evaluations of EET programs, this chapter describes findings along the lines of these four questions and offers a set of practical insights about the design and policy implications of these findings.

Summary of Findings

Who Do EET Programs Target?
This study proposes a typology for understanding the various target groups of EET programs, including: *secondary education students, higher education students, potential entrepreneurs,* and *practicing entrepreneurs.* Building upon these target groups, the analysis provides details about the characteristics of the participants that these programs target and who the individuals are that ultimately participate.

While by definition secondary entrepreneurship education (EE) programs target students at the secondary education level, the analysis indicates that there is a differentiation between programs that target "select" groups of students versus programs that target broader student populations. For example, students may participate in EE as part of curricula integrated during normal school instruction hours. By contrast, students may choose to participate in an EE program as part of an extracurricular activity, such as an after-school club.

The same holds for higher education participants in EE. Students may participate in a program as an elective course or capstone activity; students may participate in a degree/certificate-granting entrepreneurship program; or students may participate in EE as an extracurricular activity, such as a business plan competition. Depending on how the program is structured within the higher education context, sorting occurs as students make the decision to participate.

In some cases, the decision may be motivated by a deliberate interest in entrepreneurship. In other instances, the decision may be driven by available options; for example, either writing a thesis or participating in EE to develop a business plan. Program evaluations reveal little information about participants that elect not to take EE programs.

When targeting potential entrepreneurs, entrepreneurship programs aim to recruit a range of participants—from potential high-growth or opportunity-driven entrepreneurs to necessity-driven self-employed entrepreneurs. When programs are implemented as randomized controlled trials, eligibility requirements can provide a detailed picture of participants' characteristics. Outside of these cases, however, information about targeted participant characteristics is scarce. Though in some cases, the specific goals of funders or the government can influence the population a program targets; for example, residents within a post-conflict zone, rural populations, or welfare recipients.

Among entrepreneurship training programs targeting practicing entrepreneurs, interventions target a range of participants, from high-growth entrepreneurs to necessity-driven, self-employed entrepreneurs. The defining characteristics of these program participants, however, are that they are proprietors of existing enterprises. Consequently, they have a unique stake in benefiting from the time and resources invested in a program or face a unique risk if their participation doesn't benefit them. As such, the incentives for these individuals to begin to participate and to continue to participate are unique to programs targeting practicing entrepreneurs.

What Outcomes Do EET Programs Aim to Achieve?

There are a number of objectives that EET programs target within the broader domains of entrepreneurial mindsets and capabilities as well as entrepreneurial status and performance. Across program types, there is an increased emphasis on outcomes in the status and performance domains; and among EE programs, there is also a notable emphasis on mindsets (and the associated outcomes of socio-emotional skills and entrepreneurship awareness). This trend is to be expected as the target audience changes from students to practicing entrepreneurs and, in turn, as success is measured according to an individual's increased income or profitability. From an evaluation standpoint, both metrics are more practical, and from an individual's standpoint, both are potentially more urgent.

Lastly, it is worth noting that despite entrepreneurship training programs becoming comparatively less focused on entrepreneurial mindsets, some evaluations do look at the development of participants' socio-emotional skills as well as entrepreneurship awareness, suggesting that entrepreneurial mindsets are valued beyond EE students.

What Dimensions Shape These Outcomes?

Both relevant research and EET program evaluations signal the importance of context in the capacity of programs to meet their objectives. The importance of context is even discussed in evaluations that are randomized controlled trials, where it is unclear if similar outcomes would accrue if a program were implemented elsewhere. The analysis also suggests that the prominence of particular contextual factors can depend on the outcomes being measured. As an example, EE programs that focus principally on developing capabilities and mindsets are prone to be influenced by any contextual factors that may enhance or limit skills acquisition, such as the quality of a teacher/instructor or the backing of an administration to implement a program. For entrepreneurship training programs that tend to measure an individual's decision to start a business or succeed as an entrepreneur, factors affecting macroeconomic stability or access to markets tend to be of particular importance. Of interest, across program types there are examples of cultural dynamics cited as influential to shaping program outcomes; however, evaluations tend to lack specificity around what constitutes cultural resistance or embrace of entrepreneurship.

In addition to context, participants' characteristics and behaviors can influence program outcomes. Common participant characteristics cited across program types include an individual's gender and his or her skills profile (literacy and numeracy). With regard to participant behavior, there are indications that individuals electing to participate and complete a program play a role in shaping outcomes. However, few evaluations describe what becomes of those who elect not to participate or who quit. Finally, in terms of the program characteristics themselves, evaluations do not provide a discernible picture of which characteristics are most influential in shaping program outcomes. On the whole, evaluations rarely focus on testing one program characteristic approach versus another, such as a particular wrap-around service or teaching method. A notable exception is the Tier 1 evaluation of the Student Training for Promoting Entrepreneurship program in Uganda.

At What Cost Are Outcomes Achieved?

Within the literature and program evaluations, there is a paucity of information on the costs and financing of EET programs. Further, the information that is available is rarely comparable. In most cases, the costs of EET programs are a function of the institutions responsible for implementation as well as associated principles of cost recovery. How this impacts comparability is evident in evaluations that provide information on costs to the participant. For example, for one higher education program delivered in Norway, there is technically no tuition cost to the participant; whereas at one higher education program in the United States, the cost to the student is comparatively high, given that students are required to pay some form of tuition to participate in the program. These indicators can tell us very little about the actual cost to implement programs in each country or the true extent of cost recovery in the cases where students have tuition responsibilities. Ascertaining this information for programs would require a standardization of all the program inputs; rarely do evaluations provide information on the unit costs for the whole package of inputs.

Evaluations that do offer insight on unit costs—even within the same target group—range from under US$100 per participant to upwards of US$2,000 per participant. Again, little information is available about which unit costs are comprehensive. Lastly, program evaluations suggest that programs are rarely subject to cost-effectiveness analyses. Given the challenge of comparability in the cost of programs, EET program cost-effectiveness is likely better considered in comparison with other interventions or policy alternatives in that particular context, rather than in comparisons between one EE program and another.

Implications for Program Design

The analysis of programs according to program type and target group reveals a set of insights to consider about what tends to characterize programs within each category. This information can be helpful for dialogue around the options available for designing an EET program. Figure 5.1 captures a summary of what dimensions tend to characterize different types of EET programs, informed by the analysis of EET research and the sample of program evaluations summarized in chapter 4. The decision about an EET intervention's target groups and desired outcomes can ultimately inform program design.

Using the Framework to Guide Design Options

Clarity about target groups and desired outcomes can help focus program design choices that align program design to the needs of participants and their particular context. The analysis found a breadth of choices available to program designers even within a singular program input, such as instructors or wrap-around services. Details on each of these are provided in this study's corresponding database of programs. Unfortunately, the available EET research and program evaluations provide little reliable guidance about the optimal mix of program characteristic choices for certain target groups or program objectives, given the nuances of how these characteristics come together to shape program outcomes for better or worse.

That said, a useful starting point for examining program design options may be the findings from the more rigorous program evaluations, both those that engender positive results as well as those that do not. This analysis offers program designers an opportunity to understand what choices are most common for particular target groups, particular outcomes, and within particular contexts.

For example, the analysis enables a designer to move from an understanding of the general value of wrap-around services in EET to a more focused understanding about which wrap-around services are common for particular types of programs. This includes how mentorship or internship opportunities may be common wrap-around services within higher education programs; or how access to finance is a more prevalent option for programs targeting practicing entrepreneurs. In terms of program content, financial literacy and accounting are common focuses across all program types. However, this content can differ depending on the target group; for example, whether a program serves the self-employed with low literacy or high-growth potential entrepreneurs with a graduate education.

Implications for Program Design and Implementation

Figure 5.1 Summary of EET Program Analyses

	Program dimensions			Entrepreneurship education		Entrepreneurship training	
				Secondary education students	Higher education students	Potential entrepreneurs	Practicing entrepreneurs
Outcome domains	Mindsets		Socio-emotional skills				
			Entrepreneurial awareness				
	Capabilities		Management skills				
			Vocational skills				
	Status		Enterprise formation				
			Employability				
			Income and savings				
			Network formation				
	Performance		Profits and sales				
			Job creation				
			Expansion				
			Productivity				
			Formalization				
			Reinvestment				
			Implementation of innovation				
			Products and services				
Program characteristics	Program design	Design	Local partnerships				
			Selection process				
		Finance	Source of funding				
			Unit cost (program and participant)				
	Trainers and delivery	Trainers	Teacher/educator				
			Practitioner				
			Consultant				
		Delivery	Face to face				
			Online				
			Experiential				
		Class size	10 or less				
			10 to 30				
			30 to 60				
			60 to 100				
			More than 100				
		Intensity	Daily				
			Weekly/bi-weekly				
			Monthly				
		Duration	One-off				
			Less than 2 weeks				
			2 weeks to 3 months				
			3 to 6 months				
			6 months to 1 year				
			More than 1 year				
	Content and curriculum	Content	Financial literacy/accounting				
			Marketing sales				
			General business/management				
			Vocational				
			Leadership and teamwork				
			Strategic planning				
			Socio-emotional skills				
		Curricula	Mixed methods				
			Tests/assessments				
			Presentations/competitions				
	Wrap-around services	Individual	Mentoring and coaching				
			Networking				
			Job counseling				
		Firm	Access to finance				
			Technical assistance				
Moderating factors	Participants	Profile	Gender				
			Age				
			Personality and traits				
			Family background				
		Education	Education level				
			Literacy and numeracy				
		Experience	Work experience				
			Entrepreneurship experience				
		Interest and intentions	Interest in entrepreneurship				
			Intention to start/grow a business				
		Behavior	Uptake				
			Attrition				
	Context	Economic	Conditions				
			Infrastructure				
		Political	Stability				
			Entrepreneurship promotion				
		Cultural	Entrepreneurship enabling				
			Entrepreneurship constraining				

Considering Implementation

Finally, while program evaluations tend to say little about program implementation, the importance of implementation for program design should not be overlooked. Program evaluations, as well as the available literature, provide information on the context in which programs are implemented and how outcomes vary from one context to the next. Little is documented, however, about how local dynamics and the political economy can influence program implementation.

Policy Implications

When reflecting on the policy implications of the study, an initial question to consider is whether the government should be involved in the provision, financing, or promotion of EET programs. Insight is likely to be best found within the particular type of program, as reflected by its particular target group or objectives.

Entrepreneurship Education—Secondary Education Students

Among programs targeting secondary education students, the context demands some government role, at least within public institutions or institutions using national curricula. The role can vary in intensity—from promoting EE by granting its use in a curricular module to a more intensive role in making EE a requisite aspect of teacher education. Furthermore, a secondary EE program's objectives and outcomes may include the provision of socio-emotional skills and financial literacy. The relationship between labor market outcomes and socio-emotional skills (e.g., creativity, teamwork, leadership, and self-control) is documented in a body of research (Heckman and Rubinstein 2001; Jacob 2002; Heckman, Stixrud, and Urzua 2006; Becker 2007; Borghans et al. 2008; Heineck and Anger 2008), thus making it plausible for these types of programs to contribute toward a public good (beyond entrepreneurship) that may in turn justify some form of government intervention and support.

Entrepreneurship Education—Higher Education Students

At the higher education level, government intervention might be important in some contexts, particularly within public institutions, although higher education tends to operate more autonomously than secondary education. One can again return to the issue of how EE can be pointed to as a public good. Insight on this front is likely related to a government's broader rationale for supporting higher education—whether as a means to foster a productive and employable workforce or to enhance innovation and the development of a knowledge-driven economy. EE could be considered as relevant to both, whether in equipping students with relevant skills or in providing students with the capacity to innovate or bring innovative products or processes to market.

Entrepreneurship Training—Potential Entrepreneurs

Government can play an important role in potential entrepreneurship training programs. However, in comparison with EE programs, the nature and justification of its role is less straightforward. In some cases, government is a partner in allowing the use of physical space within public training institutions. However, overall, government involvement more commonly consists of directly funding—or enabling other entities to fund—entrepreneurship training programs. Since these types of programs often target specific (often vulnerable) populations that the government may already be generally interested in supporting, the public good is often more closely tied to program objectives (enhancing equity, reducing poverty) than to what the program actually delivers (knowledge and skills). In this sense, the policy implications should be grounded in the efficacy and effectiveness of policy alternatives that are present in these contexts (e.g., conditional cash transfers, fostering wage employment, promoting active labor market policies) for furthering these same objectives. Also of note, some entrepreneurship training programs suggest that there are knowledge and skills spillovers between participants and non-participants; however, there is little robust evidence about how these spillovers contribute specifically to a program's overall policy objectives.

Entrepreneurship Training—Practicing Entrepreneurs

The policy implications for programs targeting practicing entrepreneurs in vulnerable populations echo considerations for programs geared toward potential entrepreneurs of similar backgrounds. The analysis indicates that while some programs demonstrate material benefits to beneficiaries and a degree of knowledge spillover, policymakers must consider the available alternatives within the context of particular populations.

However, programs for high-growth potential entrepreneurs merit further discussion about government involvement. The analysis indicates that among these targeted programs, the government role is limited. While the objectives of these programs also tend to align with the interest of governments—including economic spillovers such as employment and innovation—these programs tend to target better educated and better-off individuals, groups for which there is limited rationale for direct government support. Furthermore, the government role with these sorts of programs is complicated by the perception of "picking winners" as well as practical limitations in identifying "the right" participants, roles that the market and investors are likely better equipped to fill. Thus, for programs targeting high-growth-potential entrepreneurs, the government's role is likely limited to creating the space for the financing, providing private entities to train, and fostering a business environment that enables entrepreneurial activity, including business registration, access to finance, and accommodative tax policies.

Conclusion

Research indicates that entrepreneurship can be tied to a number of pressing global and economic imperatives, ranging from employment creation to poverty reduction and innovation. Given the potential beneficial spillovers of entrepreneurship, there is an interest in interventions that stimulate individuals' decisions to become and succeed as entrepreneurs. Among these interventions are EET programs that aim to develop mindsets, knowledge, and skills associated with entrepreneurial success. Given that these programs represent a heterogeneous field of interventions, this study has proposed a coherent structure for the EET landscape through the development of a typology and conceptual framework.

Using available literature and program evaluations, the study also examined the range of EET programs and has sought to address four key questions about what types of program compose the global landscape and what information is available about how these programs achieve a range of outcomes. Despite a global interest in education and training for entrepreneurship, available and reliable information on program outcomes is relatively sparse. However, through an analysis of programs, this study has been able to offer a focused and structured discussion around what generally characterizes programs when they target particular groups of beneficiaries, seek to achieve certain objectives, and are delivered in various contexts. This information is intended to be helpful for practitioners and policymakers conceptualizing the design and implementation of EET programs.

Finally, while little is known about the programs' success in supporting and ultimately developing entrepreneurs, entrepreneurship is being examined as a way to cope with a number of economic realities—including the economic contributions of self-employment and small and medium enterprises (SMEs)s, the persistence of unemployment, precarious employment, the emergence of knowledge-driven economies, and the imperative of bringing innovations to market. While evaluations of EE programs can rarely draw hard, causal lines to outcomes that explain how education and training in themselves help address these issues, many EET programs appear to contribute by association—whether as a means of generating income for individuals marginalized by an evolving global economic landscape, for whom there may be few immediate alternatives, or through building foundational skills relevant to emerging knowledge-based sectors. In either case, this study illustrates the inadequacy of looking at EET as a one-dimensional, silver-bullet solution when the global landscape of programs reveals a complex and heterogeneous collection of programs.

Bibliography

Becker, G. 2007. "Intelligence and Leadership." *Posting on the Becker-Posner Blog*, June 17. http://www.beckerposner-blog.com/2007/06/intelligence-and-leadership-becker.html.

Borghans, L., A. Duckworth, J. Heckman, and B. ter Weel. 2008. "The Economics and Psychology of Personality Traits." *Journal of Human Resources* 43 (4).

Heckman, J., and Y. Rubinstein. 2001. "The Importance of Noncognitive Skills: Lessons from the GED Testing Program." *American Economic Review* 91 (2): 145–49.

Heckman, J., J. Stixrud, and S. Urzua. 2006. "The Effects of Cognitive and Noncognitive Abilities on Labor Market Outcomes and Social Behavior." *Journal of Labor Economics* 24 (3): 411–82.

Heineck, G., and S. Anger. 2008. "The Returns to Cognitive Abilities and Personality Traits in Germany." Discussion Paper 836, German Institute for Economic Research, Berlin.

Jacob, B. 2002. "Where the Boys Aren't: Non-Cognitive Skills, Returns to School and the Gender Gap in Higher Education." NBER Working Paper w8964, National Bureau of Economic Research, Cambridge, MA.

APPENDIX A

Program Outcomes

	Programs	
Program outcomes	Tier 1 and Tier 2	Tier 3
Mindsets		
Socio-emotional skills		
Persistence	BIZ	EMPRETEC
Self-efficacy	BIZ, STEP	EDU, INJAZ
Need for achievement	BIZ, EPS, EOEAS	EMPRETEC
Pro-activity	BIZ	
Creativity	BIZ	
Optimism	BPTC	
Locus of control	EPS, EOEAS	
Openness to ambiguity	EOEAS	
Opportunity recognition	DDFET, STEP	EMPRETEC
Self-confidence		10KW, EMPRETEC, JA, SIYB, ELP, WETVBI, SNP, ACTiVATE, WEMTOP
Communication and teamwork	BIZ	NET, EMPRETEC
Leadership	BIZ, JFRLP, EOEAS, STEP	NET, EMPRETEC, JA, CEA, PAVCOPA, ELP
Entrepreneurial awareness		
Entrepreneurial values, attitudes, and norms	EPS, SAIE, INT, UTES, BEP	CREA, JA, LSTVETP, SFDP, CEM, 10KW, EMPRETEC, GE, MEP, PAP, WETVBI, WEMTOP, MIT, PT, FET
Perception of entrepreneurship	SAIE, MEP, BEP	
Willingness and intention to become an entrepreneur	GE, Bødo, BEP, INT, INJAZ, BIZ, ROT, CCOE, FTDAP, STEP	ETP, SEWA, MIT, WB, APSB, ENP, EMPRETEC, NET, FEE, PAP
Capabilities		
Business and management		
General business knowledge	PRIDE, FINCA, EDC, YDP, NRSP, SAIE, EPS, Bødo, GE, GNAG, CCOE	INJAZ, CEM, ELP, 10KW
General enterprise management skills	JFRLP, FINCA, EDC, NRSP, MSMECP, UTES, PRIDE, MSETTP, MIDA-FBO, MEP, TECH, FTDAP, BPTC, FINCA	LSTVEP, SFDP, CEM, 10KW, CREA, INJAZ, ELP, SIYB, WSBP, PAVCOPA, WEMTOP, SFOP

table continues next page

Appendix A (continued)

Program outcomes	Programs	
	Tier 1 and Tier 2	Tier 3
Accounting and financial literacy		
General financial literacy	BIZ, FINCA, ROT, EDC, NRSP,	WSBP
General accounting	ROT, EDC, NRSP, EPAG	CREA, CEM, VET, CBRDP
Separation of profit and income	ROT, FINCA, EDC	
Calculation of production costs	FINCA, ULTP	CREA, PAVCOPA
Knowledge in obtaining financing	WEP	
Product pricing	FINCA	
Development of loan work-out strategies for viable companies	JRFLRP	
Marketing and sales		
General marketing	WEP, FINCA, EDC, ULTO, NRSP	CREA, CEM
Marketing plans	BIZ, EDC, NRSP	PAVCOPA, BDRDP, CEM, WETVBI
Market positioning and research	FINCA	
Strategic planning		
Business plan development	BPTC, BIZ, WEP, EDC, GE, BEP, UTES, EPS, MIDA-FBO, FTDAP, MSETTP, TECH, NRSP	PAVCOPA, WSBP, ACTiVATE
Strategic assessment	FINCA, EDC, JFLRP, DDFET	EMPRETEC
Linking theory and practice	GE, EE	
Risk assessment	EOEAS	
Prediction of problems in business	WEP	SVT
Networking skills		
	INT	10KW, CREA, EMPRETEC, NET
Vocational skills		
	AAC, ULTP, JEA, BIZ, MSETTP, GNAG	CREA, PAVCOPA, ACTiVATE, LSTVETP, SVT, LBRDP, WESDFS
Status		
Enterprise formation		
	WEP, EDC, JRFLRP, FINCA, MCSMP, TECH, MEP, Bødo, EE, DDFET, BEP, MSETTP, TECH, GATE	EMPRETEC, EDU, CREA, WSBP, CBRDP, WETVBI, ENP, ACTiVATE, DDEI, INJAZ
Employability		
Enhanced employability	EPAG, PRIDE, Bødo, NFTE, JE	BACIP, SVTP, WEMTOP, INJAZ
Employment in private sector	JEA	WEMTOP
Self-employment	BPTC, EPAG, MEP, AAC, GATE	EDU, PAP, WETVBI, WEMTOP
Income and savings		
Income	JRFLOP, ROT, WEP, FINCA, EDC, ULTP, END, INT, MEP, PBS, MIDA-FBO, FTDAP, MSMECP, MSETTP, WINGS, JE	10KW, EDU, LFTP, CREA, PAVCOPA, WESDFS, SEWA, WETVBI, SFDP, ECTFPIP, CEM

table continues next page

Appendix A *(continued)*

	Programs	
Program outcomes	Tier 1 and Tier 2	Tier 3
Savings	JRFLRP, ROT	
Increased wages	JEA, GE	
Network formation		10KW, CREA, PAVCOPA, NET
Performance		
Profits and sales		
Profits	PRIDE, AAC, WEP, EDC, END, MSMECP, MSETTP	EMPRETEC, CEM
Cash flows	FINCA	
Sales	ROT, WEP, FINCA, EDC, ULTP, END, INT, MEP, PBS, MIDA-FBO, FTDAP, MSMECP, MSETTP, GNAG	10KW, EDU, LFTP, CREA, PAVCOPA, WESDFS, SEWA, WETVBI, SFDP, ECTFPIP, CEM
Sustainability	NRSP	
Job creation		
	END, INT, PBS, MSMECEP, BEP	10KW, EMPRETEC, SFDP, CEM, ELP, CBRDP, ENP, DDEI
Expansion		
New or improved markets	WEP, PBS, MSETTP, TECH, INT, MSMCEP	EMPRETEC, PAVCOPA, ELB, WETVBI
Increased exports		PAVCOPA, ELB
Increased borrowing	EDC, NRSP, MIDA-FBO, MSMECP, MSETTP	CEM
Productivity		
	MIDA-FBO, FTDAP, MSMECP	EMPRETEC, LFTP, PAP, ECTPIP
Formalization		
	MSETTP	LFTP
Reinvestment		
	FINCA, EDC, DDFET, PBS, MSETTP, INT	EMPRETEC, CBRDP
Implementation of innovation		
	FINCA, EDC, ULTP, MSMECP, MESTTP	PAVCOPA, ACTiVATE
Products and services		
Increased customer satisfaction	WEP	
Improvements in product quality		PAVCOPA, PAP, EDP, ECTFPIP

APPENDIX B

Program Characteristics

Program characteristics	Programs		Literature	Advisory council interviews[1]	Program type	
	Tier 1 and Tier 2	Tier 3			EE	ET
Program design						
Local partnerships	JRFLP, WEP, EDC, NRSP, INJAZ, NFTE	EMPRETEC, NET, JA, SIYB	Fuchs, Werner, and Wallau (2008)	Schindehutte, Forti, Brock	X	X
Selection process	WEP, ULTP, TECH, FTDAP, GE, STEP, GATE, END	BAICP, EMPRETEC, NET	Bharadwaj, Osborne, and Falcone (2010)	Schindehutte, Heim, Forti		X
Trainers and delivery						
Trainers						
Teacher/educator	ROT, EOEAS, NFTE, STEP				X	
Trainer/consultant	PRIDE, EDC, YDP, NRSP, GNAG, JA, NFTE, MCSMP, GE, MSETTP, GATE	EMPRETEC, NET, BAICP, SIYB, JA, CREA, EDU, LFTP		Schindehutte, Brock		X
Practitioner	TECH, MSETTP					X
Blend	BPTC, BIZ, JA, Bødo, GE, BEP, MSETTP, EMPRETEC, BAICP, LSTVETP, 10KW, END		Pittaway and Cope (2007); Porter and McKibben (1988)	Mehu-Hammonds, Heim, Forti, Pfefferman, Bamkole	X	X
Includes trainer/ teacher training	NRSP, JA, NFTE	EMPRETEC, NET, JA, SIYB		Mehu-Hammonds, Forti, Brock	X	X

table continues next page

Appendix B *(continued)*

Program characteristics	Programs		Literature	Advisory council interviews[1]	Program type	
	Tier 1 and Tier 2	Tier 3			EE	ET
Delivery						
Face-to-face classroom	JFRLP, PRIDE, AAC, BTPTC, WEP, FINCA, EDC, ULTP, YDP, NRSP, JEA, BIZ, ROT, DDFET, MCSMP, Bødo, MSMECP, FTDAP, INT, TECH, SAIE, EPS, BEP, NFTE, ACTiVATE	10KW, EDU, CREA, PAVCOPA, SIYB, BACIP, WSBP, PCY, INJAZ, NET, EMPRETEC, LSTVETP, CEM, SEWA, FEE, DFCU, SVT, YEN, ENP			X	X
Online (or components of)	END, GE	BACIP, CREA			X	X
Experiential	JEA				X	
Content and curricula						
Content						
Financial literacy	PRIDE, BIZ, EPAG, FINCA, EDC, NRSP, WEP, JRFLRP, ROT, MCSMP, TECH, GE, GNAG, PBS, MIDA-FBO, BEP, NFTE, EDC, ULTP	EMPRETEC, BACIP, CREA, PAVCOPA, 10KW, LFTP, CEM, SEWA, ELP, CBRDP		Heim	X	X
Accounting	EDC, NRSP, TECH, BEP, ROT, EPAG	10KW, LFTP				X
Recordkeeping	EPAG, FINCA, EDC, MCSMP	LFTP				X
Costing	FINCA, ULTP, MCSMP					X
Marketing	FINCA, MCSMP, PRIDE, WEP, BIZ, EDC, ULTP, NRSP, TECH, BEP, MSCMP	10KW, CREA, PAVCOPA, CEM, LFTP, JA			X	X
Sales	BIZ, ROT, FINCA, ULTP	LFTP, CREA, PAVCOPA				X
General business knowledge and skills	ROT, WEP, EDC, ULTP, NRSP, JFLRP, PRIDE, EPAG, BIZ, NRSP, BEP, FTDAP, MCSMP, TECH, UTES, DDFET, GE, GNAG, PBS, MIDA, MIDA-FBO, BEP, NFTE	EMPRETEC, BACIP, CREA, PAVCOPA, 10KW, LFTP, CEM, SEWA, ELP, CBRDP	Barringer and Ireland (2010)		X	X
Vocational	EPAG, ULTP, AAC, JEA, BIZ, MIDA-FBO, DDFET, PBS, MSETTP	PAVCOPA, BACIP, PCY, LSTVETP, PAP, SVTP, VET, SVT, CBRDP			X	X

table continues next page

Appendix B *(continued)*

Program characteristics	Programs		Literature	Advisory council interviews[1]	Program type	
	Tier 1 and Tier 2	Tier 3			EE	ET
Entrepreneurship awareness/theory	BIZ, NET, WEP, NRSP, PRIDE, BPTC, AAC, EPAG, AAC, EPAG, YDP, BEP, NFTE, TECH, SAIE, EPS, PBS, NFTE	EMPRETEC, NET, 10KW, ESBP, PCY, CEM, FEE, FET, TEVET	Fuchs, Werner, and Wallau (2008)	Heim, Mehu-Hammonds	X	X
Leadership	WEP, ULTP, NFTE	EMPRETEC, JA, 10KW, NET		Mehu-Hammonds	X	X
Teamwork and networking	GE	LFTP, CREA, PAVCOPA			X	X
Strategic planning	WEP, EDC, DDFET, GE, BEP, GE, TECH, EPS	EMPRETEC				X
Business plan	BPTC, WEP, EDC, GE, MCSMP, BEP, INJAZ	10KW, CEM			X	X
General socio-emotional Skills					X	X
Customer care	PRIDE, EPAG, FINCA, ULTP					X
Life skills	EPAG, ULTP, YDP, JRFLP, AAC, TECH	EDU, PAP			X	X
Product design, production, and promotion	BIZ, FINCA, EPS, FTDAP, MCSMP, EPS, GE, PBS	PAVCOPA				X
Product quality management	ULTP, MCS, FTDAP, GE					X
Enterprise registration, trademarks	WEP, FINCA, BPTC, PCY	CREA, PAVCOPA, SFDP, WEMTOP	Barringer and Ireland (2010)		X	X
Human resource management	GE	10KW, CEM				X
Industry-specific content	MIDA-FBO	LFTP, PAVCOPA				X
Curricula						
Classroom-based lecture	WEP, BIZ, NRSP, ROT, FINCA, TECH, GE, NFTE, INJAZ	NET, EMPRETEC, JA, WSBP, PCY			X	X
Mixed methods	WEP, JEA, FINCA, NRSP, BIZ, ROT, NRSP, JA, NFTE, TECH, MSMCP, END, TECH, GE, INJAZ	NET, 10KW, EMPRETEC, JA, WSBP, PCY		Heim, Mehu-Hammonds, Bamkole, Nelson, Solomon, Davis	X	X
Company simulations	NRSP, EOEAS					

table continues next page

Appendix B (continued)

Program characteristics	Programs - Tier 1 and Tier 2	Programs - Tier 3	Literature	Advisory council interviews[1]	Program type - EE	Program type - ET
Case studies	WEP, MSMECP					X
Linking learning with real-world experience	END, NFTE, GE	EMPRETEC, NET, JA, CREA, PAVCOPA	Pittaway and Cope (2007); Porter and McKibbin (1988)	Solomon, Mehu-Hammonds, Brock		
Presentation to external audience	BIZ, WEP, NFTE, GE	EDU, EMPRETEC			X	X
Competitions and awards	BPTCC, AAC, PRIDE, INJAZ, BEP, NFTE, TECH, END, GE	EMPRETEC		Solomon, Heim, Pfefferman	X	X
Wrap-around services						
Creates linkages between students/trainees and professional community						
	WEP, YDP, NFTE, MSMECP, UTES, GE	EMPRETEC, NET, CREA, PAVCOPA	Fuchs, Werner, and Wallau (2008)	Hammonds, Heim, Bamkole	X	X
Mentoring, counseling, or coaching						
	WEP, BPTC, INT, NGTE, PCY, ENDBP, MCSMP	10KW, EMRETEC, NET, CREA, ESBP, CEM, GOWE	Sarri (2011); Wikholm, Henningson, and Hultman (2008)	Heim, Solomon, Forti, Brock, Bamkole, Nelson		X
Access to finance						
	WEP, EPAG, BPTC, AAC, PRIDE, NRSP, FINCA, EC, ULTP, MCSMP, END, PBS, END, MSMECP, MSETTP, TECH, EDC, YOP, STEP, WINGS	BACIP, CREA, PAVCOPA, WSBP, SFDP, PAP		Forti, Brock		X
Access to markets						
	JRFLP, MSMECP	BACIP, PAVCOPA		Nelson		X
Technical assistance						
	EPAG, ULTP, MCSMP, PBS, END, TECH, MSMECP, MSETTP, GE, WINGS	CREA, PAVCOPA, WSBP		Mehu-Hammonds	X	X
Access to technology						
	EPAG, NFTE, TECH		Haan (2001)	Cassup	X	X
Business plan advising						
	AAC, MSMECP, TECH	10KW, SFDP				X

table continues next page

Appendix B *(continued)*

Program characteristics	Programs		Literature	Advisory council interviews[1]	Program type	
	Tier 1 and Tier 2	Tier 3			EE	ET
Alumni network						
	WEP, NFTE, ENDBP	EMPRETEC, 10KW		Heim		X
Networking with other entrepreneurs						
	WEP, NFTE, END	EMPRETEC, 10KW, PAVCOPA, NET	Ronstadt (1985)	Mehu-Hammonds, Nelson		X
Job counseling/placement						
	JEA, YDP				X	X
Workspace/incubation centers, support centers						
		ENDBP				
Conferences, workshops, study tours, entrepreneur days						
	END, INT, EOEAS					

Note

1. Sixteen interviews were conducted with members of the study's Advisory Council to identify noteworthy research and programs. The Advisory Council includes practitioners, academics, and thought-leaders in the entrepreneurship field. A full list of Advisory Council members is provided on pp. xii.

Bibliography

Barringer, B. R., and D. Ireland. 2010. *Entrepreneurship: Successfully Launching New Ventures*, 3rd ed. Pearson Prentice Hall.

Bharadwaj, P. N., S. W. Osborne, and T. W. Falcone. 2010. "Assuring Quality in Entrepreneurship Training: A Quality Function Deployment (Qfd) Approach." *Journal of Entrepreneurship Education* 13: 107.

Fuchs, K., A. Werner, and F. Wallau. 2008. "Entrepreneurship Education in Germany and Sweden: What Role Do Different Schools Systems Play?" *Journal of Small Business and Enterprise Development* 15 (2): 365–81.

Haan, H. 2001. *Training for the World in the Informal Sector: New Evidence from Eastern and Southern Africa*. Washington, DC: International Training Center of the International Labour Organization, World Bank.

Pittaway, L., and J. Cope. 2007. "Entrepreneurship Education: A Systematic Review of the Evidence." *International Small Business Journal* 25.

Porter, L. W., and L. E. McKibbin. 1988. *Management Education and Development: Drift or Thrust into the 21st Century?* Hightown, NJ: McGraw-Hill.

Ronstadt, R. 1985. "The Educated Entrepreneurs: A New Era of Entrepreneurial Education Is Beginning." *American Journal of Small Business* 10 (1): 7–23.

Sarri, K. K. 2011. "Mentoring Female Entrepreneurs: A Mentor's Training Intervention Evaluation." *Journal of European Industrial Training* 35 (7): 721–41.

Volkmann, C., K. E. Wilson, S. Mariotti, D. Rabuzzi, S. Vyakarnam, and A. Sepulveda. 2009. *Educating the Next Wave of Entrepreneurs: Unlocking Entrepreneurial Capabilities to Meet the Global Challenges of the 21st Century*. Cologny, Switzerland: World Economic Forum.

Wikholm, J., T. Henningson, and C. M. Hultman. 2008. "Mentor and Mentee Attitudes in Mentoring for New Entrepreneurs." World Conference Proceedings, International Council for Small Business (ICSB), Washington, DC.

APPENDIX C

Moderating Factors

Moderating factors	Programs		Literature	Advisory council interviews[1]	Program type	
	Tier 1 and Tier 2	Tier 3			EE	ET
Participants						
Age						
	PRIDE, DDFET				X	X
Family background						
	NFTE, INJAZ, DDFET	10KW	Peterman and Kennedy (2003); Wang and Wong (2004)			X
Education						
	WEP, PRIDE, BPTC, FINCA, UTES, MEP, GE, WINGS		Unger et al. (2011); van der Sluis, van Praag, and Vijverberg (2005)			X
Literacy and numeracy						
	PRIDE, FINCA, MRSP					X
Work experience						
	JRFLRP, GNAG, MCSMP, ROT, MSMECP		Unger et al. (2011)		X	X
Interest and intentions						
	MEP, WEP, MSETTP, EDC, Bødo, EOEAS, MSETTP, EPAG	EMPRETEC, JA	Oosterbeek, van Praag, and Ijsselstein (2010); Rauch and Frese (2007); Krueger, Reilly, and Carsrud (2000)	Bamkole	X	X
Context						
Economic						
Conditions	AAC, WEP, NFTE, SAIE, INJAZ, MCSMP, EOEAS, EPS	NET	Bullough, Renko, and Myatt (2013); World Bank (2012)	Heim, Nelson	X	X
Infrastructure	ROT, MSMECP, MSETTP			Cassup	X	X

table continues next page

Appendix C *(continued)*

Moderating factors	Programs		Literature	Advisory council interviews[1]	Program type	
	Tier 1 and Tier 2	Tier 3			EE	ET
Political						
Stability	INJAZ				X	X
Promotion policy	JEA, JRFLP, NFTE, SAIE, MSETTP, NFTE, END	NET, SIYB, JA		Solomon, Nelson, Brock	X	X
Cultural						
Enabling		CREA	Volkmann et al. (2009)	Solomon, Brock	X	X
Constraining	WEP, NRSP, SAIE, NFTE, END, GE			Solomon, Brock, Bamkole, Nelson	X	X

Note: EE = entrepreneurship education, ET = entrepreneurship training.

Note

1. Sixteen interviews were conducted with members of the study's Advisory Council to identify noteworthy research and programs. The Advisory Council includes practitioners, academics, and thought-leaders in the entrepreneurship field. A full list of Advisory Council members is provided on pp. xii.

Bibliography

Bullough, A., M. Renko, and T. Myatt. 2013. "Danger Zone Entrepreneurs: The Importance of Resilience and Self-Efficacy for Entrepreneurial Intentions." *Entrepreneurship Theory and Practice.* doi:10.1111/etap.12006.

Krueger, N., M. D. Reilly, and A. L. Carsrud. 2000. "Competing Models of Entrepreneurial Intentions." *Journal of Business Venturing* 15 (5–6): 411–32.

Oosterbeek, H., M. van Praag, and A. Ijsselstein. 2010. "The Impact of Entrepreneurship Education on Entrepreneurship Skills and Motivation." *European Economic Review* 54: 442–54.

Peterman, N. E., and J. Kennedy. 2003. "Enterprise Education Influencing Students' Perceptions of Entrepreneurship." *Entrepreneurship Theory and Practice* 28 (2): 129–44.

Rauch, A., and M. Frese. 2007. "Let's Put the Person Back Into Entrepreneurship Research: A Meta-Analysis on the Relationship between Business Owners' Personality Traits, Business Creation and Success." *European Journal of Work and Organizational Psychology* 16 (4): 353–85.

Unger, J. M., A. Rauch, M. Frese, and N. Rosenbusch. 2011. "Human Capital and Entrepreneurial Success: A Meta-Analytical Review." *Journal of Business Venturing* 26: 341–58.

van der Sluis, J., M. van Praag, and W. Vijverberg. 2005. "Entrepreneurship Selection and Performance: A Meta-Analysis of the Impact of Education in Developing Economies." *The World Bank Economic Review* 19 (2): 225–61.

Volkmann, C., K. E. Wilson, S. Mariotti, D. Rabuzzi, S. Vyakarnam, and A. Sepulveda. 2009. *Educating the Next Wave of Entrepreneurs: Unlocking Entrepreneurial Capabilities to Meet the Global Challenges of the 21st Century.* Cologny/Geneva: World Economic Forum.

Wang, C. K., and P. K. Wong. 2004. "Entrepreneurial Interest of University Students in Singapore." *Technovation* 24 (2): 163–72.

World Bank. 2012. "Doing Business Project." http://www.doingbusiness.org.

APPENDIX D

Program Narratives

The program narratives presented in this appendix aim to give a sense of the variety of programs and audiences captured by entrepreneurship education (EE) and entrepreneurship training (ET). These programs span the developed and developing world, reaching practicing and potential entrepreneurs as well as secondary and higher education students. The programs profiled come from the EE/ET database of over 80 programs. To be profiled, the programs needed to have sufficient information to capture a complete program landscape. In many cases, these profiles show the evolution of programs—some have expanded their scope while others have narrowed it. These narratives are meant to provide a sampling of EE and ET—they highlight both good practices and areas that could be improved.

Program representatives filled in any information gaps not covered in the program evaluations or online. These same representatives reviewed the final write-ups—which include a detailed look at the program format, target audience, local partnerships, teachers, contextual factors, and an overview of the program evaluation.

BizWorld | The Netherlands

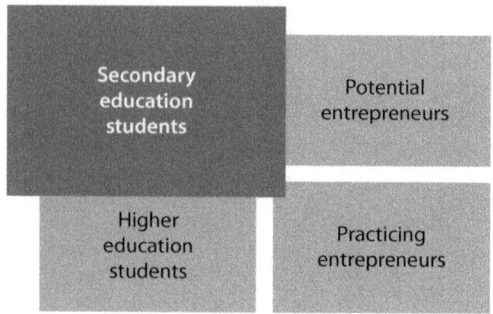

Program Overview

BizWorld launched in the Netherlands in 2004. Financed by a public-private partnership, the program takes place in hundreds of Dutch classrooms each year. Companies sponsor a class of students, typically ages 11–12, for the intensive four-day program. A businessperson from the sponsoring company co-teaches with the class's regular instructor, leading students through a business development exercise. In 2013, BizWorld's Dutch program anticipated taking place in 450 schools and reaching more than 11,000 students.[1]

Started in the United States in the late 1990s, BizWorld is a global EE program geared toward primary school students. Over 350,000 children from 84 countries have participated in the program to date.

Program Objectives

The program focuses on developing entrepreneurial mindsets, including self-efficacy, leadership, and collaboration.

Mindsets	Socio-emotional skills	✓
	Entrepreneurial willingness	
	Entrepreneurship theory	
Capabilities	Management skills	✓
	Vocational skills	
	Networking skills	
Status	Firm formation	
	Self-employment	
	Employability	
	Income and savings	
	Network formation	
Performance	Profits and sales	✓
	Job creation	
	Market expansion	
	Productivity	✓
	Reinvestment	
	Innovation	✓

Who Participates
Primary school children, typically ages 11–12, participate throughout the Netherlands if their school has opted to partner with BizWorld.

How the Program Works
A business in the community volunteers to sponsor BizWorld in a classroom. Additionally, the sponsoring business has one of its employees serve as a co-instructor during the program. Over the course of the four-day classroom-based program—typically spanning two to four weeks—the instructor and business person lead the class of 25 students through an experiential learning exercise.

The instructors divide the class into teams of about five, and each child applies to become a key member of a start-up (e.g., chief executive officer [CEO], finance director, director of product design). In each class session, which runs for three hours, the students work to create, design, market, and ultimately sell their product to buyers in the grade below. The aim is to teach the students the basics of entrepreneurship, business, and finance.

The instructor and visiting businessperson serve as judges for the competition. The teams that have the greatest revenue and perform best win a series of certificates (e.g., Best Revenue, Most Sustainable Company, Best Company to Work For).

Who Teaches the Program
Typically, a few weeks before the program starts, the primary school teachers who lead their students in BizWorld must attend a two-hour training program, where they also receive all the course materials—containing very detailed and strict guidelines about the course. For teachers who want to preview the course content, the BizWorld website provides instruction videos.

In addition to the primary school teachers, the Dutch BizWorld program also includes an entrepreneur to help lead the program and provide real world examples to the students. BizWorld trains these businesspeople in the basics of their curriculum prior to the class.

Program Partnerships
The Dutch version of BizWorld is sponsored by companies. At this time, 35 small- and medium-sized businesses as well as corporations pay 1,000 euros (US$1,300) each to sponsor at least one classroom (some larger companies sponsor up to 50 classes). The funding covers the cost of the teacher training, and the company provides one of their businesspeople to serve as a co-instructor.

The Local Context
BizWorld classes take place in a wide variety of schools in the Netherlands. Some students have parents who are entrepreneurs; other students struggle with the language barrier of being new immigrants. Schools are in dense urban areas—where there's a high likelihood students have been predisposed to business and entrepreneurship—but there are also schools in more rural areas, where these

concepts are more foreign. BizWorld's Netherlands office notes that schools with large immigrant populations perform well in design, production and sales; while schools with students who come from high-income families are much more interested in the stock exchange.

Of particular note—the Netherlands has the largest percentage of entrepreneurs of any European Union (EU) country—8.7 percent of the population owns a start-up; as compared with 6.6 percent of citizens in the EU.[2] In a 2011 survey, over 80 percent of Dutch view starting a business as a positive career development; as compared to only 59 percent of other EU citizens.

A Look at the Program Evaluation

University of Amsterdam researchers evaluated BizWorld's Dutch program using a randomized field experiment (Huber, Sloof, and Van Praag 2012) to measure the direct (short-term) effects of early EE on the development of cognitive, non-cognitive entrepreneurial skills, and entrepreneurial intentions using a randomized field experiment. The evaluation took place between February and July 2010, and over the same period in 2011.

The sample consisted of 85 schools that had signed up for the program and had consented to participating in the research (about 75 percent of all schools that signed up in 2010 and 2011), for a total of 118 classes and 2,751 students in the last year of primary school. The response rate was 87.7 percent. Since the program was delivered at the class level, the unit of analysis was the class level rather than the school.

For both randomly assigned treatment and control groups, the study applied a pretest/posttest design to allow an unbiased difference-in-differences estimate of the non-treatment effect. The study collected data on (a) non-cognitive skills, including self-efficacy, need for achievement, risk taking, social orientation, persistence, motivating, analyzing, proactivity, and creativity; (b) cognitive skills, including entrepreneurship knowledge; and (c) entrepreneurial intentions, including children's intentions to become an entrepreneur.

The treatment effect was positive and statistically significant for seven of the nine non-cognitive skills tested, namely self-efficacy (0.149***), need for achievement (0.166***), risk-taking propensity (0.114**), persistence (0.105**), analyzing (0.127***), creativity (0.096*), and proactivity (0.144***). Analysis on the heterogeneity of treatment effects showed that the treatment effects remained or increased slightly when controlling for individual, school and neighborhood characteristics, and year of data collection. Also, the size of treatment effects was substantial and comparable to being eligible to one track level in entering high school (i.e., from the baseline of pre-vocational to general secondary education).

The estimated effect on cognitive entrepreneurial skills (entrepreneurship knowledge) was positive although not significant (0.015); and the estimated effect on entrepreneurial intentions (owning a business) for children was negative and significant (−0.134***). The study acknowledged that the measures used for entrepreneurial intentions were not validated for children and could potentially alter the results.

Summary

Program details	
Program name	BizWorld
Country	Netherlands
Implementing agency	Public elementary schools under the direction of the Department of Education
Program type	Four-day experiential learning class at Dutch primary schools
Target audience	Primary school students throughout the Netherlands. The course will serve over 11,000 Dutch students in 2013.
Age	10–12 year olds
Gender	Equal mix
Objective	To improve students' collaboration, financial, and leadership skills while exposing them to the basics of business
Program maturity	In the Netherlands since 2004; originally started in the United States in the late 1990s
Contact	http://www.bizworld.org/programs/index.php
Cost	Local businesses subsidize the cost of the program—1,000 euros—to each school by sponsoring a classroom and providing a businessperson who serves as a volunteer instructor. This amount covers all classroom costs.
Evaluation	
Evaluator	Laura Rosendahl Huber, Randolph Sloof, and Mirjan Van Praag, "The Effect of Early Entrepreneurship Education: Evidence from a Randomized Field Experiment," Discussion Paper No. 6512 (IZA: 2012).
Evaluation methodology	Randomized field experiment
Evaluation tier	1

Network for Teaching Entrepreneurship (NFTE) | Boston Chapter, United States

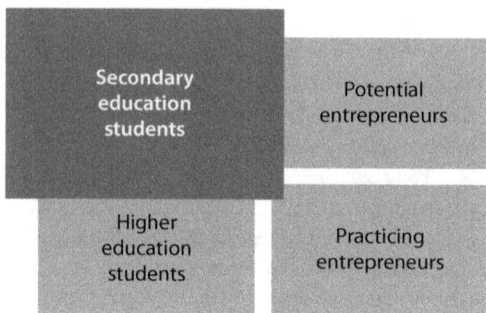

Program Overview

The Network for Teaching Entrepreneurship (NFTE)[3] program has operated in Boston since 1991 and is now working with 18 public schools there. NFTE targets high schools where at least half of the student body is eligible for free or reduced-price lunch.

During either a one-semester or year-long course, students learn entrepreneurial skills that help them create a business plan. Each student's business plan ultimately competes in a school-wide competition, with the winners advancing to a regional NFTE-wide competition and ultimately the National Youth Entrepreneurship Challenge.

NFTE is a global program that started in New York in 1987. It aims to help young people who are at risk of dropping out of school. NFTE has reached over 500,000 students and trained 5,000 teachers worldwide. In a handful of schools, students are required to take the NFTE course, but in most schools—including Boston's—students opt into the program.[4]

Who Participates

NFTE runs programs in middle schools and high schools where at least 50 percent of students are low income. The program is aimed at students who are at high risk of dropping out of school. Typically, there are an equal number of male and female participants.

Program Outcomes

NFTE focuses on participants' mindsets and capabilities, ultimately aiming to help its participants stay in school, recognize business opportunities, and plan for future employment.

Mindsets	Socio-emotional skills	✓
	Entrepreneurial willingness	✓
	Entrepreneurship theory	

Capabilities	Management skills	✓	
	Vocational skills	✓	
	Networking skills		
Status	Firm formation		
	Self-employment		
	Employability		
	Income and savings		
	Network formation		
Performance	Profits and sales		
	Job creation		
	Market expansion		
	Productivity		
	Reinvestment		
	Innovation		

How the Program Works

NFTE-certified teachers guide students for 70 hours as part of a semester or year-long class. The two possible courses are "Entrepreneurship: Owning Your Future" and "Exploring Careers for the 21st Century." Subjects range from the concepts of competitive advantage to finance and marketing. In a class of 20, students follow a curriculum that draws upon their math and literacy skills.

During the course, each student comes up with an idea for a business and works throughout the semester or year to create a business plan. To help with this process, business plan coaches visit students and help them throughout the process. These mentors are volunteers from local businesses, typically entrepreneurs or workers in the finance field.

As a capstone for the course, all students present their business plan in front of a panel of judges. The judges are volunteers who work in the local business community. The top three students in this competition then advance to a regional business plan competition, where they compete against other NFTE students. The winner of the regional competition then advances to the national competition. The top three national winners receive up to US$25,000 and prizes including two free round-trip plane tickets to anywhere in the world.

Who Teaches the Program

NFTE certifies instructors who are already teaching in the schools where their program will take place. Each teacher goes through a four-day training at the beginning of the school year (called NFTE University). NFTE provides financial incentives to their certified instructors to complete continuous professional development programs throughout their time teaching the NFTE course.

In addition to NFTE-certified instructors, mentors help students create their business plans. The mentors come to class a few times throughout the year to guide their mentees. In a handful of classes during the year, volunteer local business leaders serve as guest lecturers.

Program Partnerships

Babson College provides in-kind rent and support to NFTE's Boston administrative staff.

NFTE offers companies the ability to give back through its Adopt-a-Class program. Hollister, Inc., a Boston-based staffing business, adopts a class each year. Its staff serve as mentors to the students.

The Local Context

NFTE's students come from trying economic situations—typically from households that fall below the poverty line. Many students are the first English speakers in their families. Overwhelmingly, the students who matriculate into NFTE courses are at a high risk of dropping out—sometimes due to poor grades, other times because of the need to provide for their families. To provide context, in Boston—the largest city in Massachusetts—public high school graduation rates for 2011 were 65.9 percent, while the state-wide average was 84.7 percent.

A Look at the Program Evaluation

Researchers from Harvard University's Graduate School of Education did a multi-year analysis of NFTE's Boston program in 2004 (Nakkula *et al.* 2004). The first phase surveyed students from two large public high schools in 2001–02. The second phase expanded the universe of schools from two to six public high schools to allow the analysis of possible program impacts in a wider range of learning contexts. The sample included a total of 17 classrooms, 13 teachers, and 268 students, out of which 158 students received the NFTE program (treatment) and 110 students were selected for comparison classes (control).

The evaluation studied the role of NFTE in promoting the development of entrepreneurship, including entrepreneurship thinking and behavior. The study measured entrepreneurial behavior (EB) using an entrepreneurial activities checklist (49 activities organized around different domains and dimensions), locus of control, and applied new scales to measure healthy or positive development (using the values-in-action scale that gauges originality, curiosity, industriousness, and hopefulness).

The EB score increased for NFTE students compared to the control group, registering a significant increase of 7.5 percent ($p<0.01$). The changes in the two groups were large and significant for the starter dimension and business domain. In contrast, the EB score for comparison students did not register significant changes, although in some domains the trend declined.

Although the results for locus of control were not significant, the scores followed the hypothesized pattern. While NFTE students began with marginally lower locus-of-control scores than the comparison group, they increased their score by about 3 percent after the intervention, outscoring the control group. Similarly, immigrant students participating in the program improved in their locus of control by about 4.5 percent, while the score of similar students in the comparison group declined by approximately 2.5 percent. Locus-of-control findings were strongest for students taught by one particular teacher in one of the schools with a strong track record of effective teaching (i.e., had received recognition).

Results on students' connectedness were generally negative; and results from the values-in-action scales (originality, curiosity, industriousness, and hopefulness) were not found to be significant. Although not significant results, NFTE students scored marginally higher than the comparison group in the pretest, meanwhile the gap narrowed at posttest with the comparison group's score increasing and the NFTE students' score decreasing.

Overall, NFTE students trained by top-notch teachers showed a higher degree of general student teacher connectedness, unlike the comparison group. Similar to the findings from the first phase, relative to the comparison group, NFTE students expressed increasingly strong interest in occupations requiring advanced training or formal education, including college.

Summary

Program details	
Program name	Network for Teaching Entrepreneurship
Country	United States
Program type	Semester- or year-long entrepreneurship education class in low-income high schools
Target audience	Low-income high school students at high risk of dropping out
Age	15–18 year olds
Gender	Equal mix
Objective	To improve students' interest in staying in school—with the ultimate goal of gainful employment and potentially starting a business
Program maturity	In the United States since 1987, in Boston since 1991
Contact	http://www.nfte.com
Evaluation	
Evaluator	Michael Nakkula, Miranda Lutyens, Claudia Pineda, Amy Dray, Frank Gaytan, and Jay Huguley, "Initiating, Leading and Feeling in Control of One's Fate: Findings from the 2002–2003 Study of NFTE in Six Boston Public High Schools" (Harvard University: 2004). Recovered from: http://www.nfte.com/sites/default/files/harvard-nfte_study_02-03_full_report_6-6-04.pdf
Evaluation methodology	Quasi experimental design
Evaluation tier	2

Bødo Entrepreneurship Program | Norway

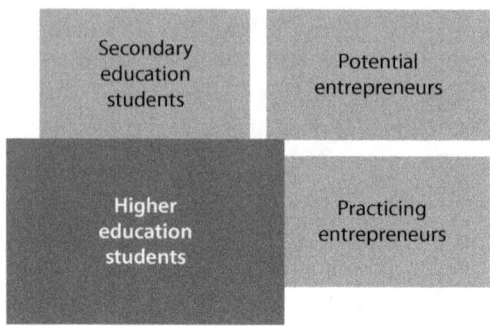

Program Overview
Founded in 1985, the Bødo Graduate School of Business in Bødo, Norway, has had more than 3,000 students graduate from its master's degree in business program. As part of the master's program, about 20 percent of Bødo students major in entrepreneurship; others choose to major in subjects like finance, management, accounting, and international business.[5]

The entrepreneurship major is a combination of course work—in topics like business formation and strategy—and thesis work on areas of entrepreneurship. The program aims to help participants develop their entrepreneurial awareness and develop skills for creating a new business when they graduate. Upon conclusion of the entrepreneurship component, students graduate with a master's in business, focusing on entrepreneurship.

Who Participates
Bødo students spend their first three years completing a bachelor's degree. To become a master's student at Bødo, students undergo a screening process based on these first three years of grades. If admitted to the master's program, they will spend two more years at Bødo completing the degree. In their fourth year (and first year as a master's student), Bødo students who have started their business master's degree select a major. For those who want to pursue entrepreneurship as a major, their fourth-year grades determine their admittance. The majority of students who apply for the entrepreneurship major are admitted.

Program Objectives
Bødo wants to prepare its graduates for gainful employment, whether self-employment or with a firm. As such, the program focuses on students' mindsets, capabilities, and status.

Mindsets	Socio-emotional skills	
	Entrepreneurial willingness	✓
	Entrepreneurship theory	✓

Capabilities	Management skills	✓
	Vocational skills	
	Networking skills	
Status	Firm formation	✓
	Self-employment	✓
	Employability	✓
	Income and savings	
	Network formation	
Performance	Profits and sales	✓
	Job creation	
	Market expansion	
	Productivity	
	Reinvestment	
	Innovation	✓

How the Program Works

The entrepreneurship major takes up the entire final year—the fifth year—of master students' course load. Most students going into the major prepare for it by taking electives in entrepreneurship in the year prior (their fourth year). This typically includes business planning, project management, and technology management. The business planning elective includes a one-week seminar where students work with real-life entrepreneurs and develop business plans.

At the start of their final year, Bødo entrepreneurship students spend half their time in the classroom taking required classes in entrepreneurship and innovation management as well as scientific method. As part of the entrepreneurship and innovation management course, students also create small enterprises in peer groups. Over the course of the year, they plan, start, and ultimately end the business—presenting on the enterprise as part of their final exams.

In conjunction with these courses, students also work on their entrepreneurship thesis. The thesis involves a theoretical and empirical study of a topic in entrepreneurship and innovation management.

Who Teaches the Program

Bødo School of Business professors teach entrepreneurship courses, in addition to classes in other areas of the school (e.g., undergraduate electives in entrepreneurship or strategy).

Program Partnerships

Local partners include Innovation Norway, Nordland County Council, SIVA, Kunnskapsparken Bodø, and Kunnskapsfondet, funding workshop seminars and experiential activities like providing housing during students' five-day business plan development seminar. Specifically, Sweden's development agency, SIVA, and the Research Council of Norway fund research on new technology-based firms in which Bødo students are involved, and some students write their master's theses about this research.

The Local Context
To be eligible to apply to the entrepreneurship program, students need to have been admitted to Bødo as undergraduates. And to be admitted to the entrepreneurship master's major, they must have sufficient grades. Given these conditions, the pool of admitted students tends to be at the top of their university.

More broadly, because of Norway's strong social programs—universal health care, education, and readily available welfare—entrepreneurs take on less of a risk when starting their own businesses. Entrepreneurship is increasingly embraced in the country—rising from 20th to 6th place among Organisation for Economic Co-operation and Development (OECD) countries among positive national attitudes toward entrepreneurs. Norway has the highest proportion of start-ups among all Nordic countries; additionally, bankruptcy laws are ranked among the best in the region for entrepreneurs, reducing the cost of failed businesses. Among OECD nations, Norway is a top provider of loans. However, Norway also ranks 10th among OECD countries in administrative burdens in starting a business—behind all Nordic countries.[6]

A Look at the Program Evaluation
In 1995, researchers from Bødo and Norway's Technical University did a tracer survey, sending surveys to entrepreneurship program participants from 1987 to 1994 (Kolvereid and Moen 1997). The evaluation focused on measuring EB and entrepreneurial intention among business school graduates. A total of 720 questionnaires were mailed, while 374 were returned. The final sample was found to be representative of the alumni.

Entrepreneurship was found to be a function of factors that can be altered through education. Further, the study found that having a major in entrepreneurship was positively associated with new firm formation (a major in entrepreneurship was the only variable that was significantly related to new firm formation $r = 0.20$ $p<0.001$); and having a major in entrepreneurship was positively associated with entrepreneurial intentions ($r = 0.26$ $p<0.001$).

Summary

Program details	
Program name	Bødo Graduate School of Business
Country	Norway
Implementing agency	Bødo Graduate School of Business
Program type	A major for master's business school students involving one year of studies and thesis writing
Target audience	Master's year students entering their fifth year
Age	20–24 years
Gender	Equal mix
Objective	To improve students' entrepreneurial awareness and prepare them for starting businesses or joining firms upon graduation
Program maturity	1985
Contact	http://www.uin.no/english/aboutus/faculties/hhb/studyprogrammes/Pages/default.aspx

Cost	None (Education is free for students in Norway.)
Evaluation details	
Evaluator	Lars Kolvereid and Oystein Moen, "Entrepreneurship among Business Graduates: Does a Major in Entrepreneurship Make a Difference?," *Journal of European Industrial Training*, Vol. 21 (1997), No. 4, pp. 154–60.
Evaluation methodology	Tracer survey
Evaluation tier	2

Business Plan Thesis Competition | Tunisia

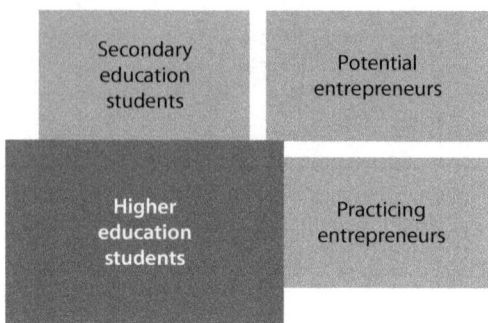

Program Overview

Introduced by Tunisia's government in the 2009–10 school year, the Business Plan Thesis Competition is intended for undergraduate, engineering, graduate, and master's students. The government created the program in the country's 12 public universities—about 700 students matriculate each year—to encourage better employment rates among college graduates. Students can choose to take this program and write a business plan to graduate instead of the traditional thesis that most Tunisian undergraduates must complete.[7]

The program is two part. First, students are trained in basic entrepreneurship skills around business creation. Then, with the help of business mentors and under the supervision of professors, students create business plans. These plans ultimately compete for seed funding in a program-wide competition. While students don't receive a degree from the program itself, they are found to be more knowledgeable about business creation and better networked in the business community.

Who Participates

The program is aimed at Tunisia's undergraduate students, as well as master's and engineering students. The program tends to enroll two-thirds women, which correlates with the demographics of the country's universities.

The typical enrollee is about 23 years old, single, has taken a previous entrepreneurship course and has a strong grasp of English. Typically, students come from middle- to low-income families, and over half have a father with at least a high school education.

Students apply to the program and are randomly admitted—there is no screening process, the only requirement being that a student be enrolled in a participating university.

Program Objectives

The program places a strong focus on status, specifically on a student's potential to become self-employed or to find gainful, sustainable employment upon graduating.

Mindsets	Socio-emotional skills	✓
	Entrepreneurial willingness	✓
	Entrepreneurship theory	
Capabilities	Management skills	✓
	Vocational skills	
	Networking skills	✓
Status	Firm formation	
	Self-employment	✓
	Employability	✓
	Income and savings	
	Network formation	
Performance	Profits and sales	
	Job creation	
	Market expansion	
	Productivity	✓
	Reinvestment	
	Innovation	

How the Program Works

The program has two parts. First, students complete a 20-day entrepreneurship course. Run by the public employment office, this course zeroes in on developing business ideas, writing a business plan, and managing a project—the skills necessary to successfully create a business. Students create an initial draft of a business plan with this information, which is then reviewed by bankers and experts. After receiving this feedback, students research implementation, estimate financials, and begin building their networks.

The second part of the program is more personalized. Each student is assigned a coach with an entrepreneurial background—with whom they meet at least eight times—who advises on finalizing their business plans. The plans include a detailed description of the enterprise, a plan for purchasing necessary inputs, and financial projections for financial viability.

Upon graduating, students can enter their finalized business plan into a competition for seed funding. An external regional jury of professors, employment agency staff, and bankers ranks the plans, with top participants advancing to a national competition where staff from federal government agencies declare a winner. The top 50 participants receive prize money to go toward setting up their enterprises.

Who Teaches the Program

Instructors from the Tunisian employment agency (ANETI) provide the ET for the first part of the program, where participants learn the basics of business creation.

In the second part of the program, experienced entrepreneurs serve as coaches, and university professors oversee students' progress in creating business plans.

Program Partnerships
The Tunisian employment agency (ANETI) runs the training program.

The World Bank has been assessing the efficacy of the program and working with ANETI to address the constraints program participants face in the postgraduation period.

The Local Context
Students choose to apply for the program. Those who enter the program with a business idea are more likely to complete the program. Those who drop out of the program are more likely to be males or students already enrolled in business-related programs, perhaps feeling that the entrepreneurship program is redundant to their current studies.

Nationally, there is a lack of access to credit—a major hindrance for new graduates. Private lending institutions require up to a 20 percent deposit, a prohibitive amount for recent graduates.[8]

A Look at the Program Evaluation
The impact evaluation used a randomized assignment among applicants to the entrepreneurship track to estimate the causal impact of the program. For the academic year of 2009–10, 1,702 students (about 9 percent of all eligible students nationwide) participated in the entrepreneurship track. Some students applied in pairs, so a total of 1,506 projects were registered. The evaluation assigned 757 projects to the treatment group and 742 to the control group. Information was collected at the beginning of the 5-month program (February 2009) and 9 to 12 months after graduation from the program (April–June 2011). Information collected included indicators on socio-economic characteristics, labor, aspirations for the future, personality traits, and behavioral skills related to entrepreneurship.

Approximately one year after graduation, graduates of the entrepreneurship track had a higher probability of being self-employed. Although the effects were small in absolute terms (ranging from 1 to 4 percentage points), given the low prevalence of self-employment in the control group, the small absolute effects imply that beneficiaries were on average 46–87 percent more likely to be self-employed compared to the control group.

There was no evidence that the program significantly affected overall employment as captured by the likelihood of being employed in the last seven days. In fact, estimates were negative and pointed to a reduction in the probability of holding wage employment; and although not significant, the decrease was of the same magnitude as the increase in self-employment, suggesting the possibility of a substitution effect from wage employment to self-employment.

The program did not promote higher-quality jobs among participants. There were no significant program impacts on employment in the formal sector, firm size, hours of work, or earnings. But the intervention produced strong impacts on participants' self-reported business skills and networking proxies.

About 77 percent of program graduates reported knowing how to produce a business plan, compared to 45 percent in the control group.

The program led to measurable, significant, and robust changes in several domains of the "Big Five" socio-emotional skills, including a decrease in agreeableness (0.23–0.25 s.d. compared to control group) and an increase in extraversion (albeit a less robust finding compared to the previous trait). There was no evidence to indicate that the ET positively affected conscientiousness and emotional stability, and other entrepreneurial traits such as tenacity or power motivation remained unchanged.

Participants were found to be more likely to be confident in obtaining credit and to have applied for credit (conditional on having a business idea), but they were neither more likely to know how to apply for credit nor to have obtained credit.

Summary

Program details	
Program name	Business Plan Thesis Competition
Country	Tunisia
Implementing agency	Ministry of Vocational Education and Employment, the Ministry of Industry, the Ministry of Higher Education, and ANETI (the public employment office)
Program type	Higher educational entrepreneurship program with a strong focus on business plan creation
Target audience	Undergraduate and master's graduate students
Age	20–25 years old
Gender	Two-thirds female
Objective	Increase self-employment among graduates by improving skills and affecting attitudes toward entrepreneurship
Program maturity	Started in Tunisia in 2009
Contact	http://www.cnentrepreunariat.mes.rnu.tn/historique.php
Evaluation details	
Evaluator	Patric Premand, Stefanie Brodmann, Rita Almeida, Rebekka Grun, and Mahdi Barouni, "Entrepreneurship Training and Self-Employment among University Graduates: Evidence from a Randomized Trial in Tunisia," Policy Research Working Paper No. 6285 (World Bank: 2012).
Evaluation methodology	Impact evaluation using a randomized assignment
Evaluation tier	1

McGuire Center for Entrepreneurship Program | United States

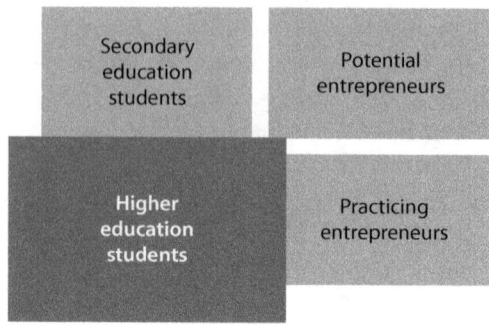

Program Overview
Started in 1983, the McGuire Entrepreneurship Program is one of the oldest entrepreneurship programs in the United States. Based at the University of Arizona's Eller College of Management, this local program attracts top tier undergraduate and graduate students from the University of Arizona. Undergraduate business students obtain a second major in entrepreneurship, master's of business administration students complete a concentration in entrepreneurship, and doctoral students from around the university complete a doctoral minor in entrepreneurship. For non-business undergraduate and graduate students, the program does not award a degree, but completing the course is a prestigious distinction and provides a strong link to the entrepreneurship community.[9]

All participants have completed at least some college and have varying degrees of business experience. They spend their year at the McGuire Program studying marketing and finance as well as venture development. These face-to-face classes complement the students' year-long focus on creating a new venture that will ultimately compete with other students' venture plans for awards totaling US$10,000.

Who Participates
Applicants from across the University of Arizona—undergraduate and graduate students alike—along with aspiring entrepreneurs can apply to be students. About 80 students matriculate each year; 65 percent are undergraduate students who are majoring in business, and the other 35 percent are completing graduate programs at the University of Arizona (e.g., business degrees; master's in engineering studies). The student body is one-quarter women.

Students who are admitted have a strong academic background with a clear interest in entrepreneurship and a commitment to collaborative learning settings.

Program Outcomes
The McGuire Entrepreneurship Program aims to prepare students to successfully apply entrepreneurial principles whether they start their own business or go

to work in a corporation. Specifically, the program focuses on students' capabilities and status.

Mindsets	Socio-emotional skills	
	Entrepreneurial willingness	
	Entrepreneurship theory	
Capabilities	Management skills	✓
	Vocational skills	
	Networking skills	
Status	Firm formation	✓
	Self-employment	✓
	Employability	✓
	Income and savings	
	Network formation	✓
Performance	Profits and sales	
	Job creation	
	Market expansion	
	Productivity	
	Reinvestment	
	Innovation	

How the Program Works

Each school year, approximately 80 students begin McGuire's year-long entrepreneurship program. The students are high-achieving, ages 20–30, who are either undergraduate or graduate students at the University of Arizona and have demonstrated strong academic credentials and an interest in enterprise. The core curriculum is very clearly defined, and students are forever part of an alumni network of entrepreneurs who also completed the McGuire program.

Within the first weeks of the program, the students form teams of 3–4 students, and each team starts formulating a new venture. Throughout the school year, their classes will help inform the elements of this venture—a marketing class, a venture finance course, and venture development classes. Classes meet twice a week in the fall and once a week in the spring semester.

Students are taught by Eller Business School professors and the McGuire program's two mentors-in-residence, successful business professionals who spend the year shepherding students through the program. Each team is also assigned one of these two mentors, with whom they check in each week to discuss the status of their venture. Additionally, each team is provided legal counsel by a team of University of Arizona students who are studying entrepreneurship law.

Throughout the year, teams compete for Heart Experiential Grants, which assist with venture testing. Students also compete for McGuire Program funding to compete in regional and national business plan competitions.

To ensure that students have learned from their time in the McGuire Program, they are put through an academic review in the spring. Each team of students must present its business plan and field questions from a panel of entrepreneurship professors from outside universities. The aim of this interaction is to ensure that students understand the material they have spent the past several months studying.

At the end of the school year, each team of students competes in an internal new-venture competition where they defend their plans. A panel of business professionals and entrepreneurs judges the students and selects first-, second-, and third-place winners. Typically, six or seven teams launch their ventures each year. To date, the McGuire Program has produced nearly 200 businesses.

Students who complete the McGuire Program receive a certificate of completion and credits that can be applied toward their degree.

Who Teaches the Program

Finance and marketing courses are taught by business school professors and adjunct faculty. The year-long venture development course, though, is team-taught by the two mentors-in-residence. Along with teaching, the mentors meet with each team of students at least once per week to review the progress of their new ventures. These are real-world entrepreneurs who found success in their own right and are now full-time McGuire Program faculty who teach and mentor students.

A communications mentor is available much of the year to advise students on the written part of their business plans and their presentation style. Occasionally, guest lecturers and domain experts present to classes.

Program Partnerships

A local angel investment group, the Desert Angels, serves as a mentoring partner. Their members occasionally guest-lecture, participate in angel mentoring workshops each semester, and are available to provide feedback to any McGuire Program teams as they develop their new ventures.

Additionally, the McGuire Program has a partnership with the entrepreneurship class at the University of Arizona's law school. Law students serve as legal advisers to each team of McGuire Program students, providing legal advice on their venture plans.

The Local Context

Self-selected students who apply for and are accepted to the McGuire Program are highly motivated and well educated. To be eligible for the program, students must be enrolled in or have completed a college degree. Students who are selected tend to be at the top of their classes—representing an upper echelon of U.S. college-educated students. Doctoral students who apply for a minor in the program are interviewed; other applicants are not.

The McGuire Program is housed within the University of Arizona's Eller College of Management. All classrooms are well equipped for learning—this is a technologically advanced campus where students can do online research anywhere and use a variety of libraries. Students can safely traverse the campus and have the option to live at the university or in nearby housing.

Entrepreneurs magazine ranked Arizona in the top 10 of U.S. states for starting a business, noting the state's large awards and tax credits for starting businesses.

A Look at the Program Evaluation

Researchers from the University of Arizona, financed by the Kauffman Center for Entrepreneurial Leadership, analyzed the McGuire Program's impact on both the University of Arizona and on the program graduates' aspirations in a 2000 publication (Charney and Libecap, 2000). A tracer survey was developed to achieve this.

The evaluation studied the trajectories of business entrepreneurship and non-business entrepreneurship cohorts from 1985 to 1998. The evaluation assessed the formation of new ventures, likelihood of self-employment, sales growth rate of emerging firms, accumulation of graduates' assets, and technology transfer from the university to the private sector. A total of 2,024 surveys were mailed to graduates from the non-entrepreneurship business school graduates and 460 entrepreneurship graduates, all of whom had graduated from the university between 1985 and 1998. The final response rate was 511 for the non-entrepreneurship business graduates and 105 for the entrepreneurship graduates.

Response rates were generally uniform across levels of degrees and types of programs, although it should be noted that the response rate was extremely low at 21 percent.

EE increased the probability of an individual being involved in a new business venture by 25 percent over non-entrepreneurship graduates. Entrepreneurship students were 11 percent more likely than non-entrepreneurship students to own their own businesses after graduation. Further, EE contributed to the growth of firms, especially smaller emerging firms. On average, smaller emerging firms that were owned by or employed entrepreneurship graduates had greater than five times the sales and employment growth than those that employed non-entrepreneurship graduates.

Entrepreneurship graduates received an average annual income that was 27 percent higher compared to the average annual income of non-entrepreneurship graduates. And entrepreneurship education increased a business school graduate's probability of being associated with a high-tech firm by nearly 13 percent and of developing new technological products by almost 9 percent.

EE enhanced the transfer of technology from the university to the private sector and promoted technology-based firms and products. Among self-employed entrepreneurship graduates, nearly 23 percent owned a high-technology firm, compared to less than 15 percent of non-entrepreneurship graduates who owned a firm.

Summary

Program details	
Program name	McGuire Center for Entrepreneurship Program
Country	United States
Program type	Year-long entrepreneurship program at the University of Arizona's Eller College of Management
Target audience	University and graduate students
Age	20–35 year olds
Gender	75 percent male
Objective	To improve students' entrepreneurial thinking and skills—preparing them for self-employment or to join a firm
Program maturity	Started in 1983
Contact	http://mcguireexperience.com/
Cost	Depending on the track of courses taken, and whether students are from Arizona, tuition rates range from US$5,200 to US$15,825. Costs to the McGuire Center to deliver the program are approximately US$900,000 annually.
Evaluation	
Evaluator	Alberta Charney and Gary D. Libecap, "Impact of Entrepreneurship Education," *Insights: Kauffman Research Series* (Kauffman Center for Entrepreneurial Leadership: 2000). Recovered from: http://entrepreneurship.eller.arizona.edu/Docs/Evaluation/Impactevaluation_Entrepreneurshipprogram_UA.Pdf
Evaluation tier	2
Evaluation methodology	Tracer survey

Entrepreneurship Development Centre | Bosnia and Herzegovina

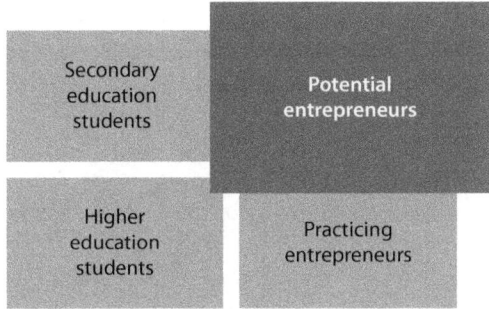

Program Overview
The Entrepreneurship Development Centre (EDC) ran a comprehensive business training program for existing and potential entrepreneurs who had loans at Partner Microcredit Foundation in 2009. Participants were young adults in Bosnia and Herzegovina who had small businesses or who were developing a new enterprise.[10]

EDC developed a curriculum around the basics of running a business and required participants to complete a strategic plan. More than 100 people participated in the nine-hour training program over three days, which culminated with a certificate.

Program Objectives
EDC focused on participants' status—how they could effectively use the capital from their loans to form or expand a promising business, with a particular focus on management skills, profit and sales, market expansion, and productivity.

Mindsets	Socio-emotional skills	
	Entrepreneurial willingness	
	Entrepreneurship theory	
Capabilities	Management skills	✓
	Vocational skills	
	Networking skills	
Status	Firm formation	✓
	Self-employment	✓
	Employability	
	Income and savings	✓
	Network formation	
Performance	Profits and sales	✓
	Job creation	
	Market expansion	✓
	Productivity	✓
	Reinvestment	
	Innovation	

Who Participates
The typical participant was between ages 18 and 35 and a resident of Tuzla. He or she either owned a business or was trying to start one with a Partner Microcredit Foundation loan. Potential participants were called to see if they were interested in taking part in the training.

How the Program Works
EDC ran its ET in seven locations around Tuzla in 2009. EDC consultants, including professors from the University of Tuzla, served as instructors. Class size was between 6 and 10 participants.

The training took place over three days, with three-hour intensive meetings each day. Participants learned the basics of running a small business—accounting, investment, and growth strategies. During the course, each participant developed a business plan. If participants completed the business plan and abided by the mandatory attendance rule, they received a certificate of completion.

Who Teaches the Program
EDC trainers and consultants served as instructors. They came from a variety of backgrounds—accounting, marketing, and business—and some were professors from the University of Tuzla. EDC gave instructors a curriculum to follow.

Program Partnerships
The EDC trainings were held at seven different locations, including the Tuzla Chamber of Commerce, in order to limit traveling for the project beneficiaries.

The Local Context
Participants had varying degrees of business knowledge. Many already owned small businesses, and others were new to entrepreneurship.

Bosnia and Herzegovina has high youth unemployment—61 percent.[11] Further, the economy is post-conflict and is still struggling. The country has a difficult climate for new or developing businesses. The International Finance Corporation ranks Bosnia and Herzegovina the lowest in Eastern Europe for small and medium-sized enterprises per capita, and the World Bank ranks the country 110th for doing business.

A Look at the Program Evaluation
The evaluation aimed to study the impact of a comprehensive business and financial literacy program on firm outcomes, specifically among young entrepreneurs in emerging post-conflict economy. A randomized control trial took place in 2009 (Bruhn and Zia 2011), using a sample size of 445 active business loan clients—all between 18 and 35 years old—who were interested in the training at the initial phone screening.

The evaluation design suffered some changes over time, and by the end, the treatment group was composed of 117 individuals (39 percent of the individuals who were invited to the training) and 148 in the control group.

A baseline survey was conducted in April and May 2009, and the implementation of the business training was carried out between June and December 2009.

An exit test was administered at the end of the training to all participants. Finally, a follow-up survey was conducted in May and June 2010, one year after the baseline survey. Outcomes were based on business creation and survival, business performance, business growth, business practices and investments, and loan behavior.

The training program did not influence the business survival. Training did improve the business practices, investments, and loan terms for businesses, as well as improving business and financial knowledge on average (after the training, the total score of the exit test had increased from a baseline of 2.6–2.9). At follow-up, the average treatment effect of the training in business and financial knowledge was positive, but not statistically significant.

The strongest effects of the training were on improvements in business practices and investments: the treatment group was 17 percent more likely to implement new production processes than the control group, and 11 percent more likely to inject new investment into the business.

The training also increased business profits for entrepreneurs with above median financial literacy at baseline by 54 percent, although the results were not statistically significant at conventional levels.

No impact was found on loan amounts, but there were significant impacts on loan restructuring. The treatment group was 3.4 percent more likely than the control group to refinance its loans. This effect was large, indicating that the treatment almost doubled the likelihood of refinancing loans.

Summary

Program details	
Program name	Entrepreneurship Development Centre
Country	Bosnia and Herzegovina
Implementing agency	Partner Microcredit Foundation
Program type	Entrepreneurial training program for young adults
Target audience	Potential and practicing entrepreneurs, many of whom were exiting loan clients of Partner Microcredit Foundation
Age	18–35 years
Gender	One-third women
Objective	To help participants create an effective business plan for implementation after receipt of loan
Program maturity	Two-month program run in 2009
Contact	office@cerpod-tuzla.org
Cost and financing	The World Bank, Kaufman Foundation, and Partner Microcredit Foundation provided financing. It was free for beneficiaries, who were also provided a stipend of US$35 for the cost of their time and received transportation to and from the program location.
Evaluation details	
Evaluator	Miriam Bruhn and Bilal Zia, "Stimulating Managerial Capital in Emerging Markets: The Impact of Business and Financial Literacy for Young Entrepreneurs," Policy Research Working Paper No. 5642 (Washington, DC: World Bank, 2011).
Evaluation methodology	Randomized control trial
Evaluation tier	1

Economic Empowerment of Adolescent Girls and Young Women | Liberia

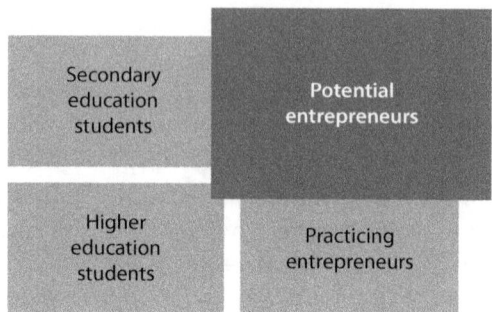

Program Overview

Mindsets	Socio-emotional skills	✓
	Entrepreneurial willingness	✓
	Entrepreneurship theory	
Capabilities	Management skills	✓
	Vocational skills	✓
	Networking skills	✓
Status	Firm formation	
	Self-employment	✓
	Employability	✓
	Income and savings	✓
	Network formation	
Performance	Profits and sales	
	Job creation	
	Market expansion	
	Productivity	
	Reinvestment	
	Innovation	

Led by the Liberian Ministry of Gender and Development, the Economic Empowerment of Adolescent Girls and Young Women (EPAG) focuses on improving young women's employment opportunities. Over six months of classroom training and a subsequent six months of placement and support, participants receive life skills training and learn business development or job skills.[12]

EPAG started in December 2009, and has trained 2,500 women—1,000 more were anticipated in the summer of 2013. EPAG's first two years were financed by the Nike Foundation and the Danish International Development Agency; its incoming group of trainees will be supported by the World Bank's Umbrella Facility for Gender Empowerment.

Who Participates
Selection criteria for EPAG participants are that women:

- be between ages 16 and 27;
- not have been in school the past six months (this requirement has since become more flexible if potential participants have returned to school);
- have basic literacy; and
- live in 1 of the 11 EPAG communities. (The first years of EPAG included nine communities around Monrovia and Kakata City. In 2013, trainings were to also take place in Grand Bassa County.)

In its current form, prospective participants apply for the program and, if they meet the criteria, are placed in a training session.

Program Objectives
The program focuses on participants' mindsets, capabilities, and status—the program wants more young women who are employable or prepared to open their own businesses.

How the Program Works
The program is structured to ensure seamless transition from training to job placement. The training takes places over six months and includes a classroom component of life skills training followed by segmentation of the class into training in business development skills (70 percent of participants) and job/entrepreneurial skills (30 percent of participants). Those receiving job skills training have their curriculum specifically tailored to sectors that are hiring. Throughout the training, participants receive stipends, contingent upon their attendance.

Upon completion of the classroom component, trainees receive six months of job and internship placement assistance as well as micro-enterprise advice. Further, participants receive a bonus of US$20 if they've completed the training, which goes towards opening a savings account. Each classroom has an instructor as well as an EPAG coach, a local businesswoman who volunteered to mentor students. Additionally, EPAG participants form peer groups to mentor each other throughout the year.

To accommodate participants' outside jobs and family demands, classroom sessions are held in the morning and afternoon, with free childcare on site. Throughout the six-month training, there is a series of incentives to ensure attendance—prizes, business plan competitions, contests, and so on.

Who Teaches the Program
In the most recent iteration of the program, four nongovernmental organization (NGO) service providers supplied the instructors for the trainings and helped lead the job placement among participants. The instructors have extensive training in this kind of teaching, and their pay is withheld until they place their participants in jobs.

Program Partnerships

The service providers have strong ties to the private sector to ensure job placement of participants. Further, in the most recent iterations of the program, the coach in each class is a practicing businesswoman in the community.

The Local Context

In Liberia, EPAG decided that literacy would be a requirement for selection because international experience suggests that youth training programs are generally more effective for beneficiaries with some basic literacy skills. However, the girls who are interested in the program are mostly illiterate. As a result, the project piloted a literacy and numeracy component in the second round of training.

In 2010, Liberia ranked 11th out of 47 countries in the corruption index; the country is also hindered by poor infrastructure and expensive electrical power. Liberia ranked 151 out of 183 in the World Bank's 2012 *Doing Business* report.

Liberia's difficult job market is especially prohibitive for women. Society prioritizes young men's education over women's, meaning women are more likely to be illiterate. According to the United Nations Educational, Scientific, and Cultural Organization, young women have a 57 percent literacy rate, compared to 65 percent among Liberian men. Further, gender-based vulnerabilities are prevalent throughout Liberia. Schools are often unsafe for young women. Almost one-third of 15- to 24-year old women have reported physical violence, and rape is the most documented crime in Liberia.

A Look at the Program Evaluation

A World Bank study used a randomized pipeline research design to assess EPAG, randomly assigning beneficiaries to receive training in either the first round (March 2010–February 2011) or the second round (July 2011–June 2012).

Approximately 2,500 young women were accepted to participate in the program for the evaluation. The evaluation randomized participants into a control group and a treatment group, which included two types of treatment: (a) training package on business development and life skills and (b) training package on job, entrepreneurship, and life skills.

Impact was defined as the change in outcomes between the time the program started and six months after the classroom training ended, as compared to a statistically similar control group (the second-round trainees). The evaluation measured the impacts of the skills packages on employment, behaviors, empowerment and agency, and family welfare.

The study revealed that the program was well received—the retention rate was 95 percent and attendance averaged 90 percent. Further, EPAG increased employment among trainees by 50 percent, compared to those in the control group.

Positive employment outcomes were driven primarily by the business development skills trainees, whose monthly income increased by US$75 per month. Additionally, EPAG increased the girls' savings compared to the control group. At midline, the treatment group had a total of US$44 more in savings compared to the control group. However, there were no significant changes to borrowing or lending among beneficiaries.

Summary

Program details	
Program name	Economic Empowerment of Adolescent Girls and Young Women
Country	Liberia
Implementing agency	Liberian Ministry of Gender and Development
Program type	Six-month course that included business or entrepreneurial skills training in a classroom, microenterprise counseling, and job placement services
Target audience	Young Liberian women who aren't in school and who live in Monrovia, Kakata City, or Grand Bassa County
Age	16–27 year olds
Gender	All women
Objective	To improve participants' employability by sharpening business and/or entrepreneurial skills
Program maturity	In Liberia since 2009
Contact	www.worldbank.org/gender/agi
Cost and financing	The program costs between US$1,220 and US$1,700 per participant, depending on their track
Evaluation details	
Evaluator	World Bank, "Can Skills Training Programs Increase Employment for Young Women? The Case of Liberia," Adolescent Girls Initiative, Results Series (Washington, DC: 2012)
Evaluation methodology	Randomized pipeline research design
Evaluation tier	1

TechnoServe | El Salvador

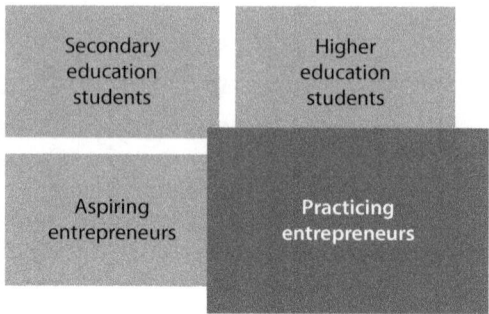

Program Overview

In 2002, TechnoServe started to do work in El Salvador, creating a business plan competition to promote entrepreneurship. Existing entrepreneurs who wanted to grow their businesses and potential entrepreneurs who wanted to create new businesses entered a 40-hour training course to learn the basics of creating a business plan. Upon completion of the course, the participants entered a business plan competition, with the potential to win seed funding. Originally, 296 participants took the course, with 114 completing a business plan.

Soon, TechnoServe will be launching a revised version of its ET program in El Salvador, training existing entrepreneurs in writing business plans and ultimately assigning them business advisers to help in the implementation of the plan.

Started in 1968, TechnoServe is a global NGO that aims to promote private enterprise in areas with rural poverty. Its business plan competition component spread from El Salvador throughout Central America and into Africa. In addition to business plan competitions, TechnoServe has a series of tailored ET programs for developing countries around the world.[13]

Who Participates

In its original business plan program in El Salvador, potential participants applied to the program and were selected if they exhibited the potential of growing their business through the program. The basic requirements were that participants had to own a small business—with no more than five employees—and have less than US$20,000 in assets. Participants were from across the country, including San Salvador, Santa Ana, Sonsonate, Cabanas, and Libertad.

Program Objectives

The program focuses on taking small businesses to the next level—specifically zeroing in on participants' performance.

Mindsets	Socio-emotional skills	
	Entrepreneurial willingness	
	Entrepreneurship theory	
Capabilities	Management skills	
	Vocational skills	
	Networking skills	
Status	Firm formation	
	Self-employment	
	Employability	
	Income and savings	
	Network formation	
Performance	Profits and sales	✓
	Job creation	
	Market expansion	✓
	Productivity	✓
	Reinvestment	
	Innovation	✓

How the Program Works
Over six months, participants completed a 40-hour training over seven days in how to create a business plan. The training focused on developing both technical business skills and core EBs. During this time, participants worked to create their own plan—a 30–40 page document. Each class's business plans were judged, one against the other, and the top 30 scoring plans proceeded into a third phase of the program.

In the program's final phase, participants received one-on-one assistance from volunteer consultants, who helped them refine their business plans. This last phase concluded with another business plan competition, this time segmented by sector, with the top-placing participants receiving between US$6,000 and US$15,000 to go toward the implementation of their businesses.

Who Teaches the Program
TechnoServe typically chooses instructors—whom they call *business advisers*—with strong backgrounds in education and business. Business advisers are typically from the region and have been trained by TechnoServe in the curriculum.

Program Partnerships
In the original version of the El Salvador program, TechnoServe partnered with the United Nations Council on Trade and Development's EMPRETEC to implement the curriculum.

The Local Context
In its initial format, participants chose to apply, and needed to match criteria that indicated a likelihood of being able to expand an existing business (or create a new one). This self-selection indicated a more ambitious baseline among participants.

TechnoServe programs take place in rural, poverty-ridden areas. This makes the formation and sustainment of new businesses difficult. El Salvador in particular is a difficult economic climate for entrepreneurs—crime is high in the region, adversely affecting businesses. World Bank data indicate that losses from theft, robbery, vandalism, or arson represent 2.6 percent of company sales in El Salvador, the highest rate in Latin America and the 10th highest in the world.[14]

A Look at the Program Evaluation

Researchers looked at the results of past competitions in Latin America between 2002 and 2005 (Klinger and Schündlen 2007). The evaluation assessed whether business training for small and medium enterprise entrepreneurs or potential entrepreneurs could lead to an increase in the number of business start-ups or an expansion in the size of existing businesses. The methodology exploited a quasi-experimental approach (regression discontinuity), where the number of participants was fixed exogenously and provided a cut-off in the scoring of applications. The sample size was 655 applications in the three countries, where 377 received at least some training, and 278 were rejected applicants who did not receive any training. The outcomes measured were related to starting or expanding businesses.

The evidence suggested that receiving business training significantly increased the probability of business start-ups and expanded existing business. TechnoServe led to a higher probability—9–11 percentage points—of opening a business (for individuals without a business before the start of the program) in the treatment group and a 23–26 percentage point higher probability of expanding a business (for individuals with an existing business before the program) in the treatment group.

Winning TechnoServe's business plan competition led to economically significant changes in the probability of starting or expanding a business, suggesting the presence of financial constraints. Of note, financial constraints were more important for women who wished to start or expand a business than for men.

Summary

Program details	
Program name	TechnoServe
Country	El Salvador
Implementing agency	TechnoServe
Program type	Week-long training session for potential and practicing entrepreneurs, followed by a business plan competition
Target audience	Potential and practicing entrepreneurs
Age	All ages
Gender	More males than females
Objective	To improve participants' business skills and core entrepreneurial competencies so they can grow their businesses
Program maturity	In El Salvador in 2002; subsequent program anticipated to begin in late 2013

Contact	http://www.technoserve.org/
Cost and financing	Participants paid an application fee of US$15. The implementation cost to run the initial program was US$343,420.
Evaluation details	
Evaluator	Bailey Klinger and Matthias Schündlen, "Can Entrepreneurial Activity be Taught? Quasi-Experimental Evidence from Central America," CID Working Paper No. 153 (Harvard University: 2007).
Evaluation methodology	Quasi-experimental (Regression discontinuity)
Evaluation tier	1

FINCA Entrepreneurship Program | Peru

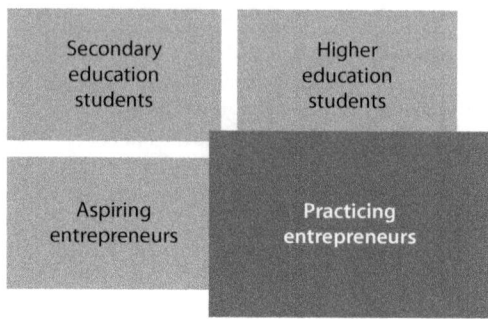

Program Overview

Operating in Peru since 1993, FINCA-Peru is a micro-finance institution that trains low-income entrepreneurs using a village-banking methodology. FINCA-Peru clients receive loans and meet once or twice a month to repay their installments and receive training. Participants use their loan money to invest in their businesses and are required to save money each month. FINCA's ultimate goal is to provide clients with financial and non-financial services while helping them develop their businesses.[15]

Each FINCA-Peru client has some experience running a business and comes to FINCA-Peru for loans and training in small business fundamentals. The program uses both experiential and peer-based education, and participants are required to make biweekly or monthly deposits into their savings accounts.

FINCA-Peru has over 16,000 clients throughout Peru, operating a 3,000 client program in the low-income neighborhoods of Lima and larger programs throughout two high-poverty Andean provinces, Ayacucho and Huancavelica. Participants are predominantly female—82 percent of whom lack formal education beyond secondary school. FINCA-Peru maintains that women who are able to achieve a higher level of income will be able to pass along their earnings directly to all members of their families. In addition to its entrepreneurship micro-finance program, FINCA-Peru also offers trainings on preventive health care, gender equality, and personal development.

Who Participates

FINCA-Peru primarily serves women who run small businesses in one of their three regions. To become eligible for the program, a participant needs to have overseen her business for at least six months.

Women apply for the FINCA-Peru loan and become a FINCA-Peru client once they've presented a copy of their identification and a utility receipt to confirm where they live, as well as gone through a site visit to verify they live there and have a business.

Program Objectives

The program hopes to impact its clients' status and to some extent their mindsets. The biggest focus is on participants' capabilities around saving and reinvesting in their companies.

Mindsets	Socio-emotional skills	
	Entrepreneurial willingness	
	Entrepreneurship theory	
Capabilities	Management skills	✓
	Vocational skills	
	Networking skills	
Status	Firm formation	
	Self-employment	
	Employability	
	Income and savings	✓
	Network formation	✓
Performance	Profits and sales	✓
	Job creation	
	Market expansion	✓
	Productivity	
	Reinvestment	✓
	Innovation	

How the Program Works

When a client joins FINCA-Peru, she is given a small loan to help her business. The loan amount varies by region—the initial disbursement ranging from US$80 to US$360. The group of women in each region who gather for instruction and bank disbursements is called a "village bank." In each of these FINCA-Peru banks, clients elect a board of their peers to oversee the bank's finances. This board helps guide their bank's functioning and leads group decision making.

Once or twice a month, groups of about 18 clients meet for a 45-minute training session about a topic relevant to growing a business. A case study is discussed, and then the clients break into small groups to weigh questions put forward by the instructor. The session then reconvenes to hear the three to four take-aways from the session, which will again be discussed at the next meeting.

After each training session concludes, clients take turns discussing problems in their businesses and seeking advice from their colleagues. Every month or two, clients receive internal loan disbursements from their bank at the conclusion of the day's session.

The length of the training modules varies by region but can go from six months to a year. Clients receive trainings that focus on improving their basic business practices in subject areas like how to treat clients, how to use profits, where to sell, how to use special discounts, and how to conduct credit sales. FINCA-Peru places a strong emphasis on saving money; at each meeting, clients are encouraged to add to their savings.

Who Teaches the Program

FINCA-Peru identifies potential instructors (called "promoters" by FINCA) based on their ability to work with a group and facilitate training sessions. Instructors are frequently chosen from a pool of former FINCA-Peru clients and are trained in the basics of being a loan officer, since they will also serve in this role with the village banks.

FINCA-Peru training coordinators teach the instructors group facilitation skills, the materials covered in FINCA modules, and financial preparedness.

FINCA-Peru's instructors receive a bonus for the quality and number of sessions they deliver each month, as well as financial indicators of growth and past-due loans.

Program Partnerships

FINCA-Peru partners with organizations in certain communities that can provide technical assistance. In rural areas, alliances provide assistance on how to better produce crops. In quasi-rural or urban areas, FINCA partners with universities where students help carry out evaluations of the program's efficacy. Volunteers also provide significant help with evaluations.

The Local Context

There is significant variation in education and literacy levels among participants in Lima and the two other regions. In Lima, the majority of clients have at least completed secondary school, whereas in Ayacucho and Huancavelica, some of the clients are illiterate.

Clients participate at varying levels. Some find it hard to attend training sessions because of family concerns. Some cannot always take the time to leave their business and travel for the once or twice-monthly sessions.

There is no cost to take the program. Instead, the interest rate for each participant's loan covers the cost of participation.

There is significant economic variation among FINCA's regions. The job market in Lima is strong and well developed—in 2011, unemployment fell to 7 percent in the capital city.[16] However, rural Peru is a different story—in 2008, an overwhelming 49 percent of rural female workers were unpaid family members (Peruvian Ministry of Labour 2008). Further, Ayacucho and Huancavelica—two of FINCA's outposts—have struggled with terrorist activities, creating a more trying setting to start or enhance a business.

A Look at the Program Evaluation

The evaluation (Karlan and Valdivia 2012) looked at whether micro-entrepreneurs were maximizing their profits, given the resources available to them, and whether lessons on business development improved FINCA-Peru clients' profits. A randomized control trial was conducted to evaluate the effectiveness of integrating business training with microfinance services, using a sample of FINCA Peru's preexisting lending clients.

Typically, the clients were organized into groups of 20 women randomly assigned to control and treatment groups, stratified by credit officer. The distribution included 139 groups assigned to the treatment and 101 to the control. The evaluation used three key data sources: FINCA financial transaction data, a baseline survey before the randomization results were announced, and a follow-up survey up to two years later.

The response rate was 76 percent for the follow-up survey, somewhat lower in the treatment group (75.2 percent) compared to the control group (77.9 percent). The results of the analysis were divided into four categories: (a) business outcomes, (b) business processes and knowledge, (c) household outcomes, and (d) microfinance institutional outcomes.

Basic business training to preexisting clients did not lead to higher profits or revenues on average. However, difference-in-difference specifications found a positive but small impact on enterprise revenues.

Positive changes in four business skills and practices outcomes were significant at 95 percent (keeping records, an index of business knowledge, the use of profits for business growth, and implementation of innovations in the business). But no training impact was found on household decision making.

The training led to a 4 percentage point increase in the client retention rate—generating an increase in net revenue for FINCA. But the training had no effect on loan size or accumulated savings. Further, sometimes the stronger training effects were found for those clients who expressed less interest in the training in the baseline survey.

Summary

Program details	
Program name	FINCA Entrepreneurship Program
Country	Peru
Program type	Classroom-based microfinance and entrepreneurial training program for existing small business owners
Target audience	Small business owners of at least 6 months; serving 16,000 practicing entrepreneurs around Peru
Age	Adults of mixed ages
Gender	90 percent women
Objective	To improve business outcomes and overall welfare for clients and to improve institutional outcomes for the microfinance institution
Program maturity	Evaluation in 2002–03
Contact	http://www.fincaperu.net/cms/index.php/es/
Evaluation	
Evaluator	Dean Karlan and Martin Valdivia, "Teaching Entrepreneurship: Impact of Business Training on Microfinance Clients and Institutions," *The Review of Economics and Statistics,* Vol. 93 (2012), No. 2, pp. 510–27.
Evaluation methodology	Randomized control trial
Evaluation tier	1

National Rural Savings Programme | Pakistan

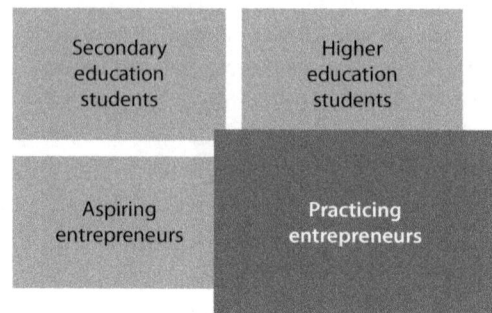

Program Overview

At the time of its evaluation in 2007, the National Rural Support Programme (NRSP) in Pakistan tied a series of its micro-loans to entrepreneurial training sessions. During 46 hours of training, participants studied business planning, marketing, and financial management. Upon completion of the training modules, NRSP identified the participants who were eligible to apply for a larger loan size.[17]

NRSP's approach to microfinance lending includes a requirement that its members join community organizations (COs). These local organizations typically have between 15 and 30 members and number over 150,000 across Pakistan, occupying nearly one-third of Pakistan's microfinance market. NRSP members must meet regularly with their COs, contribute towards their group's savings as well as their own, and both receive and repay their loans.

With a presence in 54 districts in Pakistan, NRSP now works with more than two million low-income households in the country. Started in 1991 with a focus on reducing poverty and increasing rural development, NRSP works within rural regions of Pakistan to help communities implement a variety of programs aimed at increasing productive employment, alleviating poverty, and improving the quality of life.

Who Participates

NRSP works in low-income, rural communities. The participants are more likely to be male, who run at least one business.

Program Outcomes

NRSP is strongly focused on its participants' firm performance and their capabilities in saving and around business development. By participating in group learning and saving sessions, NRSP also values participants' status, specifically regarding network formation.

Mindsets	Socio-emotional skills
	Entrepreneurial willingness
	Entrepreneurship theory

Capabilities	Management skills	✓
	Vocational skills	
	Networking skills	
Status	Firm formation	
	Self-employment	
	Employability	
	Income and savings	
	Network formation	✓
Performance	Profits and sales	✓
	Job creation	
	Market expansion	✓
	Productivity	
	Reinvestment	✓
	Innovation	

How the Program Works

In 2007, NRSP randomly selected over 1,200 rural Pakistanis who had applied for loans. These participants each received a loan of US$1,000 and were required to attend a series of trainings on better business practices. Over several weeks, they attended sessions on expenditures, financial outlook, marketing, and business planning.

Participants were given a travel allowance and a snack and lunch for the six-day session that ran daily from 9 am to 4 pm. The training took place in a classroom, involving a series of group work activities and an off-site field visit to local markets, area suppliers, and wholesalers. The final day of the training included a business creation exercise, where participants created a micro-business plan. The training concluded with an awards ceremony.

Loan officers followed up with each participant after the training was completed to make sure their businesses were still running, and to ensure that the loan money was going toward business development. With the completion of the business training, the sign-off of loan officers, and proof of being in good financial standing (i.e., having successfully met loan repayment deadlines), participants were eligible to apply for another, larger loan.

Among all the participants in the 2007 training and microfinance program, no one has had a loan delinquency.

Who Teaches the Program

NRSP staff members—who had a background in classroom instruction—underwent a 31-day training session, organized by ECI, a local firm specializing in capacity-building activities for micro-entrepreneurs.

Program Partnerships

NRSP worked with ECI to train instructors and create an appropriate curriculum for the micro-lending/training program in 2007.

The Local Context

Participants were randomly selected to be part of the program. As such, there is significant variation in education and literacy levels. Further, male and female participants had remarkably different levels of success upon completing the program—despite having an increase in business knowledge (87 percent), women reported being unable to put into practice their newly acquired knowledge. Similarly, the training had positive effects on men's business failures but no effect on women's businesses—perhaps indicating that a future intervention might need to have a more intense focus on engaging women entrepreneurs.

The focus of this program on rural populations created barriers to providing vast, equitable trainings. Some participants had to travel long distances to participate, making regular access of trainings more difficult and creating variation in the amount learned.

A Look at the Program Evaluation

University researchers from the World Bank conducted a field experiment to understand the main barriers to entrepreneurship in a country, specifically around access to human capital and credit for entrepreneurship. Taking place in rural Pakistan with a subset of male and female microfinance clients of NRSP organized in COs, the experiment offered training to a randomly selected group—half of the 747 COs from five different branches of three different districts (treatment group)—while the other half did not receive training (control group).

A baseline survey was conducted in November 2006, and the business training sessions were held in 2007. A follow-up survey was conducted in December 2008, 6 months after the loan lottery concluded and about 13 months after the loan orientation meetings. The attrition rate between the baseline and follow-up (about two years after) was 16 percent. The evaluation focused on intent-to-treat estimates, and the outcomes were related to business knowledge, creation, and performance.

Business training led to increased business knowledge (estimate value of 0.058, with significance at 10 percent level), but no business training effect was found on business creation either with or without access to the larger loan (estimate value of –0.006). Business training offers did lead to improvements in business practices, such as recording the sales on paper, as well as separating business from household accounts.

Female CO members who had lower levels of business knowledge at baseline increased their business knowledge by about 87 percent (p-value 0.12). However, unlike the men, they were unable to put into practice their newly acquired knowledge. Further, business training led to a reduction in business failure by 6.1 percent among male business owners, compared to the control group, but there was no effect among businesswomen (p-value of 0.98). Access to the larger loan, in contrast, had little effect on anyone.

Summary

Program details	
Program name	National Rural Savings Programme (NRSP)
Country	Pakistan
Program type	Six-day intensive entrepreneurial skills training for existing entrepreneurs who wanted to take a loan
Target audience	Rural Pakistanis who own at least one business
Age	Mixed ages
Gender	60 percent male
Objective	To hone skills around financial management and business planning to enhance effective use of micro-loans and timely repayment
Program maturity	One-time program in 2007. NRSP plans to run similar programs in the near future.
Contact	http://nrsp.org.pk/index.htm
Cost and finance	Pakistan Poverty Alleviation Fund financed the training
Evaluation	
Evaluator	Xavier Giné and Ghazala Mansuri, "Money or Ideas? A Field Experiment on Constraints to Entrepreneurship in Rural Pakistan," Mimeo (Washington, DC: World Bank, 2013).
Evaluation methodology	Field experiment
Evaluation tier	1

Interise | United States

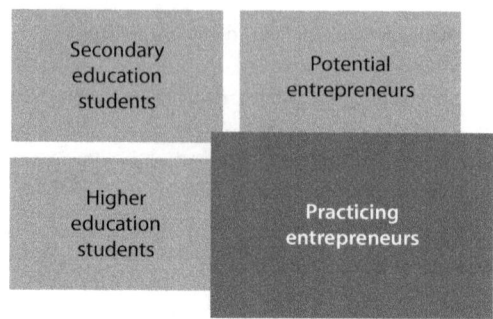

Program Overview

Interise is a nonprofit organization that teaches small business owners how to sustain and grow their businesses. Through an interactive peer-based curriculum, the program aims to help business owners grow their enterprises, create jobs, and strengthen their communities.[18]

Initially started as a regional program in Massachusetts in 2004, Interise is now a national program in the United States, imbedded in over 35 communities. Interise promotes the economic revitalization of lower income communities through its StreetWise 'MBA'™ curriculum. By the end of 2015, Interise will be serving approximately 1,000 practicing entrepreneurs per year.

Program Objectives

Interise wants its participants to grow their businesses—placing a strong emphasis on performance.

Mindsets	Socio-emotional skills	
	Entrepreneurial willingness	
	Entrepreneurship theory	
Capabilities	Management skills	✓
	Vocational skills	
	Networking skills	
Status	Firm formation	
	Self-employment	
	Employability	
	Income and savings	
	Network formation	
Performance	Profits and sales	✓
	Job creation	✓
	Market expansion	✓
	Productivity	✓
	Reinvestment	✓
	Innovation	

Who Participates

Interise's executive education program is intended for small business owners. Potential participants apply and frequently go through an interview process before selection. Further, every participant's business must meet these criteria:

- It needs to have achieved initial growth but have then hit barriers that prevented second-stage growth;
- Its annual revenues must be between US$250,000 and US$10 million;
- At least one employee must be on the payroll, other than the CEO/owner; and
- It must have been in business for a minimum of three years.

Interise aims to help underserved populations. Over 90 percent of Interise's clients are minorities, Native Americans, recent immigrants, or business owners located in lower-income communities. Between one-third and one-half of participants are women.

How the Program Works

Interise uses a peer-based learning model with a case-study-based curriculum. Participants meet for three hours biweekly for 13 sessions in class sizes of 15–18. Participants also form peer-mentoring groups during the first session. These groups allow for further in-depth discussion of classroom materials and individuals' particular business concerns.

The case studies are based on each participant's business—a kind of live case study. The class analyzes one of their colleagues' business situations, providing real-time feedback. Throughout the course, each participant will present about their business.

By the end of the course, each participant has a three-year strategic growth action plan, which they present to colleagues and business experts.

After completion of the curriculum, each participant receives a Certificate in Small Business Entrepreneurship from Boston University's Entrepreneurial Management Institute. Participants become part of Interise's membership, through which they can identify volunteer business experts who can coach them as they implement their growth plans. Also of note—in 2011, among the 600 past Interise participants who completed the annual survey, more than US$13 million worth of business was done through their Interise contacts.

Who Teaches the Program

Interise selects instructors through a network of referral partners and local agencies. They look for people who have a track record of successful small business growth and of enabling adult learning or facilitative instruction.

Program Partnerships

Interise licenses the use of StreetWise 'MBA'™ to a network of partners, selecting the partner that is best for that locale. Partners can be universities, government agencies, or trade associations, among others. Interise trains and supports its partners in the delivery of the curriculum and also provides annual impact data. Since 2008, the U.S. Small Business Administration has contracted with Interise to be the instructional provider for an emerging leader's initiative.

The Local Context

Participants come from a variety of industries and backgrounds. While all have built successful businesses, they can vary greatly in the extent of their personal networks, in their formal education, and in their access to capital.

Interise's StreetWise MBA program is limited to Massachusetts, ranked as the best U.S. state in 2012 for starting a business.[19] Massachusetts received a 3.01 score—each state was ranked on a one-point scale for a state's percentage growth and per capita growth of business establishments, its business formation rate, the number of patents per thousand residents, and income per non-farm proprietor in each state. Nearby states ranked 7th (New Hampshire, at 1.55), 12th (Connecticut, at 1.44), and 19th (Rhode Island, at 1.191).

A Look at the Program Evaluation

Interise does an extensive evaluation of its program each year. In 2011, an annual survey[20] was sent out to past participants to get a sense of the social and economic impact of the program. Of the 451 alumni that received the surveys, 61 percent responded.

The responses to the survey conducted in 2011 indicated that 62 percent of Interise participants had added jobs to their companies or maintained all jobs; and 61 percent of businesses offered health insurance to their employees and gave out an average salary to new employees of about US$41,000.

Over half of Interise participants also reported a growing business—with increased revenue (57 percent) and government grants averaging US$325,000 per business (47 percent of the businesses). Further, nearly 80 percent of Interise participants reported being actively involved in the community—and the majority (58 percent) encouraged their employees to be active as well.

Summary

Program details	
Program name	Interise
Country	United States
Implementing agency	Interise
Program type	Classroom-based peer learning course for existing entrepreneurs
Target audience	Small business owners with annual revenues between US$250,000 and US$10 million and at least two employees; over 90 percent from underserved communities. In 2013, Interise anticipates 700 participants.
Age	22–65 years old
Gender	One-third to one-half female
Objective	To help participants grow their businesses and become more active leaders in their communities
Program maturity	2004

Contact	www.interise.org
Cost and financing	Each partner sets their own tuition rate, ranging from US$500 to US$2,000 per participant. Corporations, foundations, and government agencies provide organizational support for Interise. Partners secure their own local funding.
Evaluation details	
Evaluator	Interise, "Interise 2011 Report Card: Creating Jobs, Growing Business, Building Communities" (Boston: 2011).
Evaluation methodology	Survey of participants
Evaluation tier	3

Notes

1. Current program information gathered from discussions with BizWorld's Catherine Markwell (CEO) and Pauline van Dulken (commercial director, Jong Ondernemen, BizWorld Licensee).
2. http://www.ondernemerschap.nl/sys/cftags/assetnow/design/widgets/site/ctm_getFile.cfm?file=A201211.pdf&perId=0
3. Originally, NFTE was the National Foundation for Teaching Entrepreneurship.
4. Current NFTE information gathered from discussions with Ms. Jennifer Green, New England executive director, and Ms. Tracy Mehu-Hammonds, former NFTE program officer.
5. Current program information drawn from discussions with Bodø Graduate School of Business's Gry Agnete Alsos (associate professor, University of Nordland).
6. The Nordic Institute for Studies in Innovation, Research and Education's *Nordic Growth Entrepreneurship Review 2012.* http://www.nordicinnovation.org/Global/_Publications/Reports/2013/NGER_2012_noApp.pdf
7. Information about the program drawn from discussions with Stefanie Brodmann (economist, World Bank).
8. http://www.tunisia-live.net/2012/01/16/tunisian-entrepreneurism-and-innovation-the-road-ahead/#sthash.VcNzY1nd.dpuf
9. Current program information gathered from discussions with Ms. Patty Sias, McGuire Entrepreneurship Program director.
10. Current program information gathered from discussions with Entrepreneurship Development Centre's Selma Cilimkovic (market research officer, Partner Microcredit Foundation).
11. KILM, Key Indicators Labour Market Youth, Beta version 2008.
12. Information about the current program drawn from discussions with Sarah Elizabeth Haddock (knowledge management officer, World Bank) and Peter Darvas (senior education economist, World Bank).
13. Information about current and past TechnoServe programs in El Salvador provided from interviews with TechnoServe's Andrew Eder (marketing and communications officer) and Oscar Artiga (Central American regional director).
14. World Bank's 2013 *Doing Business* in El Salvador. http://www.doingbusiness.org/data/exploreeconomies/el-salvador/

15. Current program information gathered from discussions with Ms. Iris Lanao Flores (CEO) and Ms. Viviana Salinas (manager of solutions for human development), FINCA-Peru.
16. http://www.goinglobal.com/articles/1041/
17. Information about the program drawn from discussions with Mr. Rashid Bajwa, NRSP CEO.
18. Information about the current program drawn from discussions with Ms. Jean Horstman, Interise CEO.
19. University of Nebraska's Bureau of Business Research and Department of Economics State of Entrepreneurship rankings. http://newsroom.unl.edu/blog/?p=1354
20. Interise.org, "Interise 2011 Report Card" (Boston: Interise.org: 2011).

References

Bruhn, M., and B. Zia. 2011. "Stimulating Managerial Capital in Emerging Markets: The Impact of Business and Financial Literacy for Young Entrepreneurs," Policy Research Working Paper 5642, World Bank, Washington, DC.

Charney, A., and G. D. Libecap. 2000. *Impact of Entrepreneurship Education, Insights: Kauffman Research Series*. Kauffman Center for Entrepreneurial Leadership. http://entrepreneurship.eller.arizona.edu/Docs/Evaluation/Impactevaluation _Entrepreneurshipprogram_UA.Pdf.

Gine, X., and G. Mansuri. 2013. "Money or Ideas? A Field Experiment on Constraints to Entrepreneurship in Rural Pakistan." Mimeo. World Bank, Washington, DC.

Huber, L. R., R. Sloof, and M. van Praag. 2012. "The Effect of Early Entrepreneurship Education: Evidence from a Randomized Field Experiment." Discussion Paper 6512, Institute for the Study of Labor (IZA), Bonn, Germany.

Interise. 2011. "Interise 2011 Report Card: Creating Jobs, Growing Business, Building Communities." Interise, Boston.

Karlan, D., and M. Valdivia. 2012. "Teaching Entrepreneurship: Impact of Business Training on Microfinance Clients and Institutions," *The Review of Economics and Statistics* 93 (2): 510–27.

Klinger, B., and M. Schündlen. 2007. "Can Entrepreneurial Activity be Taught? Quasi-Experimental Evidence from Central America," CID Working Paper 153, Harvard University, Cambridge, MA.

Kolvereid, L., and O. Moen. 1997. "Entrepreneurship among Business Graduates: Does a Major in Entrepreneurship Make a Difference?" *Journal of European Industrial Training* 21 (4): 154–60.

Nakkula, M., M. Lutyens, C. Pineda, A. Dray, F. Gaytan, and J. Huguley. 2004. *Initiating, Leading and Feeling in Control of One's Fate: Findings from the 2002–2003 Study of NFTE in Six Boston Public High Schools*. Cambridge, MA: Harvard University. http:// www.nfte.com/sites/default/files/harvard-nfte_study_02-03_full_report_6-6x-04.pdf.

Peruvian Ministry of Labour. 2008. Annual Report, "La mujer en el mercado laboral peruano" as cited in Janina V. León, "Peruvian Women and Microenterprises," Canadian Foundation for the Americas (FOCAL). http://www.focal.ca/en/publications /focalpoint/368-december-2010-janina-v-leon-en.

Premand, P., Brodmann, S., Almeida, R., Grun, R., and Barouni, M. 2012. "Entrepreneurship Training and Self-Employment among University Graduates: Evidence from a Randomized Trial in Tunisia." Policy Research Working Paper No. 6285, World Bank, Washington, DC.

World Bank. 2011. "Can Skills Training Programs Increase Employment for Young Women? The Case of Liberia." Adolescent Girls Initiative, Results Series, World Bank, Washington, DC.

APPENDIX E

Program Descriptions

Table E.1 Entrepreneurship Education—Secondary Education Students (EESE)

Name	Country/region	Program	Program evaluation	Reference
BIZ—BizWorld	Netherlands	**Beneficiaries** Children in the final grade of primary school **Description** The program aims to teach children ages 11–12 the basics of business and entrepreneurship as well as to promote teamwork and leadership in the classroom through an experiential learning program that takes five days. BizWorld launched in Netherlands in 2004 and is a global entrepreneurship education program geared toward primary school students. Over 350,000 children from 84 countries have participated in the program to date. The program includes five lessons with a practical orientation, and also facilitates student groups through a firm's business cycle from start-up to liquidation. Jointly financed by a public-private partnership, the program takes places in hundreds of Dutch classrooms each year. Companies sponsor a class of students—typically ages 11–12—for the intensive four-day program. A businessperson from the sponsoring company co-teaches with the class's regular instructor, leading students through a business development exercise. In 2013, BizWorld's Dutch program anticipates taking place in 450 schools and reaching over 11,000 students. The BizWorld curriculum is standard across countries, with a few adjustments made. In the case of BizWorld in the Netherlands the program is delivered by an entrepreneur in cooperation with the classroom teacher rather than by the classroom teacher alone, as is the case in other countries.	Evaluation Tier 1 The study evaluated the direct (short-term) effects of early entrepreneurship education on the development of cognitive, non-cognitive entrepreneurial skills, and entrepreneurial intentions using a randomized field experiment. The evaluation took place between February and July 2010, and over the same period in 2011. The sample consisted of 85 schools (which had signed up for the program and had consented to participating in the research; about 75 percent of all schools that signed up in 2010 and 2011)—a total of 118 classes and 2,751 students in the last year of primary school. The response rate was 87.7 percent. Since the program was delivered at the class level, the unit of analysis was the class level rather than the school. The schools and classes were assigned to a treatment or a control group. For both groups, the study applied a pretest/posttest design to allow an unbiased difference-in-differences estimate of the non-treatment effect. The study collected data on (a) non-cognitive skills including self-efficacy, need for achievement, risk taking, social orientation, persistence, motivating, analyzing, proactivity, and creativity; (b) cognitive skills including entrepreneurship knowledge; and (c) entrepreneurial intentions, including children's intentions to become an entrepreneur. Highlights: • The treatment effect was positive and statistically significant for seven of the nine non-cognitive skills tested, namely self-efficacy (0.149***), need for achievement (0.166***), risk-taking propensity (0.114**), persistence (0.105**), analyzing (0.127***), creativity (0.096*), and proactivity (0.144***). Analysis on the heterogeneity of treatment effects showed that the treatment effects remained or increased slightly when	Rosendahl-Huber, Sloof, and van Praag (2012)

table continues next page

Table E.1 Entrepreneurship Education—Secondary Education Students (EESE) *(continued)*

Name	Country/region	Program	Program evaluation	Reference
		Costs: US$1,300 for each school (sponsoring a classroom and providing a businessperson who serves as a volunteer instructor	controlling for individual, school, and neighborhood characteristics and year of data collection. Also, the size of treatment effects was substantial and comparable to being eligible to one track level in entering high school (i.e., from the baseline of pre-vocational to general secondary education); • The estimated effect on cognitive entrepreneurial skills (entrepreneurship knowledge) was positive although not significant (0.015); and • The estimated effect on entrepreneurial intentions (owning business) for children was negative and significant (0.134***). The study acknowledged that the measures used for entrepreneurial intentions were not validated for children and could potentially alter the results.	
EOEAS—Entrepreneurial Orientation and Education in Austrian Secondary Schools Study	Austria	**Beneficiaries** Students at general and vocational secondary education schools (focusing on business, technical careers, trades and commerce) **Description** The EOEAS program aims to enhance students' start-up-related instruction and entrepreneurial knowledge by improving students' attitudes toward entrepreneurship. Searches for information on whether the program is still under implementation did not yield information. At a variety of secondary schools in Austria—among both general and technical schools—students found a company and sold their products in a school market.	Evaluation Tier 2 The study assessed how entrepreneurial thinking was promoted in vocational and general secondary education and the extent to which targeted instruction in start-up-related and entrepreneurial knowledge supported the development of a positive attitude toward entrepreneurship as a goal in life. The study focused on the following outcomes: (a) personality (achievement, motivation, locus of control, innovative orientation); (b) resources (attention to business and economics, knowledge of business and organization, network and activities inside and outside school; (c) start-up inclination (start-up probability); (d) environment (entrepreneurs in the student's surroundings, use of technology, supportive upbringing); and (e) process (entrepreneurship orientation of the school, independence/criticism as values in instruction, entrepreneurship-oriented instruction methods, and team oriented methods.	Frank *et al.* (2005)

table continues next page

Table E.1 Entrepreneurship Education—Secondary Education Students (EESE) *(continued)*

Name	Country/region	Program	Program evaluation	Reference
			The study was conceived as an interdisciplinary project and designed to include various types of secondary schools. The sample included six general secondary schools, four commercial academies, three secondary technical schools, and one secondary school for technical and business professionals. In addition, a sample of Austrian participants in an international junior entrepreneur contest ("Junior") was selected. A total of 875 students and 36 contest participants were surveyed in 2001. Survey participants were 15–18 years old. *Highlights:* • Self-employment was the least-preferred option in all school types; • Commercial academy and secondary technical school graduates were more likely to start a career after graduation; • Commercial academy students had more opportunities to gain practical experience and demonstrated the strongest entrepreneurship orientation, although these conditions did not lead to higher start-up inclinations or a pronounced entrepreneurial orientation; and • Education processes seemed to fulfill an important function in the development of entrepreneurial orientation. Schools could influence this effect by reinforcing business and economics knowledge. However, the development of start-up inclinations seemed to be more closely linked to social influences in the microsocial environment. For example, the most important predictors of start-up inclinations included: entrepreneurs in the surroundings (0.31***); innovative orientation (0.27***); experience in leadership and organization (0.19***); and team-oriented instruction methods (0.11***).	

table continues next page

Table E.1 Entrepreneurship Education—Secondary Education Students (EESE) (continued)

Name	Country/region	Program	Program evaluation	Reference
INJAZ—Junior Achievement for Youth in Middle East	Morocco, Lebanon, Jordan, Saudi Arabia, United Arab Emirates, and Egypt, Arab Rep.	**Beneficiaries** Students in upper secondary that participated in the INJAZ Company Program. **Description** The Junior Achievement (JA) program aims to provide basic business skills and financial literacy to students to start up and run their own businesses and to promote work readiness among students. The beneficiaries are upper secondary students in Morocco, Lebanon, Jordan, Saudi Arabia, United Arab Emirates and the Arab Republic of Egypt. The program is delivered as part of either the school curriculum or through extracurricular activities by private sector volunteers in coordination with school administrators and ministries of education. The JA program delivery method, the Company Program, is based on experiential learning—students develop a business idea and a business plan design, ultimately producing a product and service, marketing them, and closing the business. This all takes place over the course of 4–6 months.	Evaluation Tier 2 The evaluation assessed the impact of entrepreneurship education on producing skills to initiate and sustain a business. The methodology was based on matching pre- and postsurveys of treatment and comparison groups. Interested beneficiaries were not randomly assigned to either group, and due to limitations in implementation, they could only match pre- and postsurveys in limited cases. The pool of students came from a small number of cities in six countries. Its total size was 1,454, of which 617 were interviewed for the baseline of the comparison group and 837 for the treatment group. The baseline questionnaire was collected in December 2010 and January 2011, and the follow-up survey was collected in July and November 2011. The outcomes studied included student knowledge, skills and attitudes, and behavioral intentions about entrepreneurship. *Highlights:* • Participants in the JA programs had very high levels of access to entrepreneurs in their lives. Around 80 percent had siblings who were entrepreneurs, and 30–74 percent indicated that their parents or neighbors were entrepreneurs; • Participants had medium levels of knowledge of basic entrepreneurial concepts; • Participants had high and positive aspirations, views of self and others, self-efficacy, and interest in business creation; and • Participants had favorable attitudes towards entrepreneurship and business.	Reimers, Dyer, and Ortega (2012)

table continues next page

Table E.1 Entrepreneurship Education—Secondary Education Students (EESE) *(continued)*

Name	Country/region	Program	Program evaluation	Reference
JACP—Junior Achievement Company Program	Sweden	**Beneficiaries** Upper-secondary-level students in Swedish schools **Description** The program objective is to provide opportunities to train and develop creativity, entrepreneurship, and practical business skills. The beneficiaries are students at the upper secondary level in Swedish schools. The training and materials are provided by the Swedish branch of Junior Achievement, a voluntary organization that works with schools to promote entrepreneurship and encourage connections between enterprises and schools. The program focuses on "learning by doing" the tasks of entrepreneurs in the context of setting up, organizing, producing and selling a product, and closing a firm. The same type of educational concept is applied in other nations that are members of Junior Achievement.	Evaluation Tier 2 The evaluation assessed the relative effects (in the long term) of entrepreneurial performance, relative to those who did not participate. The methodology was a quasi-experimental design based on Propensity Score Matching (PSM) of individuals who participated in JACP during the mid-1990s with those who did not by using publicly available databases. The pool of individuals for the treatment group was around 166,606. The sample size was 224,838 individuals, of whom 10,103 comprise the treatment group (individuals who participated in the JACP between 1994 and 1996) and 214,735 comparable non-participant individuals. The outcomes measured were the probability of starting a business, entrepreneurial income, and firm survival. *Highlights*: • Participation increased the likelihood of starting a new business by at least 20 percent ($p<0.1$) when compared to the non-participants of JACP; • JACP participation had a positive effect on expected income in the range of 7 percent ($p<0.05$) to 18 percent ($p<0.001$); and • There was no significant effect on firm survival due to JACP participation.	Elert, Andersson, and Wennberg (2013)
JAN—Junior Achievement	Namibia	**Beneficiaries** Upper-secondary-level students in Namibian schools **Description** The program objective is to educate and inspire youth around entrepreneurship, financial literacy, and work-related life skills. The program reached 32,000 students in 2007. The JA Company Program is based on learning by doing the whole business cycle.	Evaluation tier 3 The study's objective was to appraise the impact of entrepreneurship education among Namibian youth in areas of entrepreneurship, financial literacy, and work-related life skills acquisition. The methodology involved qualitative and quantitative analysis through structured questionnaires. The scope of the study was six regions in Namibia; information was gathered from parents, teachers, and learners from randomly selected schools from each region. In total, 13 schools participated, including	Mahohoma and Muyambo (2008)

table continues next page

Table E.1 Entrepreneurship Education—Secondary Education Students (EESE) *(continued)*

Name	Country/region	Program	Program evaluation	Reference
			13 teachers, 130 learners, and 90 parents. The outcomes were assessed in terms of entrepreneurship education, financial literacy, and work-related life skills from the teachers, learners, and parents' perspective. *Highlights:* • 82 percent of the teachers acknowledged that students were learning entrepreneurship abilities, social and financial skills, and employability, as well as responsibility, social involvement, and critical thinking; • Parents indicated that benefits from the programs were derived from learning the use of money, budgeting, business-related subjects, intentions, and appreciation skills. Parents also acknowledged helping the students with their own businesses in bookkeeping, start-ups, and business-related needs; • 86 percent of parents indicated that the program led to positive changes in their child's behavior; and • 80 percent of students joined the program to learn skills and knowledge on starting their own businesses, and 93 percent confirmed that they learned entrepreneurship abilities, financial literacy, and work-related skills. Seventy-two percent indicated a positive impact on their life in the same areas they learned skills.	
KAB—Know About Business	Syrian Arab Republic	**Tier** 3 **Beneficiaries** Vocational secondary schools in five governorates **Description** KAB aims to help its participants seamlessly transition from school to labor force by building entrepreneurial and business skills; as well as raising awareness about	The evaluation assessed the programs' efficacy in training students in entrepreneurial and business skills. Using a two-part impact analysis of KAB in the Syrian Arab Republic, students were given a questionnaire before the program and after, using a sample of 871 students (591 female) from four governorates. Further, the focus groups provided a better understanding of the program's effects by interviewing KAB instructors, parents, alumni, and current students.	Bikhazi and Kabbani (2010)

table continues next page

Table E.1 Entrepreneurship Education—Secondary Education Students (EESE) *(continued)*

Name	Country/region	Program	Program evaluation	Reference
		self-employment. Active in eight Arab countries since 2008, KAB's Syria program has reached over 66,000 young people. In 2007–08, KAB was integrated into the curriculum of vocational secondary schools and intermediate institutes in 5 governorates. KAB is an interactive, classroom-based entrepreneurship education program.	*Highlights:* • KAB participants reported on the program's positive impact on their knowledge, skills, and attitudes towards starting a business 18 months after completing the program; • KAB participants were more aware of self-employment as a future career option and had a greater knowledge about the basics of sustainable enterprises. There was, however, no significant difference in participants' labor force outcomes; and • For former KAB participants, only 11 percent said the program was not helpful.	
NFTE—Network for Teaching Entrepreneurship (Previously National Foundation for Teaching Entrepreneurship)	United States	**Beneficiaries** Currently in 18 high schools in Boston, Massachusetts. The program targets high schools where at least half of the student body is eligible for free or reduced-price lunch. **Description** NFTE aims to teach students entrepreneurial skills that help them create a business plan. A global program that started in New York in 1987, students are taught over a semester or year-long course. NFTE targets high schools where at least half of the student body is eligible for free or reduced-price lunch, having reached over 500,000 students who are typically at risk of dropping out of school. Lessons include the concepts of competitive advantage, ownership, opportunity recognition, marketing, finance, and product development—and all tie back to core math and literacy skills. NFTE trains existing teachers to teach its curriculum, and relies on local	Evaluation Tier 2 The evaluation of the NFTE program in Boston, Massachusetts, was carried out in two phases. The first phase surveyed students from two large public high schools in 2001–02. The second phase expanded the universe of schools from two to six public high schools to allow the analysis of possible program impacts in a wider range of learning contexts. The sample included a total of 17 classrooms, 13 teachers, and 268 students, out of which 158 students received the NFTE program (treatment) and 110 students were selected for comparison classes (control). The evaluation studied the role of NFTE in promoting the development of entrepreneurship, including entrepreneurship thinking and behavior. The study measured entrepreneurial behavior (EB) using an entrepreneurial activities checklist (49 activities organized around different domains and dimensions), locus of control, and it applied new scales to measure healthy or positive development (using the values-in-action scale that gauges originality, curiosity, industriousness, and hopefulness).	Nakkula et al. (2004)

table continues next page

Table E.1 Entrepreneurship Education—Secondary Education Students (EESE) *(continued)*

Name	Country/region	Program	Program evaluation	Reference
		business people to serve as volunteer mentors to students as they create their business plans. Each student's business plan is ultimately presented to a panel of judges for a chance to win seed capital.	*Highlights:* • The EB score increased for NFTE students compared to the control group. The EB score for NFTE students registered a significant increase of 7.5 percent ($p<0.01$). The changes in the two groups were large and significant for the starter dimension and business domain; • In contrast, the EB score for comparison students did not register significant changes, although in some domains, the trend declined; • Although the results for locus of control were not significant, the scores followed the hypothesized pattern. While NFTE students began with marginally lower locus-of-control scores than the comparison group, they increased their score by about 3 percent after the intervention, outscoring the control group. Similarly, immigrant students participating in the program improved in their locus of control by about 4.5 percent while the score of similar students in the comparison group declined by approximately 2.5 percent; • Locus-of-control findings were strongest for students taught by one particular teacher in one of the schools with a strong track record of effective teaching (i.e., who had received recognition); • Results on students' connectedness were generally negative; • Results from the values-in-action scales (originality, curiosity, industriousness, and hopefulness) were not found to be significant. Although not significant results, NFTE students scored marginally higher than the comparison group in the pretest; meanwhile, the gap narrowed at posttest with the comparison group's score increasing and the NFTE students' score decreasing;	

table continues next page

Table E.1 Entrepreneurship Education—Secondary Education Students (EESE) *(continued)*

Name	Country/region	Program	Program evaluation	Reference
			• Overall, NFTE students trained by top-notch teachers showed a higher degree of general student-teacher connectedness, unlike the comparison group; and • Similar to the findings from the first phase, relative to the comparison group, NFTE students expressed increasingly strong interest in occupations requiring advanced training or formal education, including college.	
SAIE—South African Institute for Entrepreneurship	South Africa	**Beneficiaries** Primary and secondary school students in South Africa **Description** SAIE aims to influence students' entrepreneurial knowledge, skills, and attitudes by improving the educational process through quality materials and educator training. Started in 1996, SAIE has developed and implemented entrepreneurship education programs in over 2,500 South African schools. To date, a total of 5,676 schools have implemented the Business Ventures (BV) course. About one-third of the schools are primary and two-thirds are secondary schools.	Evaluation tier 3 Two evaluations were carried out to test entrepreneurial knowledge, skills, and attitudes for those using the business ventures course in the economic management and science curriculum. The first evaluation took place in 2003 using a sample of five schools in the greater Cape Town metro area. The second evaluation took place in 2005 using a sample of 41 schools in two provinces. The evaluations included a treatment group (business venture curricula delivered over a period of time) and a control group (no intervention). There is no information on whether there was randomization in the assignment to the treatment. *Highlights:* • The 2003 evaluation showed that, compared to a control group, schools implementing the Business Venture curricula had significant positive effects on students' entrepreneurial knowledge, skills, and attitudes; and • The 2005 study confirmed the 2003 results, but pointed to a picture far more complex than originally thought. The results showed that (a) extraneous factors (socioeconomic profile) were a powerful influence on student performance, at times more influential than teaching materials; (b) entrepreneurial skill acquisition was not a neat, linear process, but proceeded haphazardly over a longer period of time than originally thought—stronger	South African Institute for Entrepreneurship (2006)

table continues next page

Table E.1 Entrepreneurship Education—Secondary Education Students (EESE) *(continued)*

Name	Country/region	Program	Program evaluation	Reference
			performance improvements were associated with the use of BV after a two-year period than with the use of BV over a one-year period; and (c) schools were complex, fluid, and challenging environments for educational interventions; therefore, implementation issues were critical to improving student performance.	
YE—Young Enterprise	Denmark	**Beneficiaries** Secondary school students **Description** The entrepreneurship education model is expanding in Denmark—with a focus on students' own ideas and thus strongly connected to emotional experience as the problems are felt, not only conceived. Currently, the Danish system has project-based education and entrepreneurship education in secondary schools. Many schools use both teaching methods.	Evaluation tier 3 The evaluation assessed the effects of entrepreneurship education among secondary students in Denmark using a stepwise regression among 2,000 randomly selected 15-year-old students' 2011 surveys. *Highlights:* • At the earlier secondary level of the education system, the effects of entrepreneurship education are mediated by its effects on students' self-conception; and • Entrepreneurship education by itself has an impact on students' personal development. But when entrepreneurship and project-based education are combined, the effect of these two approaches becomes negative.	Moberg (2012)

Note: * = $p<0.1$, ** = $p<0.05$, *** = $p<0.001$.

Table E.2 Entrepreneurship Education—Higher Education Students (EEHE)

Name	Country/region	Program	Program evaluation	Reference
APSB—Auchi Polytechnic School of Business	Edo State, Nigeria	**Beneficiaries** Tertiary students at Auchi Polytechnic **Description** APSB aims to teach students the skills around managing a small-scale business as a way of preparing them for gainful employment after graduating. This is an initiative of the Nigerian federal government to introduce entrepreneurship education programs in tertiary schools.	Evaluation Tier 3 The evaluation assessed the efficacy of entrepreneurship education on students' employability. The study used a sample of 300 final-year tertiary school students who had filled out surveys. *Highlights:* • A positive correlation was found between entrepreneurship education and managerial skill development; and • Students who received instruction in entrepreneurship education showed a greater desire to set up small-scale businesses after graduation.	Idogho and Ainabor (2011)
BEP—Berger Entrepreneurship Program (McGuire Entrepreneurship Program)	United States	**Beneficiaries** Business undergraduate and graduate students at the University of Arizona **Description** The McGuire Entrepreneurship Program aims to prepare students to successfully apply entrepreneurial principles, whether they start their own business or go to work in a corporation. Specifically, the program focuses on students' capabilities and status. Based at the University of Arizona's Eller College of Management, the program attracts top-tier undergraduate and graduate students from the university who wish to major in entrepreneurship (if undergraduates) or receive a concentration in entrepreneurship (if master's of business administration students). All participants—about 80 each year—spend their two semesters taking marketing and finance, as well as a venture development course. These face-to-face classes complement the students'	Evaluation Tier 3 A tracer survey was developed to assess how BEP affected the entrepreneurial intentions and achievements of students it graduated over the years. The evaluation studied the trajectories of business entrepreneurship and non-business entrepreneurship cohorts from 1985 to 1998. The evaluation assessed the formation of new ventures, likelihood of self-employment, sales growth rate of emerging firms, accumulation of graduates' assets, and technology transfer from the university to the private sector. A total of 2,024 surveys were mailed to graduates from the non-entrepreneurship business school graduates and 460 entrepreneurship graduates, all of whom had graduated from the university between 1985 and 1998. The final response rate was 511 for the non-entrepreneurship business graduates and 105 for the entrepreneurship graduates. Response rates were generally uniform	Charney and Libecap (2000)

table continues next page

Table E.2 Entrepreneurship Education—Higher Education Students (EEHE) *(continued)*

Name	Country/region	Program	Program evaluation	Reference
		year-long focus on creating a new venture that will ultimately compete with other students' plans for awards totaling US$10,000. *Costs:* Tuition rates range from US$5,200–US$15,825, depending on the track of courses taken, and whether students are from Arizona. Costs to deliver the program are approximately US$900,000 annually.	across levels of degrees and types of programs; however, it should be noted the response rate was extremely low at 21 percent. *Highlights:* • Entrepreneurship education increased the probability of an individual being involved in a new business venture by 25 percent over non-entrepreneurship graduates. Entrepreneurship students were 11 percent more likely than non-entrepreneurship students to own their own businesses after graduation; • Entrepreneurship education contributed to the growth of firms, especially smaller emerging firms. On average, smaller emerging firms that were owned by or employed entrepreneurship graduates had greater than five times the sales and employment growth than those that employed non-entrepreneurship graduates; • Entrepreneurship graduates received an average annual income that was 27 percent higher compared to the average annual income of non-entrepreneurship graduates; • Entrepreneurship education increased a business school graduate's probability of being associated with a high-tech firm by nearly 13 percent and of developing new technological products by almost 9 percent; and • Entrepreneurship education enhanced the transfer of technology from the university to the private sector and promoted technology-based firms and products. Among self-employed entrepreneurship graduates, nearly 23 percent owned a high-technology firm, compared to less than 15 percent of non-entrepreneurship graduates who owned a firm.	

table continues next page

Table E.2 Entrepreneurship Education—Higher Education Students (EEHE) *(continued)*

Name	Country/region	Program	Program evaluation	Reference
BPTC—University Entrepreneurship Track/Business Plan Thesis Competi-tion	Tunisia	**Beneficiaries** Undergraduate students enrolled in Tunisian universities **Description** BPTC is aimed primarily at increasing self-employment, fostering an entrepreneurship culture among university graduates, and more broadly improving participants' employment outcomes. In 2009, the Government of Tunisia introduced this entrepreneurship track in the tertiary education curriculum. Students may opt into the entrepreneurship track, which consists of business training (from a local employment office), coaching to develop a business plan (from entrepreneurs), and supervision from university faculty. The business plan is an alternative option to the thesis requirement that all undergraduate students must complete to graduate. Students who opt to participate in this track can submit their business plan to a competition with a chance to win seed capital to finance their venture.	Evaluation Tier 1 The evaluation used a randomized control trial methodology to estimate the impact of the program. For the academic year of 2009–10, 1,702 students (about 9 percent of all eligible students nationwide) participated in the entrepreneurship track—some students applied in pairs so a total of 1,506 projects were registered. The evaluation assigned 757 projects to the treatment group and 742 to the control group. Information was collected at the beginning of the 5-month program (February 2009) and 9 to 12 months after graduation from the program (April–June 2011). Information collected included indicators on socioeconomic characteristics, labor, aspirations for the future, personality traits, and behavioral skills related to entrepreneurship. *Highlights:* • Approximately one year after graduation, graduates of the entrepreneurship track had a higher probability of being self-employed. Although the effects were small in absolute terms (ranging from 1 to 4 percentage points), given the low prevalence of self-employment in the control group, the small absolute effects imply that beneficiaries were on average 46–87 percent more likely to be self-employed compared to the control group; • There was no evidence that the program significantly affected overall employment as captured by the likelihood of being employed in the last seven days. In fact, estimates were negative and pointed to a reduction in the probability of holding wage employment;	Premand et al. (2012)

table continues next page

Table E.2 Entrepreneurship Education—Higher Education Students (EEHE) *(continued)*

Name	Country/region	Program	Program evaluation	Reference
			and although not significant, the decrease was of the same magnitude as the increase in self-employment, suggesting the possibility of substitution effect from wage employment to self-employment; • The program did not promote higher quality jobs among participants. There were no significant program impacts on employment in the formal sector, firm size, hours of work, or earnings; • The intervention produced strong impacts on participants' self-reported business skills and networking proxies. About 77 percent of program graduates reported knowing how to produce a business plan, compared to 45 percent in the control group; • Intervention led to measurable, significant and robust changes in several domains of the "Big Five," including a decrease in agreeableness (0.23–0.25 s.d. compared to control group) and an increase in extraversion (albeit a less robust finding compared to the previous trait). There was no evidence to indicate that the entrepreneurship training positively affected conscientiousness and emotional stability, and other entrepreneurial traits such as tenacity or power motivation remained unchanged; and • Participants were found to be more likely to be confident in obtaining credit and to have applied for credit (conditional on having a business idea), but they were neither more likely to know how to apply for credit nor to have obtained credit.	

table continues next page

Table E.2 **Entrepreneurship Education—Higher Education Students (EEHE)** (continued)

Name	Country/region	Program	Program evaluation	Reference
Bødo—Bødo Graduate School of Business	Norway	**Beneficiaries** Business school students entering their fifth year **Description** The objectives of the Bødo entrepreneurship major are entrepreneurship awareness and small business development. Founded in 1985, the Bødo entrepreneurship track offers a major in entrepreneurship to its students enrolled in the master's degree in business program. Since 1987, the annual number of students selecting the entrepreneurship major has ranged from 15 to 30. Costs: Public post-secondary education in Norway is at no cost to students.	Evaluation Tier 3 The evaluation assessed entrepreneurial behavior and entrepreneurial intention among business school graduates. The methodology consisted of a tracer survey of alumni who graduated from the business school between 1987 and 1994. A total of 720 questionnaires were mailed and 374 were returned. The final sample was found to be representative of the alumni. *Highlights:* • Entrepreneurship was found to be a function of factors that can be altered through education; • Having a major in entrepreneurship was positively associated with new firm formation (a major in entrepreneurship was the only variable that was significantly related to new firm formation ($r = 0.20$ $p<0.001$); and • Having a major in entrepreneurship was positively associated with entrepreneurial intentions ($r = 0.26$ $p<0.001$).	Kolvereid and Moen (1997)
CCOE—College Carve-Out Education	China	**Beneficiaries** Undergraduates in China **Description** In Chinese universities, carve-out education aims to encourage students to start their own businesses. A big component of carve-out education is to impact entrepreneurial intention among students.	Evaluation Tier 3 The evaluation analyzed five variables, including carve-out education, business knowledge, entrepreneurial abilities, psychological quality, and entrepreneur intention. A survey was designed for undergraduates in universities and colleges in China. A total of 300 questionnaires were distributed and 214 were completed, of which 200 were valid (response rate of 93 percent). The evaluation used a structure equation model (SEM) to study the complex relations among these five variables. The SEM consisted of two models; one was an equation model, which was used to verify the linear	Zhang et al. (2012)

table continues next page

Table E.2 Entrepreneurship Education—Higher Education Students (EEHE) *(continued)*

Name	Country/region	Program	Program evaluation	Reference
			relationship between potential independent variables (education, business knowledge, ability, psychological quality) and potential dependent variables (business knowledge, ability, psychology quality, and intention), while another measurement model was used to verify the linear relationship between potential variables and real variables. *Highlights:* • The evaluation found positive and significant correlations (a) between college carve-out education and business knowledge (estimate 0.513***), entrepreneurial ability (0.641***), and psychological quality (0.385***); (b) between business knowledge and intention (0.0243***); (c) between entrepreneurial ability and intention (0.201***); and (d) between psychological quality and intention (0.276***). The evaluation did not find a significant correlation between education and intention (0.077) or between knowledge and ability (0.006).	
FEE—Finland Entrepreneurial Education	Finland	**Beneficiaries** Students at business colleges in Finland **Description** Two Finnish business colleges in the same town aim to teach entrepreneurship skills to students. Searches for information on whether the program is still under implementation did not yield information. There are two notable differences between the schools. First, the language of instruction differs:	Evaluation Tier 3 The evaluation assessed students' interest in entrepreneurship and likelihood of starting a business. In the two Finnish schools, undergraduate business students in 2004 were sent surveys—among school A students, 237 questionnaires were sent out (191 returned, an 80.6 percent response rate) and among school B students, 74 questionnaires were sent out (72 returned, a 97 percent response rate).	Brannback et al. (2005)

table continues next page

Table E.2 Entrepreneurship Education—Higher Education Students (EEHE) *(continued)*

Name	Country/region	Program	Program evaluation	Reference
		At School A, instruction is in Finnish and at School B, it is in Swedish. Second, the course options vary widely: School A requires that every student take two entrepreneurship courses, offers an entrepreneurship major, and has a Small Business Research and Development Center on campus. At School B, students have the option of one course on entrepreneurship (30 students may enroll).	*Highlights:* • The students who took entrepreneurship classes seemed to have an opportunistic view, whereas the other groups only saw entrepreneurship as a necessary, last-resort alternative; • The probability that any of the respondents would start a firm within five years was very low among both types of respondents; and • The study could not determine whether entrepreneurship education would increase the probability of students' starting a firm, only that education appeared to impact the perception of entrepreneurship.	
GE—*Grande École*	France	**Beneficiaries** Undergraduate and master's students in France **Description** The *École Supérieure de Commerce* (ESC) in Rouen offers three types of entrepreneurship courses that differ in both content and duration—all of which aim to expand students' familiarity with entrepreneurship. The first program is the *Projet Entreprendre*, which is geared toward first-year students—they use the course to turn a business idea into a business plan. The focus is on getting students to develop a blend of knowledge, skills, and attitudes to enable them to recognize the links between management theory and entrepreneurial practice. The second is a *dominante* program consisting of an 11-week intensive course (180 hours) that aims to deepen the entrepreneurship knowledge among third-year master's students. Finally, the third one is comprised of short courses (6–12 hours) focusing	Evaluation Tier 3 The study evaluated students' attitudes toward entrepreneurship and entrepreneurs as well as their desired career choices, with the intention to identify differences between first- and second-year ESC students. Between December 2002 and February 2003, two groups of young people were surveyed. The sample consisted of a group of undergraduates, between ages 19 and 22, who were either about to enter the program (first-year students) or had just completed the program (second-year students). The survey was sent to 280 first-year students, of whom 82 responded, and 276 second-year students, of whom 60 students responded. The evaluation investigated students' perspectives on entrepreneurs and entrepreneurship, students' attitudes toward entrepreneurship, and the influence of entrepreneurs as family members on the career choice of students.	Klaper (2004)

table continues next page

Table E.2 Entrepreneurship Education—Higher Education Students (EEHE) *(continued)*

Name	Country/region	Program	Program evaluation	Reference
		on topics such as "Entrepreneurship in Europe" and "Female Entrepreneurship." These courses are part of the general ESC program and/or specialized master's program.	*Highlights:* • There was an upward shift in students' attitudes toward entrepreneurship as a career choice between first- and second-year students. While only 26.5 percent of first-year students surveyed saw themselves as potential entrepreneurs, the percentage for second-year students surveyed was 50.0. Similarly, while 30.9 percent of first-year students could envisage setting up their own businesses, 53 percent of second-year students imagined setting up their own businesses; • About 81 percent of first-year students surveyed mentioned wanting to work in a large organization upon completion of their studies, compared to 60 percent for second-year students; and • The proportion of students who mentioned wanting to work in a small and medium enterprise dropped from 54.0 percent for first-year students to 31.7 percent for second-year students.	
STEP—Student Training for Promoting Entrepreneurship	Uganda	**Beneficiaries** Undergraduate students in their final semester **Description** The STEP program aims to shape students' psychological skills—such as leadership, the psychology of planning, personal initiative, and persuasion and negotiation. STEP targets undergraduate students from all disciplines (except business administration) who are in the last semester of their undergraduate studies at Makerere University (University A)	Evaluation Tier 1 The evaluation investigated how action-based entrepreneurship training transmitted its effects to entrepreneurial action and the creation of a start-up. A randomized controlled field experiment evaluated the effectiveness of an action-based entrepreneurship training program on entrepreneurial self-efficacy, action knowledge, action planning, entrepreneurial goals, entrepreneurial action, business opportunity identification, and business ownership.	Gielnik et al. (2013)

table continues next page

Table E.2 Entrepreneurship Education—Higher Education Students (EEHE) *(continued)*

Name	Country/region	Program	Program evaluation	Reference
		and Uganda Christian University (University B). To participate in the training, students apply and, if accepted, pay a US$10 deposit that is refunded at the end of the training to students who attend all modules. The training features 12 modules on entrepreneurship taught on a weekly basis. Two experienced lecturers from the two universities deliver the program using methodologies based on action-regulatory theory. During the course, teams of four to six students start a real business using US$100 for start-up capital. The training is not part of the regular university program—participants do not receive any credits or grades for participation but receive a certificate at the end of the training.	Of the 651 applications received, 200 were selected to receive the training immediately (treatment group) and 200 were placed in a waiting group (control group) that received the training after the completion of the study. The data were collected using a pretest/posttest design at three points in time. The first measurement (T1) took place the month prior to the training, the second measurement (T2) took place in the month after the training, and the third measurement (T3) took place 12 months after the first measurement. All data were collected using personal interviews and questionnaires. Highlights: • Action knowledge was a central factor promoting the initiation and maintenance of entrepreneurial activity. Compared to the control group, the training increased the likelihood of starting a business by 50 percent, and compared to initial status in the training group, the training increased the likelihood of starting a business by 219 percent; • The training had a positive and significant effect on (a) entrepreneurial self-efficacy ($F = 10.44$, $p<0.01$, interaction effect = 0.03 and group effect after training 0.44); (b) action knowledge ($F = 17.65$, $p<0.01$, interaction effect = 0.05 and group effect after training 0.61); (c) action planning ($F = 5.53$, $p<0.05$, interaction effect = 0.02 and group effect after training 0.47) and (d) business opportunity identification ($F = 7.70$, $p<0.01$, interaction effect = 0.02 and group effect after training 0.42). The effect of training on	

table continues next page

Table E.2 Entrepreneurship Education—Higher Education Students (EEHE) *(continued)*

Name	Country/region	Program	Program evaluation	Reference
			entrepreneurial goals was marginally supported ($F = 2.88$, $p<0.10$, interaction effect = 0.01 and group effect after training 0.31); and • Entrepreneurial action at T2 had a significant effect on entrepreneurial action at T3 ($\beta = 0.26$; $p<0.01$), and action knowledge had a significant and positive effect on entrepreneurial action ($\beta = 0.13$; $p<0.05$). The coefficient on entrepreneurial self-efficacy on entrepreneurial action was not significant.	
UTES—University Training for Entrepreneurs	Sweden	**Beneficiaries** Business undergraduate and engineering graduate students at two Swedish universities **Description** The program, as tested for in the evaluation, aimed to influence entrepreneurial action capability, locus of control, and entrepreneurial values. The program was intended for business administration undergraduate students at Vaxjo and Halmstad universities, engineering students at Halmstad University, and small-business owners.	Evaluation Tier 2 The evaluation used three tests to assess entrepreneurial action capability (EAC), locus of control (LoC), and an entrepreneurial value index (EVI). Between 1994 and 1995, the tests were administered to 265 business students at Vaxjo and Halmstad universities, 110 engineering students at Halmstad University, and 213 business owner-managers of small firms (less than 20 employees)—the latter group was subdivided into traditional or single-venture owner-managers and genuine or multiple-venture owner-managers. The LoC test was not applied to the owner-managers. *Highlights:* • Contrary to expectations, no significant differences in EAC were found between single owner-managers and multiple owner-managers • The EAC and EVI results were highest for business students participating in entrepreneurship programs (7.11 and 3.28, respectively), followed	Johannisson, Landström, and Rosenberg (1998)

table continues next page

Table E.2 Entrepreneurship Education—Higher Education Students (EEHE) *(continued)*

Name	Country/region	Program	Program evaluation	Reference
			by engineering students (6.51 and 2.47, respectively) and lastly, by owner-managers (6.03 and 2.29, respectively); the differences between business students and owner-managers were significant at p<0.01, and between engineering students and owner managers significant at p<0.10; • Business students enrolled in entrepreneurship programs showed higher EAC compared to business students from conventional programs (significant at p<0.01). However, business students in conventional programs scored higher on the EVI and LoC, suggesting that showing entrepreneurial value did not necessarily lead to orientation in entrepreneurial action (LoC was significant at p<0.01); • Contrary to expectations, there was no evidence that students in entrepreneurial programs with an engineering orientation had higher scores on EAC compared to students enrolled in parallel business programs (significant at p<0.01); and • Academic training had an impact on students' EAC; however, the short-term effects were stronger than the long-range effects.	

Table E.3 Entrepreneurship Training—Potential Entrepreneurs (ETPo)

Name	Country/region	Program	Evaluation	Reference
AAC–*Atención a Crisis*	Nicaragua	**Beneficiaries** Agricultural households that faced increased exposure to weather shocks linked to changes in rainfall and temperature patterns. The program was targeted primarily toward women. **Description** The *Atención a Crisis* program was a one-year pilot program that combined a traditional safety net with interventions to improve households' ex ante risk management through income diversification. The program had two objectives: (a) to serve as a short-term safety net by providing cash transfers to reduce the need for adverse coping mechanisms and (b) to promote long-run upward mobility and poverty reduction by enhancing households' income diversification and risk-management capacity. The program targeted agricultural households that faced increased exposure to weather shocks linked to changes in rainfall and temperature patterns. The program was targeted primarily to women and complemented an ongoing conditional cash transfer program with two interventions to promote income diversification: (a) a vocational training scholarship and (b) a productive investment grant. The program targeted a total of 3,000 households for a one-year period in six municipalities.	Evaluation Tier 1 The evaluation design consisted of a randomized control trial to estimate the program impacts on consumption, income, income diversification, participation, and returns in nonagricultural activities. The sample included 3,002 eligible households in the treatment communities (56) and a random sample of 1,019 eligible households in the control communities (50). Eligible households were assigned to one of three packages: (a) the basic conditional cash transfer (CCT) (US$145 plus US$90 per household for households that had children between 7 and 15 years old attending primary school plus an additional US$25 per child); (b) the basic CCT plus a scholarship for vocational training (training focused on diversification outside subsistence farming as well as the labor market, and business skills training workshops), and (c) the basic CCT plus the productive investment grant (US$200 to encourage starting nonagricultural activities). Baseline data was collected in April–May 2005; the first follow-up took place in July–August 2006, nine months after the receipt of payments but before the full implementation of the training and the productive grant components. A second follow-up took place in August 2008 and May 2009, or on average about two years after households had stopped receiving payments. *Highlights:* • Two years after the end of the intervention, both the productive investment grant and the training helped to protect against the negative impact of shocks and reduce the variability of consumption and income,	Macours, Premand, and Vakis (2012)

table continues next page

Table E.3 Entrepreneurship Training—Potential Entrepreneurs (ETPo) *(continued)*

Name	Country/region	Program	Evaluation	Reference
			while the basic CCT package did not offer protection against the negative effect of shocks; • The productive investment grant and training showed positive and significant results in increasing consumption (12 percent and 9 percent, respectively) as shock intensity increased by one standard deviation; • The effect of only the training package on consumption showed a strong positive and significant impact. Conversely, there was no significant impact on consumption found for only the vocational training package; and • In terms of household participation and returns to nonagricultural activities, results showed that the households that received the productive investment grant package were 13 percentage points more likely to engage in nonagricultural self-employment, though no significant impact was found on nonagricultural wage employment. The magnitude of the impact on returns was large, amounting to a 15–20 percent annual return on the initial investment of US$200. For households that received the training package the increases shown were not significant.	
EPAG—Economic Empowerment of Adolescent Girls and Young Women	Liberia	**Beneficiaries** About 2,500 beneficiaries in nine communities in Monrovia and Kakata City **Description** EPAG's objective is to smooth young women's transition from school to wage or self-employment. The program offers a six-month classroom training component (business development skills or job skills,	**Evaluation Tier 1** The evaluation measured the impacts of the skills packages on employment, behaviors, empowerment and agency, and family welfare. The study used a randomized pipeline research design—randomly assigning beneficiaries to receive training in either the first round (March 2010–February 2011) or the second round (July 2011 to June 2012). Approximately 2,500 young women were accepted	World Bank (2012)

table continues next page

Table E.3 Entrepreneurship Training—Potential Entrepreneurs (ETPo) *(continued)*

Name	Country/region	Program	Evaluation	Reference
		life skills, and entrepreneurship skills; followed by six months of job placement and support. The program is targeted to young women ages 16–27 who are not currently in school and reside in one of the nine target communities in and around Monrovia and Kakata City. Participants receive small stipends contingent on classroom attendance and a small bonus for completing the training program (US$20). *Costs:* Per unit costs range from US$1,221 (business skills training) to US$1,678 (job skills training).	to participate in the program. The evaluation randomized participants into a treatment group, which included two types of treatments: (a) training package on business development and life skills or (b) training package on job, entrepreneurship, and life skills—and a control group. Impact was defined as the change in outcomes between the time the program started and six months after the classroom training ended, as compared to a statistically similar control group (the second-round trainees). *Highlights:* • The program was well received—the retention rate was 95 percent and attendance averaged 90 percent; • The program increased employment among trainees by 50 percent, compared to those in the control group; • Positive employment outcomes were driven primarily by the business development skills trainees, whose monthly income increased by US$75 per month; • The program increased girls' savings compared to the control group. At midline, the treatment group had a total of US$44 more in savings compared to the control group; and • There were no significant changes to borrowing or lending among beneficiaries.	
JE—*Juventud y Empleo*	Dominican Republic	**Beneficiaries** Young people ages 16–29 from disadvantaged backgrounds who did not have secondary education **Description** The program objective was to increase employment opportunities for the low-income population, achieved by facilitating	Evaluation Tier 1 The study evaluated the impact of job training interventions on reducing the time of unemployment and the search time for employment, increasing employability, income and the duration of employment. The evaluation applied an experimental design where the eligible population	Ibarrarán, Rosas, and Soares (2006)

table continues next page

Table E.3 Entrepreneurship Training—Potential Entrepreneurs (ETPo) *(continued)*

Name	Country/region	Program	Evaluation	Reference
		access to the labor market through training, counseling, and modernization of the country's labor regulations. The program aimed to (a) increase the employability of the beneficiaries by adapting to the labor demands of employers; (b) assess the effectiveness of different job and training programs; (c) establish ongoing dialogue on policies to modernize the labor market; and (d) strengthen the capacity of the Ministry of Labor to improve its policy and program effectiveness. The program trained 27,000 low-income young people ages 16–29 who did not have secondary education. Training institutions interested in providing training were selected through bidding processes that started with a call for proposals. A total of 121 training institutions participated in the program. Costs: About US$700 per person (estimate).	was randomly selected for training. The sample consisted of 786 individuals in the treatment group and 563 in the control group. About 93 percent of the individuals who started the training completed it, and of these, 84 percent started an internship. Baseline data were collected in May–July 2005 and a follow-up interview was carried out, on average, about 13 months after completion of the program. *Highlights:* • There was no impact found on the employment rate of participants. Employment rate post-intervention was 57 percent for the treatment and 56 percent for the controls; • Although there were caveats in the estimation, the treatment group had higher monthly labor earnings—about 17 percent higher than the control group (about 10 percent on average). The earnings effects were larger for the youngest age group, for residents of Santo Domingo, and for those with some secondary education; • There were no large or systematic effects on hours worked per week in the overall sample or by subgroups; and • There was no evidence of a large or systematic quality effect in terms of training institutions.	
JEA—*Jóvenes en Acción*	Colombia	**Beneficiaries** Young people between the ages of 18 and 25 in the two lowest socioeconomic strata of the population, living in the seven largest cities, were eligible for the program (Barranquilla, Bogota, Bucaramanga, Cali, Cartagena, Manizales and Medellin).	Evaluation Tier 1 The evaluation assessed the impact of the program on employment and earning effects as well as formal-sector employment and earnings. A randomized control trial was conducted; the total sample consisted of 3,300 individuals broken down into a treatment group (1,650 individuals) and a control	Attanasio, Kugler, and Meghir (2009)

table continues next page

Table E.3 Entrepreneurship Training—Potential Entrepreneurs (ETPo) *(continued)*

Name	Country/region	Program	Evaluation	Reference
		Description *Jóvenes en Acción* had the objective of providing a combination of in-classroom training and on-the-job training to urban young people between the ages of 18 and 25 in the two lowest socioeconomic strata. Run between 2001 and 2005, the training institutions in Colombia's seven largest cities chose their respective programs. Each institution was asked to select more applicants than they had the capacity to enroll. From this pool of applicants, the program randomly offered the available slots. Remaining applicants were placed in a control group and were not offered the training. The program reached 80,000 over the 2001–05 period (approximately 50 percent of the target population). Training providers were selected through a bidding process that included the following criteria: legal registration, economic solvency, quality of teaching, and ability to place trainees in internships with registered employers. In 2005, there were 114 training institutions (43 percent private) offering 441 types of courses and 989 classes with total slots for 26,615 trainees. Training providers were paid according to market prices, and payment was conditional on trainees' completion of the course. A total of 1,009 companies participated in the program, many offering internships for an average of 2 hours of training per day. The program provided a cash transfer of US$2.20 per day	group (1,650 individuals). Anticipating a level of attrition of 24 percent for program participants and 40 percent for non-program participants, the samples were increased to 2,040 for the treatment and 2,310 for the control group. Baseline data were collected in 2005 and a follow-up individual interview was carried out between August and October 2006. Telephone updates were done 4 months after completion of the program, and the individual interviews were carried out between 9 and 11 months after the telephone update. *Highlights:* • Individuals who were offered the training did better in the labor market. They were more likely to be employed, to show an increase in paid employment of about 6.8 percent, and to have about 12 percent higher wage and salary earnings compared to those not offered training; • Women offered training were more likely to have paid employment and to be employed in the formal sector and earn higher overall and formal wages (results for men were estimated imprecisely); • Training increased the probability of having a formal-sector job by 0.053 and a written contract by 0.066; • Training increased wage and salary earnings in the formal sector but not in the informal sector; and • A cost-benefit analysis using an average monthly increase in earnings of 25,500 Colombian pesos for men and 30,000 Colombian pesos for women, and a discount rate of 5 percent over a 40-year period yielded a net gain of US$2,344 for men and US$2,749 for women. Using a 5 percent discount rate and depreciation in earnings of 10 percent annually, the results were still positive for men (gain of US$906) and women (US$1,066).	

table continues next page

Table E.3 Entrepreneurship Training—Potential Entrepreneurs (ETPo) *(continued)*

Name	Country/region	Program	Evaluation	Reference
		for six months to young men and women without children and US$3.00 per day for young women with children under the age of 7. This transfer was conditional on participation in the program. Costs: US$750 per participant.		
WINGS—Women's Income Generating Support Program	Uganda	**Beneficiaries** 1,800 beneficiaries (86 percent poor women) in 120 villages across two districts in Northern Uganda **Description** The objective of the program was to help beneficiaries create small businesses that generated earnings and to serve as an earnings opportunity for the women of the household. WINGS was implemented as a collaboration between AVSI Uganda (the implementers) and Innovations for Poverty Action (IPA) (the researchers). It was an innovative 3-year program of economic assistance and social support for the young women and their children who were most severely affected by conflict in northern Uganda. AVSI Uganda has been active in Northern Uganda for almost three decades. The WINGS core program package consisted of (a) a few days of business skills training (5 days), (b) an individual start-up grant of US$150 (on average) to be used for approved business plans, and (c) regular follow-up visits by trained community workers (3 visits). Optional components of the program included: (a) group training (a cross-cutting design component)	Evaluation Tier 1 The program evaluated the impacts of providing beneficiaries with business skills training, a cash grant, and follow-up support (home visits). A randomized control experiment with mixed-methods data collection was used to gather information on beneficiaries at different points in time, starting in April 2009 and ending in August 2012. The sample consisted of 1,800 mostly poor women, ages 14–30, from 120 villages (15 beneficiaries per village). The evaluation built a wait-list control group whereby 900 of the beneficiaries were randomized in the program in phase 1 (mid-2009) and another 900 in phase 2 (early 2011). For phase 1, the program evaluation randomized participants into three groups: one group received the WINGS program, another group received the core package plus the cross-cutting design package (support for business networks), and the last group acted as the wait-listed control group. The evaluation measured program impacts on earnings, earnings opportunities, distribution of poverty impacts, savings, characteristics of individual success, health (sick days, hunger, health status, index of depression and anxiety), empowerment (indexes of economic decision making, gender attitudes, interpersonal violence, independence, household support), and social capital (groups and networks, trust, social cohesion, collective action).	Blattman et al. (2013)

table continues next page

Table E.3 Entrepreneurship Training—Potential Entrepreneurs (ETPo) *(continued)*

Name	Country/region	Program	Evaluation	Reference
		and (b) spousal training to support participants in their new endeavors. *Costs:* Total cost per participant was approximately US$688. The breakdown of this unit cost per person: grant US$120, targeting and disbursement costs US$100, business training US$99, group dynamics training US$65, follow-up US$279, and overhead US$25.	*Highlights:* • A year after the intervention, monthly cash earnings doubled from 16,500 to 31,300 Uganda shillings (US$6.60–US$12.52), cash savings tripled, and short-term expenditure on goods and services, and durable assets increased 30–50 percent relative to the control group (the average treatment effect is 16,200 Uganda shillings per month and the median treatment effect is 9,700 Uganda shillings per month); • The treatment had the greatest impact on the people with the lowest initial levels of capital and access to credit; • Among those who responded to treatment with more economic success (rather than average levels of economic success), the study found that women had lower success, and individuals with higher levels of access to credit at baseline saw fewer gains; • There was no large positive effect of skills/ education, patience, or good health on response to treatment; • There were only small health and social effects (positive or negative) of the intervention on beneficiaries; • There was little effect on psychological or social well-being from the observed reduction in poverty; • There was no effect found on women's independence, status in the community, or freedom from intimate partner violence; • Involving male partners and training the couples brought more positive results on the couples' interactions and on women's physical and mental health, but not on women's empowerment;	

table continues next page

Table E.3 Entrepreneurship Training—Potential Entrepreneurs (ETPo) *(continued)*

Name	Country/region	Program	Evaluation	Reference
			• There were large spillovers in the small village economies, including more women becoming traders, an increase in imports from major trading centers and a fall in the consumer price index; • Close supervision and advising by the NGO led to slight increases in economic success; and • The rate of return calculated for the WINGS full package plus administration (using an increase in income of 6,200 Uganda shillings per month for 15 years) was −33 percent when applying a discount rate of 15 percent for 15 years, and +36 percent when applying a 3 percent discount rate for 15 years. Although the return of the intervention using the average income effect was positive at a lower discount rate, it was not possible to determine whether the inputs that went into the program were the most appropriate or optimal combination, versus their individual contribution to the outcome.	
YOP—Youth Opportunities Program	Uganda	**Beneficiaries** Poor and underemployed youth ages 16–35 in Uganda's north **Description** The program aims to expand skilled nonagricultural employment, reduce poverty and spur the north's economic catch-up with the rest of Uganda. The beneficiaries are young adults ages 16–35. The government of Uganda administers the program, with groups submitting proposals to receive grants. The program is a one-time transfer of US$7,487 per group (in 2008 dollars), and only one group is financed by the community. A church, government extension office, or an NGO provides training.	Evaluation Tier 1 The evaluation looked at whether capital market imperfections hold back occupational choice, income, and employment growth, and play a role in the shift from agriculture to nonagriculture. The methodology was a randomized control trial; the treatment group received a one-time transfer (and the survey indicated those funds were not diverted by district officials). From the pool of 535 groups, 265 were randomly assigned to the intervention (treatment) and the remaining 279 to the control. They surveyed 2,675 treatment and control youth three times: at baseline, two, and four years postintervention, with an attrition rate of 9 percent after two years and 16 percent after four years. The outcomes were measured in terms of investment,	Blattman, Fiala, and Martinez (2013)

table continues next page

Table E.3 Entrepreneurship Training—Potential Entrepreneurs (ETPo) *(continued)*

Name	Country/region	Program	Evaluation	Reference
			occupational choice/levels, and income. Additional outcomes in social issues were also measured. **Highlights:** • Treated youth invested most of the grant in skills and business assets, and after four years they were 65 percent more likely to practice the skilled trade; • Earnings were 49 percent greater than for the control group and 41 percent greater after four years; • The treatment group was more likely to engage in business practices such as keeping records and registering and paying taxes; • There was a shift in occupational choice towards skilled work, where the treatment group was around 38 percent higher than the control, and it was larger for women; • Labor supply increased in response to the increase in capital for both men and women; • Earnings were larger for the treatment group and for both genders, but there was a catch-up by the control group after four years, primarily among men; • Wealth index was 0.2 s.d. greater for the treated group than for the control group; and • There was limited and weak evidence of a positive social impact after two years and none after four.	
GATE—Growing America Through Entrepreneurship Project	United States	**Beneficiaries** Potential entrepreneurs within seven sites in three states. **Description** The program objective is to provide training to individuals interested in start-ups or improving their own business. The program was delivered by Small Business Development Centers and nonprofit community-based organizations (up to	**Evaluation Tier 1** The evaluation aimed to test the effectiveness of offering free training on business start-ups or improving its performance. The methodology was based on a randomized control trial. The sample consisted of 4,197 individuals seeking training who had to attend an orientation meeting, which made them eligible. They all had to fill a baseline application form. The applications were reviewed and randomly assigned—2,094 to treatment and	Karlan, Fairlie, and Zinman (2012)

table continues next page

Table E.3 Entrepreneurship Training—Potential Entrepreneurs (ETPo) *(continued)*

Name	Country/region	Program	Evaluation	Reference
		14 organizations total) in eight cities serving both rural and urban population: Philadelphia, Pittsburgh, Minneapolis/St. Paul, Duluth (Minnesota), Virginia (Minnesota), Portland (Maine), Lewiston (Maine), and Bangor (Maine). The program delivered a one-on-one assessment and a "bundle" of training by business consultants in classrooms and one-on-one settings. *Costs:* The estimated cost of providing training to GATE recipients was around US$850–US$1,300 per person.	2,103 to control. Attrition was not big, but it was larger for the control group than for the treatment. Applications and interventions were administered between September 2003 and July 2005, and follow-up surveys were gathered at 6, 18, and 60 months after the intervention. The outcomes measured were related to business ownership, business performance and size, and the labor market (employment, household income, and work satisfaction). Additionally, it looked at heterogeneous treatment effects over various rationales for providing training subsidies (credit constraints, human and managerial capital constraints, labor market discrimination, and unemployment insurance frictions). *Highlights:* • Training significantly increased short-run business ownership and employment, but these effects vanished over the long term; • Business-ownership impacts are mainly driven by differences in business starts only, and not by business exits; • There is no evidence that entrepreneurship training had an effect on the firm size distribution in the sense of producing high-revenue or high-employment firms after five years of intervention; • There was no evidence of significant effects on business performance, household income, and work satisfaction in the short, medium, or long term; • There was no evidence of lasting effects of the provision of training on credit constraints effects, nor on human and managerial capital constraints, nor on labor market discrimination; and • However, the provision of entrepreneurship training had a significant effect in the short term on business ownership for those who were unemployed, but the effect disappeared over the long run.	

table continues next page

Table E.3 Entrepreneurship Training—Potential Entrepreneurs (ETPo) *(continued)*

Name	Country/region	Program	Evaluation	Reference
MEP—*Microempren-dimientos Productivos*	Argentina	**Beneficiaries** All beneficiaries of *Jefes*, a large-scale workfare program in Argentina **Description** The program objective is to promote the development of productive activities as part of an exit strategy from the workfare program. The beneficiaries are all eligible member of *Jefes*, a workfare program that provides direct income support to heads of households with dependents. The program is delivered nationwide through the municipalities and is administered by the Ministry of Social Development. It provides grants to purchase inputs and equipment; local institutions (e.g., universities, technical institutes, and NGOs) deliver the technical assistance.	Evaluation Tier 2 The evaluation assessed the short-term effects of promoting self-employment as part of an exit strategy of a safety net program. The evaluation methodology was a quasi-experimental design, exploiting administrative delays or cancelations to construct comparable groups. The sample covered 553 beneficiaries, of whom 309 are program participants (301 households and a total of 1,340 individuals) and 244 are non-participants (244 households and a total of 1,116 individuals). The attrition rate was 14 percent, and the final sample was 476 beneficiaries, of whom 279 were program participants and 197 were non-participants. A baseline survey was gathered in 2004 with a follow-up survey in 2005. The outcomes measured were labor market related (labor market participation, hours of work, individual and household income). *Highlights:* • Program participants substituted away from other jobs and significantly increased their total weekly work hours; however, this did not happen for other household members; • There was no evidence of a significant increase in individual income or total household income; • Effects were differentiated across gender, where women were more likely to combine self-employment with other jobs; and • Income effects were targeted to a subset of younger and more educated beneficiaries and those for whom the self-employment was related to an ongoing activity.	Almeida and Galasso (2007)

table continues next page

Table E.3 Entrepreneurship Training—Potential Entrepreneurs (ETPo) *(continued)*

Name	Country/region	Program	Evaluation	Reference
ACTIVATE—Achieving the Commercialization of Technology in Ventures through Applied Training for Entrepreneurs	United States	**Beneficiaries** Each year, 30 mid-career women from either technology or business backgrounds in Maryland **Description** ACTIVATE's objective is to help mid-career women start new businesses after learning new technologies. Started at the University of Maryland Baltimore County (UMBC) in 2005, ACTIVATE recruits about 30 qualified women from either technology or business backgrounds in Maryland each year. They meet at least once a week in a classroom, separated into diverse interdisciplinary teams. Up to three instructors lead sections on business plan development, the market of emerging technologies, and the actual formation of companies.	Evaluation Tier 3 The ACTIVATE evaluation assessed the firm achievements of its past participants, drawing on data for the classes from 2005 through 2009. *Highlights:* • At the time of the 2010 publication, each of these classes had generated between five and six companies; and • As of 2010, at least 77 jobs had been created by ACTIVATE companies, leading the report writer to deduce that the very low cost of the program (about US$200,000 a year in Maryland) creates a remarkable number of jobs.	Sage Policy Group and Nearing Group (2010)
BACIP—Building & Construction Improvement Programme	Pakistan	**Beneficiaries** 545 unemployed youth and young people **Description** The program aimed to teach participants how to construct and repair better homes, with the objective of becoming housing entrepreneurs and thereby decreasing unemployment rates. BACIP trainings were held in 39 villages around Pakistan from 2004 to 2007. Focused on improving the life quality of unemployed youth and young adults (aged 16–35) in remote and poor villages with marginal literacy rate, BACIP focused on enterprise development and promotion related to the housing sector.	Evaluation Tier 3 The project evaluation assessed BACIP's impact on unemployment rates and income for youth and women in Pakistan as well as housing construction. The study concluded that the BACIP program was successful in achieving its objectives. *Highlights:* • The project added to the skill set of youth participants, helping them generate incomes; • Many participants who would have otherwise been unemployed are now employed either as entrepreneurs or skilled laborers in the area; and • The community benefited from having more house builders—bringing down the cost of home building and fixing.	Zia (2007)

table continues next page

Table E.3 Entrepreneurship Training—Potential Entrepreneurs (ETPo) *(continued)*

Name	Country/region	Program	Evaluation	Reference
		There were three training tracks for the 545 participants. The first track was in manual labor, including carpentry, masonry, electrical wiring, stove making, plumbing, and painting. The second track was in home maintenance. The third track—for 33 participants—was in serving as sales agents of BACIP houses. From this pool of 545 participants, 60 were given money to start their own home improvement or sales businesses.		
DCEI—Dade County Entrepreneurial Institute	United States	**Beneficiaries** Minority business owners in Dade County **Description** DCEI aims to reduce the disparity among the African-American community in such areas as housing, education, economic development, and the criminal justice system. Searches for information on whether the program is still under implementation did not yield information. The program provides small business training and technical assistance to minority business owners and operators in Dade County (Florida, US). Started in 1983 and supported by Metro-Dade County, the three five-week courses each year, costing participants US$15 (that goes towards course materials), are designed specifically to train participants in becoming entrepreneurs. Upon completion, participants receive an institute certificate listing all courses completed. A second component of the	Evaluation Tier 3 There was no thorough evaluation of the program; however, Metropolitan Dade County evaluates the program each year and has continued to fund it. Seven separate institutions of higher education have worked together seamlessly to carry out the program.	Mann (1990)

table continues next page

Table E.3 Entrepreneurship Training—Potential Entrepreneurs (ETPo) *(continued)*

Name	Country/region	Program	Evaluation	Reference
		institute is providing direct technical assistance to six African-American-owned businesses each year, drawing on the expertise of the Dade County Office of Business Development as well as three public/private sector seed capital funds.		
ENBDP— Entrepre-neurship and New Business Development Programme	Sweden	**Beneficiaries** Potential entrepreneurs in technology-based enterprises **Description** The program aims to train individuals in the start-up of new technology-based or knowledge-intensive enterprises. Financed by public money from the Swedish National Board for Technical Development and the Technology Bridge Foundation in Linkoping in 1994, ENBDP has its participants develop a business plan and attend workshops on the process of developing a business. Participants have a senior entrepreneur serve as a mentor, check in with a program manager to discuss their progress, network through formalized groups, have the ability to rent space in an incubator space at a nearby science park, and have access to seed financing in the form of grants or soft loans.	Evaluation Tier 3 The evaluation assessed the possibility of stimulating entrepreneurial behaviors in a way that will lead to positive outcomes, like an improvement in the quality of new projects or firms. The evaluation was carried out using a series of follow-up surveys of past program participants. *Highlights:* - Participants noted that the program benefited them by providing a better structure in their business because their business plan had been gone through thoroughly; and - Participants pointed to a supportive environment with ample pressure to perform; a network that stimulated development; and the ability to analyze a business idea and/or plan.	Klofsten (2000)
SEWA—SEWA Banks	India	**Beneficiaries** 597 female SEWA Bank clients **Description** The program aimed to teach participants the basics of financial literacy and business skills to spur improvements in their businesses.	Evaluation Tier 3 The evaluation assessed the program's impact on participants' financial literacy, business skills, and firm development. For the experiment, 597 women were surveyed, all of whom had actively saved with SEWA in the past two years and were employed (drawn	Field, Jayachandran, and Pande (2010)

table continues next page

Table E.3 Entrepreneurship Training—Potential Entrepreneurs (ETPo) *(continued)*

Name	Country/region	Program	Evaluation	Reference
		This was a one-time intervention in 2006–07. Participants were SEWA Bank clients who had a savings account and took a two-day training course that covered financial literacy (including basic accounting skills, interest rates, and life-cycle planning), business skills (cost reduction, investment, customer service), and an aspirational module (including a short film highlighting successful SEWA members who used good financial practices to pull themselves out of poverty). For homework, participants filled out a worksheet identifying a financial goal they wanted to achieve over the next six months, and during the second day, participants broke it into short-run steps.	from a random pool that met this criterion). Two-thirds of the women were placed in the treatment groups. All participating women were categorized into sub-castes based on their surnames (Muslims, Hindu sub-castes (SCs), Hindu upper-castes (UCs), non-scheduled castes, and others). *Highlights:* • Training led to a significant increase—13 percentage points—in taking out loans within four months of training among UCs, and none borrowed beyond their means; • Training had no effect on savings; • There was a positive and significant effect of the training on business income only among UCs, suggesting that the new loans were put toward business investments; • UC women were more likely to talk frequently with family members about their business plans; and • The evaluation suggested that the training encouraged UCs to start or expand their microenterprises.	
SIYB—Start and Improve Your Business Program	Vietnam	**Beneficiaries** Over 1 million farmers **Description** The original program aimed to train micro and small business owners in basic business management and helped them—as well as aspirational entrepreneurs—start up or improve the performance of their businesses. The students had regular course work, refresher training, and post-training support.	Evaluation Tier 3 The evaluation assessed the program's efficacy in helping participants improve their business performances. The evaluation included a visit to a dozen locations where SIYB programs took place during 2006, with interviews of at least 10 different beneficiary entrepreneurs in each location. The participants had positive things to say about the program; however, the program's consistency and rigor were noted as limitations.	Goppers and Coung (2007)

table continues next page

Table E.3 Entrepreneurship Training—Potential Entrepreneurs (ETPo) *(continued)*

Name	Country/region	Program	Evaluation	Reference
		From 1998 to 2004, the Vietnam Chamber of Commerce and Industry (VCCI) and the International Labour Organization (ILO) implemented Start and Improve Your Business (SIYB) program in Vietnam. Today, SIYB has partnered with Vietnam's General Department for Vocational Training (under the Ministry of Labor) to deliver the program to more than one million farmers over the next seven years. Participants will get skill training around agriculture and rural occupations in one of 800 vocational outlet training locations around the country.	*Highlights:* • Available information indicated that the SIYB training program helped the businesses of participants; and • While increased profits weren't always recorded, the majority of firms benefited from being better run, from owners having a better understanding of the market, and from an increase in confidence and business outlook among participants.	
WEMTOP—Women's Enterprise Management Training Opportunity Program	India	**Beneficiaries** Over 1,000 rural producer women **Description** The program aimed to improve the enterprises of rural producer women in India. A pilot program, WEMTOP ran from 1992 until 1996. WEMTOP training was in credit, market linkages, technical skills training, and management training as well as empowerment. Women learned in groups around the country—by the end of 1995, over 1,000 women had participated in the program. The Economic Development Institute designed the training, bringing in expertise on Indian development, and ultimately partnering with 21 NGOs to carry out the training.	Evaluation Tier 3 The study assessed the program's impact on women's soft and business skills. Evaluated in 1996, staff interviews from across WEMTOP and participating NGOs were used to understand the program, as were the findings of a pilot impact survey, monitoring, and evaluation data that had been prepared about the 1,077 women who took part in the pilot program. *Highlights:* • A large proportion of the participating women became more self-confident and more involved in group decision making; and • Women benefiting from WEMTOP were those who hadn't previously been part of a group, women who have since organized themselves for income-generating activity for the first time, and women who were already working on enterprises and have become more systematic in their efforts.	Neill, Sreedhar, and Kapadia (1998)

table continues next page

Table E.3 Entrepreneurship Training—Potential Entrepreneurs (ETPo) (continued)

Name	Country/region	Program	Evaluation	Reference
WSBP/MBDP—Women's Small Business Program and Micro Business Development Program	Vermont, United States	**Beneficiaries** Women in Vermont with business ideas (WSBP); low-income Vermonters who want to start their own businesses (MBDP) **Description** Mercy Connections Women's Small Business Program (WSBP)'s objective is to train women in the skills needed to own, run, and staff a business. Women participating in the WSBP seek help at different stages of their business—some have a concept, others have an enterprise but need help with marketing, financing, etc. WSPB accepts women trainees of all income levels. The Micro Business Development Program (MBDP) of the Vermont Community Action Agencies aims to provide technical assistance and training to low- to moderate-income Vermonters who want to start or expand a small business. For the purposes of evaluation, participants from both programs were trained in interviewing skills—with practice questions and coaching provided by mentors and instructors.	Evaluation Tier 3 The evaluation assessed participants' motivation to start their own businesses, participants' definitions of success, the barriers they faced, and the trainings' impact on their interviewing skills. A qualitative approach was used, with area college students interviewing 27 graduates of WSBP and 16 graduates of MBDP in 2008. *Highlights:* • Participants were extremely positive about their entrepreneurship trainings; • The skills the majority emphasized having gained were ability to write a solid business plan, financial training, some education in marketing education, and a higher confidence level; • The most common negative responses were that the bulk of experience-based teaching was directed towards those who only had an idea for a business even though many of the women participants had already opened their business and were looking to refine their skills; and • Another gap was inadequate preparation for dealing with labor issues.	Bauer (2011)

Table E.4 **Entrepreneurship Training—Practicing Entrepreneurs (ETPr)**

Name	Country/region	Program	Evaluation	Reference
EDC—Entrepreneurship Development Center	Bosnia and Herzegovina	**Beneficiaries** 18–35-year-old clients of Partner Microcredit Foundation around Tuzla, Bosnia and Herzegovina **Description** The objective of the program was to identify the determinants of entrepreneurship in emerging market economies where there are stringent constraints on business growth. Carried out in 2009, participants were young adults in Bosnia and Herzegovina who had small businesses or who were developing a new enterprise. The program was run in partnership with Partner Microcredit Foundation (a group that operates within and near the city of Tuzla). It consisted of comprehensive business training for existing and potential entrepreneurs who had loans at Partner Microcredit Foundation. The training was provided by Entrepreneurship Development Center, a local NGO in Tuzla. The training included six comprehensive modules; and participants were provided a stipend of US$35 and given free transportation to the training location. *Costs:* free for beneficiaries.	Evaluation Tier 1 The evaluation assessed the impact of a comprehensive business and financial literacy program on firm outcomes of young entrepreneurs in emerging post-conflict economy. The methodology consisted of a randomized control trial with a sample size of 445 active business loan clients—between ages 18 and 35—who were interested in the training at the initial phone screening. The evaluation design suffered some changes over time. By the end, the treatment group was composed of 117 individuals (39 percent of the individuals who were invited to the training) and 148 in the control group. A baseline survey was conducted in April and May 2009. The implementation of the business training was carried out between June and December 2009. An exit test was administered at the end of the training to all participants. Finally, a follow-up survey was conducted in May and June 2010, one year after the baseline survey. Outcomes were based on business creation and survival, business performance, business growth, business practices and investments, and loan behavior. *Highlights:* - The training program did not influence business survival; it did improve business practices, investments, and loan terms for businesses; - The training improved business and financial knowledge on average (after the training, the total score of the exit test had increased from a baseline of 2.6–2.9). At follow-up, the average treatment effect of the training on business and financial knowledge was positive, but not statistically significant; - The strongest effects of the training were on improvements in business practices and	Bruhn and Zia (2011)

table continues next page

Table E.4 Entrepreneurship Training—Practicing Entrepreneurs (ETPr) *(continued)*

Name	Country/region	Program	Evaluation	Reference
			investments: the treatment group was 17 percent more likely to implement new production processes than the control group and 11 percent more likely to inject new investment into the business; • The training increased business profits for entrepreneurs with above-median financial literacy at baseline by 54 percent, although the results were not statistically significant at conventional levels; and • No impact was found on loan amounts, but there were significant impacts on loan restructuring. The treatment group was 3.4 percent more likely than the control group to refinance its loans. This effect was large, indicating that the treatment almost doubled the likelihood of refinancing loans.	
END—Endeavor	South Africa	**Beneficiaries** The target is mostly small and medium enterprises that are particularly conducive to innovation in South Africa **Description** The program objective is to support small and medium enterprises in order to promote economic development and job growth. Endeavor, headquartered in New York City, launched its operations in 1997 in Latin America and now has operations around the world. Its South African program started in 2003. As with all Endeavor programs, participants go through a highly selective vetting process ensuring that only potentially high-impact entrepreneurs take part in the training. On average, four to six entrepreneurs are selected each year; they are supported by successful entrepreneurs, business school professors, and students in business plan and strategy	Evaluation Tier 1 An external evaluation of Endeavor South Africa was completed in March 2007, assessing if programs supporting high-growth entrepreneurs worked. The evaluation was based on a quasi-experimental design, in which the 19 selected enterprises (Ees) comprised the treatment group (those who received the whole arrange of Endeavor's services) and 33 non-selected applicants (non-Ees) were the control group. The review included an online survey, interviews with Ees, and with other applicants who were rejected (non-Ees). The surveys and interviews provided quantitative and qualitative information. The outcomes aimed to estimate the effect of being chosen as a program participant on firms; as well as assessing total sales, export sales, number of employees, and income. *Highlights:* • The program had positive effects on sales growth; • On average, sales for Ees increased by approximately R2-R3 million more than they did for non-Ees;	IFC Monitor (2008)

table continues next page

Table E.4 Entrepreneurship Training—Practicing Entrepreneurs (ETPr) *(continued)*

Name	Country/region	Program	Evaluation	Reference
		development, as well as being assisted by their mentorship as they develop their businesses. The non-profit Endeavor Global delivers the program.	• The effect on the percentage of export sales was not statistically significant; and • Ees' most used services were the mentoring, training course, and networking opportunities, but not all the services were used, showing that achieving all program objectives required some additional effort.	
FINCA—Entrepreneurship Program	Peru	**Beneficiaries** Clients of FINCA microfinance institution (approx. total of 16,000 clients in Lima and two Andean provinces) **Description** The program aims to teach entrepreneurial skills that improve business practices to clients of FINCA-Peru, a micro-finance institution that trains low-income female entrepreneurs using a village-banking methodology. In Peru since 1993, FINCA-Peru provides training sessions for 16,000 clients. Participants use the money to invest in their businesses and are required to save money each month. FINCA's ultimate goal is to provide clients a financial service while helping them develop their businesses. Training typically lasts 22 weeks and is in Lima and two more rural provinces. The training materials were developed by FINCA, Atinchick, and Freedom from Hunger; training was timed with the loan cycles.	Evaluation Tier 1 The study tested whether micro-entrepreneurs were maximizing their profits given the resources available to them, and whether lessons on business development improved FINCA-Peru clients' profits. A randomized control trial was conducted to evaluate the effectiveness of integrating business training with microfinance services, using a sample of FINCA Peru's preexisting lending clients. On average, they were organized in groups of 20 women randomly assigned to control and treatment groups, stratified by credit officer. Regarding distribution, 139 groups were assigned to treatment and 101 to control. The evaluation used three key data sources: FINCA financial transaction data, a baseline survey before the randomization results were announced, and a follow-up survey up to two years later. The response rate was 76 percent for the follow-up survey; it was lower in the treatment group (75.2 percent) compared to the control group (77.9 percent).	Karlan, and Valdivia (2011)

table continues next page

Table E.4 Entrepreneurship Training—Practicing Entrepreneurs (ETPr) *(continued)*

Name	Country/region	Program	Evaluation	Reference
			The results of the analysis were divided into four categories: (a) business outcomes, (b) business processes and knowledge, (c) household outcomes, and (d) microfinance institutional outcomes. *Highlights:* • Basic business training to preexisting clients did not lead to higher profits or revenues on average. However, difference-in-difference specifications found a positive but small impact on enterprise revenues; • Positive changes in four business skills and practices outcomes were significant at 95 percent (keeping records, an index of business knowledge, the use of profits for business growth, and implementation of innovations in the business); • No training impact was found on household decision making; • The training led to a 4 percentage point increase in the client retention rate, generating an increased net revenue for FINCA; • The training had no effect on loan size or accumulated savings; and • Sometimes the stronger training effects were found for those clients who expressed less interest in the training in the baseline survey.	
GNAG—Ghana National Association of Garages	Ghana	**Beneficiaries** Aprox. 1,000 metalwork entrepreneurs in the Suame Magazine, located in the city of Kumasi, Ghana **Description** The program objective was to provide management training to micro and	Evaluation Tier 1 The evaluation assessed how micro and small enterprises in Sub-Saharan Africa could become more productive. The pool of entrepreneurs was 167 metalwork entrepreneurs randomly selected from the GNAG member list. However, due to attrition and implementation problems, the final sample	Mano et al. (2011)

table continues next page

Table E.4 Entrepreneurship Training—Practicing Entrepreneurs (ETPr) *(continued)*

Name	Country/region	Program	Evaluation	Reference
		small enterprises in order to become more productive. The program ended in 2007. The beneficiaries were individuals from Suame Magazine, a large cluster of garage mechanics and of metalwork enterprises that produce a variety of metal products in Kumasi, Ghana. The program was funded by the Policy and Human Resource Development Trust Fund from the Government of Japan, and the training was modeled on the Business Course provided by the Japan international Cooperation Agency. The training was delivered by the Suame Branch of the National Vocational Training Institute. The program consisted of three modules of classroom training; each module lasted for five weekdays, 2.5 hours per day. *Costs:* US$40,000 to set up and to run the program ($740 per participant).	was 113 entrepreneurs. The treatment group had 47 entrepreneurs while the control consisted of 66. The data were gathered before and after the management training. A survey of metalwork entrepreneurs was conducted in early 2005, with a follow-up study in November 2008, about a year after the training sessions were completed. The outcomes were measured in terms of practice adoption and financial outcomes. *Highlights:* • The training had a strong impact on the adoption of the recommended practices, although the firms experienced decreased profitability due to new competition; • After the training, the percentage of firms in the treatment group keeping records increased by 36 percentage points whereas the increase was 6 percentage points in the control group; • Similarly, the percentage of firms in the treatment group analyzing business records increased by 34 percentage points while the increase was about 3 percentage points in the control group; • However, these effects were not homogeneous because between a third and a half of participants did not adopt these practices; • The decrease in the sales and gross profits after the training were somewhat smaller for the treatment group than for the control group, respectively,	

table continues next page

Table E.4 Entrepreneurship Training—Practicing Entrepreneurs (ETPr) *(continued)*

Name	Country/region	Program	Evaluation	Reference
			−12.9 percentage points compared to −19.6 points for the sales, and −2.8 percentage points compared to −6.9 for the gross profits. Also, the effects of the training on the gross profits were much more significant than the effects of the training on sales revenues; and • Participation in the training program increased the probability of survival by 8 or 9 percentage points.	
MIDA-FBO Millennium Development Authority—Farm-Based Organization Training	Ghana	**Beneficiaries** Farm-based organizations (FBOs) in 30 districts in the Northern Agricultural Zone, the Central African Basin Zone, and the Southern Horticultural Belt **Description** The program aimed to increase the production and productivity of high-value cash and food crops while enhancing the competitiveness of these crops in targeted geographical local and international markets from 2006 to 2011. The beneficiaries were the farmers in the Northern Agricultural Zone, Central African Basin Zone, and Southern Horticultural Belt in Ghana. The program organized the farmers in farm-based organizations (FBOs), composed of five farmers each. The FBO training sessions lasted 27 days and was conducted three days a week. The training was performed by the Millennium Development Authority (MiDA). Every farmer who was trained received a starter pack to pilot the knowledge and skills acquired during the training. The content of the starter pack included fertilizer, seeds for an acre, protective clothing, and some cash amount for land preparation, all valued at US$230.	Evaluation Tier 1 The evaluation aimed to measure the impact of the FBO training program on farmers' farm productivity and crop income. The evaluation methodology was a randomized phase-in approach, where farmers were put into early and late treatment categories to enable the estimation of program impact. Approximately 1,200 FBOs were ex ante to be interviewed as part of the evaluation. The surveys were conducted over a three-year period during the lifespan of the program, from November 2008 through January 2011. Under the evaluation design, each farmer was to be interviewed twice—in rounds one (baseline) and two (follow-up). The overall attrition rate was about 10 percent over the baseline and follow-up. The outcomes measured were loan access and estimates of behavior (cultivated land size, chemical use and value, labor hours, and seed use). *Highlights:* • There was no evidence of intervention impact on crop yields and crop incomes overall, but there were significant zonal differences on crop incomes; • Training positively impacted the loan amounts that households received, but were driven by MiDA loans; • Training increased farmers' use of more formal sources for loans; and	Institute of Statistical, Social and Economic Research (2012)

table continues next page

Table E.4 Entrepreneurship Training—Practicing Entrepreneurs (ETPr) *(continued)*

Name	Country/region	Program	Evaluation	Reference
			• The intervention led to an increase in the use of improved seeds and fertilizers by farmers, but that was mainly driven by the starter pack that participants received.	
NRSP—National Rural Support Program	Pakistan	**Beneficiaries** Over 300 groups of borrowers (community organizations or COs) at five branches of a microfinance institution in three districts of rural Pakistan **Description** The program's objective is to enhance participants' business knowledge and their firms' creation and performance. At the time of its evaluation in 2007, NRSP tied a series of its microloans to entrepreneurial training sessions. The program developed a field experiment where a subset of male and female NRSP clients in rural Pakistan were offered eight full-time days of business training and the opportunity to participate in a lottery to access business loans of up to 100,000 Rs (US$1,700—about seven times the average loan size). Over 46 hours of training, participants studied business planning, marketing, and financial management. Upon completion of the training modules, NRSP identified the participants that were eligible to apply for a larger loan size. NRSP's more typical approach to microfinance lending includes a requirement that its members join community organizations. NRSP members must meet regularly with	Evaluation Tier 1 The evaluation assessed the main barriers to entrepreneurship in a country, specifically around access to human capital and credit for entrepreneurship. The methodology consisted of a field experiment in rural Pakistan with a subset of male and female microfinance clients of NRSP organized in COs. The experiment offered training to a randomly selected half of the 747 groups of borrowers (COs) from five different branches of three different districts (treatment group), while the other half did not receive training (control group). A baseline survey was conducted in November 2006, and the business training sessions were held in 2007. A follow-up survey was conducted in December 2008, 6 months after the loan lottery concluded and about 13 months after the loan orientation meetings. The attrition rate between the baseline and follow-up about two years after was 16 percent. The evaluation focused on intent-to-treat estimates. The outcomes were related to business knowledge, creation, and performance. *Highlights:* • Business training led to increased business knowledge (estimate value of 0.058, with significance at 10 percent level); • No effect of business training was found on business creation either with or without access to the larger loan (estimate value of −0.006);	Giné and Mansuri (2011)

table continues next page

Table E.4 Entrepreneurship Training—Practicing Entrepreneurs (ETPr) *(continued)*

Name	Country/region	Program	Evaluation	Reference
		their community organization, contribute towards the group's savings as well as their own, and both receive and repay their loans. With a presence in 54 districts in Pakistan and started in 1991, NRSP now works with more than two million low-income households in the country—providing uncollateralized microloans to individual clients, who then must become members of a CO. Additionally, NRSP offers training in vocational skills and provides up to 80 percent financing for infrastructure projects in the villages.	• Offer of business training led to improvements in business practices such as recording the sales on paper as well as separating business from household accounts; • Female CO members who had lower levels of business knowledge at baseline increased business knowledge by about 87 percent (p-value 0.12), but unlike men, they were unable to put into practice their newly acquired knowledge; • Business training led to a reduction in business failure by 6.1 percent among male business owners, compared to the control group, but there was no effect among business women (p-value of 0.98); and • Access to the larger loan, in contrast, had little effect on anyone.	
PRIDE	Tanzania	**Beneficiaries** The more than 300 clients of PRIDE microfinance in Dar es Salaam, Tanzania **Description** The program objective was to help clients' business results. Run in Tanzania between 2008 and 2009, PRIDE Bank provided microfinance training to 300 small-scale entrepreneurs in Dar es Salaam. Participants attended 21 sessions lasting 45 minutes after each client's weekly loan meeting. In total, 319 clients were offered free training, and 325 clients were placed in the control group. Clients who attended at least 10 out of the 21 sessions received a diploma from the University of Dar es Salaam's Entrepreneurship Centre (who had helped developed the training). *Costs:* Free for participants.	Evaluation Tier 1 The evaluation aimed to answer the question "what is the impact of training on small-scale entrepreneurs in terms of business skills?" The evaluation included a randomized control trial, conducted in 2009, approximately six weeks after completion of the training program. Clients were randomly placed in treatment and control groups from the pool of clients at intermediary loan levels (500,000 to 1 million Tanzanian shillings [T Sh], or US$300–600). A randomly selected subset was drawn from the pool of clients who were offered training. The sample size included 126 in the treated group and 126 in the control group. There was an attrition rate of 15 percent for the treatment group and 13 percent for the control group, but it did not affect the randomization. The final sample was 107 for the treatment and 104 for the control. Monetary incentives helped keep the response bias low.	Bjorvatn and Tungodden (2010)

table continues next page

Table E.4 Entrepreneurship Training—Practicing Entrepreneurs (ETPr) *(continued)*

Name	Country/region	Program	Evaluation	Reference
			The evaluation focused on two criteria: participation and performance (the latter measured as entrepreneur business skills). *Highlights:* • The mean attendance for the subsample of the treated participants was 15.9 out of 21 sessions (76 percent), indicating that the training was perceived as beneficial for the businesses; • More schooled, more skilled (in terms of math), and more experienced (in terms of age) entrepreneurs had higher attendance than those who scored lower on these dimensions. The values of attendance were, respectively, 1.70 (significant at 10 percent), 1.62 (significant at 10 percent), and 2.26 (significant at 5 percent); • On average, the treatment group had a 9 percent higher score on the business knowledge test than the control group; and • The effect of training appeared to be highest for entrepreneurs who participated frequently in the course, who initially did not have a lot of formal education, but who did have strong cognitive skills.	
ROT- Rules of Thumb	Dominican Republic	**Beneficiaries** 1,200 clients of ADOPEM microfinance institution in Santo Domingo, Dominican Republic **Description** ROT's objective was to improve participants' business practices and firm performance. Between November 2006 and July 2008 in Santo Domingo, 1,200 loan clients from ADOPEM (one of the Dominican Republic's largest banks) were randomly assigned a	Evaluation Tier 1 The evaluation assessed the impact of different financial accounting classes on firm-level and individual outcomes. A randomized control trial was constructed with two treatment groups (one for each type of course offered) and a control group. The 1,200-person sample was selected out of the existing clients of ADOPEM who had expressed an interest in training. A baseline survey was conducted in November 2006 and, due to errors, the sample was reduced to 1,193 people. The distribution across the	Drexler, Fischer, and Schoar (2010)

table continues next page

Table E.4 Entrepreneurship Training—Practicing Entrepreneurs (ETPr) *(continued)*

Name	Country/region	Program	Evaluation	Reference
		basic accounting course, a Rule of Thumb entrepreneurship course, or no training. The Rule of Thumb course was about simplifying financial decision making without explaining the motivation—separating out personal and business expenses. The course—held once a week for three hours over five weeks—taught participants how to estimate business profits, how to pay oneself a fixed salary, and how to reconcile accounts when business funds have been used for personal purposes (and vice versa). Additionally, in order to understand the potential limitations to classroom-based financial training, some of the participants (randomly chosen) received in-person financial trainer visits to the micro-entrepreneur's business. The follow-up visits ensured that individuals understood the material and were capable of implementing their newly acquired financial accounting skills in their businesses. The courses were offered at seven schools throughout Santo Domingo. *Costs:* The overall program cost was approximately US$17 per participant. Some fees were randomly assigned (up to US$5) to test for selection effects among the participants.	groups was 402 assigned to accounting courses, 404 to ROT courses, and 387 to the control group. The baseline survey collected information on household and business characteristics, business practices and performance, business skills, training history, and interest in future training. An ex-post survey was conducted during the summer of 2008, at least 12 months after training was completed. The attrition rate for this survey was 13 percent. The outcomes were based on business practices and performance. *Highlights:* • The impact of financial literacy training varied by its delivery method: the training program based on simple rules of thumb led to significant improvements in the way SMEs managed their finances relative to groups not offered training or offered the standard accounting training; • ROT training increased by 6–12 percent the likelihood that individuals reported separating business and personal cash and accounts, kept accounting records, and calculated revenues formally, in comparison with the control group, which did not receive training. The estimates were significant at the 5 percent level. No statistically significant effects were found on the business practices of those assigned to the accounting treatment; • Individuals assigned to the ROT treatment reported a substantial increase (about US$31) in revenues during bad weeks. This value was significant at the 5 percent-level. No discernible effects of the accounting program were found on revenues;	

table continues next page

Table E.4 Entrepreneurship Training—Practicing Entrepreneurs (ETPr) *(continued)*

Name	Country/region	Program	Evaluation	Reference
			• Economically large increases in savings (6 percent) were found for the participants in the ROT trainings, and they were significant at the 10 percent level. No effect on savings was found for the group that received the basic accounting training; and • Follow-up visits did not affect the outcomes for clients in the rule-of-thumb-based training. In contrast, the follow-up visits to the participants of the basic accounting training showed a significant increase in savings levels of about 10 percent and an increase in the probability of implementing the accounting practices taught in class. But no improvements on real outcomes of the businesses, such as sales, were found. This suggested that effectiveness might be a matter of delivery method or the likelihood of implementing techniques conditional on understanding them.	
SIYB—SL ILO's Start and Improve Your Business training program	Sri Lanka	**Beneficiaries** Women who operate subsistence enterprises and have been out of the labor force but are interested in starting a business **Description** The program aims to help women start new businesses and to make existing businesses more productive. The beneficiaries are women who operate subsistence enterprises and those who are out of the labor force but are interested in starting a business. The program is the ILO's Start and Improve Your Business (SIYB), which provides five- to six-day training courses designed to help potential entrepreneurs set up a new business (e.g., selection of products, pricing, organization of staff, purchasing of equipment,	Evaluation Tier 1 The evaluation assessed how business training and grants affect the running of a business and their profitability. The methodology was based on a randomized experiment conducted among women in urban Sri Lanka. The sample included: (a) 628 current business owners, a random sample of women working full-time in businesses and earning below the median profit level (5,000 Rs, or about US$40/month); and (b) 628 potential business owners, a random sample of women ages 25–45 who were out of the labor force and were planning on starting a business in the next year. Each of the two samples was randomly allocated into three groups: (a) training only: 200 individuals invited to training; (b) training plus grant:	de Mel, McKenzie, and Woodruff (2012)

table continues next page

Table E.4 Entrepreneurship Training—Practicing Entrepreneurs (ETPr) *(continued)*

Name	Country/region	Program	Evaluation	Reference
		and other inputs) and to help existing businesses grow (e.g., marketing, buying, costing, stock control, record-keeping, financial planning). The training was provided by the Sri Lanka Business Development Centre. *Costs:* The training is offered for free. The training cost for the program is US$126–US$131 per current business owner and US$133–US$140 per potential business owner.	200 individuals invited to training, who received a grant of 15,000 Rs (US$130) conditional on finishing training; and (c) a control group of 228 individuals. Four follow-up surveys were conducted, at time intervals corresponding to 4, 8, 16, and 25 months after training. Attrition rates were relatively low, ranging from 6–12 percent, with information on business ownership available for 97 percent of firms. Measurements were done on business practices and business outcomes for both sets of groups (business owners and potential business owners). *Highlights:* • Training alone did not appear to be enough to get subsistence businesses run by women to grow, although results were more encouraging for using business training to help women out of the labor force as well as for improving profits and management of these businesses; • Training led to improvements in business practices for existing firms, although the magnitude was relatively small; • Training (with or without grants) had no impact on the survival of existing firms; • Training along with grants had no significant impact on the profits or sales of existing firms; • Training sped up the creation of new businesses; and • Businesses started by trained entrepreneurs were more profitable up to two years later, with profits and sales that were up to 40 percent higher.	
TECH—TechnoServe	Central America	**Beneficiaries** Individuals or existing small and medium-scale enterprises in Central America who are interested in setting up a new business or expanding business services	Evaluation Tier 2 The evaluation assessed whether business training for SME entrepreneurs or potential entrepreneurs could lead to an increase in the number of business start-ups or an expansion in the size of existing businesses.	Klinger and Schündlen (2007)

table continues next page

Table E.4 Entrepreneurship Training—Practicing Entrepreneurs (ETPr) *(continued)*

Name	Country/region	Program	Evaluation	Reference
		Description The program aims to promote entrepreneurship and competitiveness at the national level through a Business Plan Competition. The beneficiaries are individuals or existing small and medium-scale enterprises who are interested in setting up a new business or gaining the necessary skills and abilities to expand their current businesses. In Central America, the program attracts entrepreneurs with existing businesses of about 10 employees on average. TechnoServe offers business training programs in Central America (Guatemala, Nicaragua, and El Salvador). The program that previously ran in El Salvador included a business plan development component, with the potential to win seed funding. The financial prize was between US$6,000 and US$15,000 (depending on country and year), conditional on investment in the business, plus some additional business development services. The number of applicants admitted into the program and the number of participants that subsequently progressed to each stage was fixed before the competition began. *Costs:* Participants paid an application fee of US$15. The implementation cost to run the initial program was US$343,420.	The methodology exploited a quasi-experimental approach (regression discontinuity) where the number of participants was fixed exogenously and provided a cut-off in the scoring of applications. The sample size was 655 applications in the three countries, where 377 received at least some training, and 278 were rejected applicants who did not receive any training. The outcomes measured were related to starting or expanding businesses. *Highlights:* • The evidence suggested that receiving business training significantly increased the probability of business start-ups and expanded existing business; • The training program led to an effect of a higher probability—9–11 percentage points—of opening a business (for individuals without a business before the start of the program) in the treatment group and a 23–26 percentage point higher probability of expanding a business (for individuals with an existing business before the program) in the treatment group; • Winning the competition led to economically significant changes in the probability of starting or expanding a business, suggesting the presence of financial constraints; and • Financial constraints were more important for women who wished to start or expand a business than for men.	
ULTP—Urban Land Titling Program	Peru	**Beneficiaries** Micro-entrepreneurs who were beneficiaries of a titling program in Lima	Evaluation Tier 1 The evaluation aimed to understand whether a business training program can complement titling	Valdivia (2011)

table continues next page

Table E.4 Entrepreneurship Training—Practicing Entrepreneurs (ETPr) *(continued)*

Name	Country/region	Program	Evaluation	Reference
		Description The objective of ULTP was to help women grow their businesses and emerge from poverty. This was a pilot intervention of the program, and searches for information on whether the program is still under implementation did not yield information. Eligibility for the training was based on women having a family business and a titled plot and expressing interest in participating in the training program. The training was organized into two components: a general training component (GT) and a technical assistance component (TA). The GT included 36 three-hour sessions over approximately 12 weeks (regular training). In addition, half of the women who received the GT were offered an individualized support in the form of TA over a period of three extra months. The GT focused on best practices, with modules on personal development; business development and management; and management and productivity improvement. The program was done in consortium with three organizations: Centro de Servicios para la Capacitación Laboral y el Desarrollo, Centro Latinoamericano de Trabajo Social, and Instituto de Promoción del Desarrollo Solidario.	to improve female micro-entrepreneurs' access to credit and increase their possibilities to escape from poverty. A randomized control trial was conducted in which eligible female micro-entrepreneurs were randomly assigned to control and treatment groups. Eligibility was based on women having family businesses, a titled plot, and an expressed interest in participating in the training program. There were 1,983 eligible women who were placed in two treatment and one control groups. The distribution of women was 709 in Treatment 1 (T1), the group that received only the GT component; 709 in Treatment 2 (T2), the group that received both the general training component (first) and the TA component; and the remaining 565 who were assigned to the control group. A baseline survey was applied before randomization and a follow-up survey completed about four months after the end of the treatment. Follow-up surveys went from March to November of 2010. A total of 1,627 women were interviewed, which implies an attrition rate of 18 percent, although attrition was slightly higher for the control group (21 percent). A method of intention to treat (ITT) was adopted. The outcomes were in terms of business practices. *Highlights:* • Treatment induced women to make important adjustments to their business practices, although they differed across the type of treatment; • Positive differences in business sales were found among the treated micro-entrepreneurs, but they were not statistically different from zero. The sales	

table continues next page

Table E.4 Entrepreneurship Training—Practicing Entrepreneurs (ETPr) *(continued)*

Name	Country/region	Program	Evaluation	Reference
			increases came mainly from those for whom the treatment included GT+TA. In a normal month, those treated with GT+TA sold 19 percent more than their control counterparts; • No significant employment effect was found due to the training, so the sales increases imply a productivity gain for the GT+TA treatment group; • GT+TA-trained women were 5.7 percentage points more likely to participate in business-related associations; • GT-treated women were more likely to close their old businesses (3.5 percentage points) once they realized that they were not profitable, while those who received GT+TA were more prone to plan and implement innovations in their current business (about 3.5 percentage points); • Business results effects accrued among the businesses run by single women (0.34 s.d.), with a more entrepreneurial attitude index (0.36 s.d.), in households with titled dwellings (0.09 s.d.), and where the woman´s business was relatively more important for the household's budget (0.25 s.d.), and for larger businesses (0.11 s.d.); • The aggregate standardized index for business practices showed statistically significant positive average effects of the training (0.037 s.d.), in particular, for those who received full treatment (0.049 s.d.); and • Increased participation in savings/borrowing for family or personal purposes was found.	
WEP—Women Entrepreneurship Program	South Africa	**Beneficiaries** Women who want to start their own business or have one and seek to improve their entrepreneurial and management skills.	**Evaluation Tier 1** An evaluation, conducted in 2004–05, assessed the effectiveness of the training program on potential, new, and established women entrepreneurs	Botha (2006)

table continues next page

Table E.4 Entrepreneurship Training—Practicing Entrepreneurs (ETPr) *(continued)*

Name	Country/region	Program	Evaluation	Reference
		Description The Women Entrepreneurship Program (WEP) aims to promote and encourage women entrepreneurs in South Africa and address the lack of entrepreneurial training and education. The beneficiaries are women who want to start their own business or have one and seek to improve their entrepreneurial and management skills. The program involves screening, profiling, selecting, training, developing business plans, mentoring, and providing access to finance to beneficiaries; this was done in different phases. The training phase is 6 days long and carried out through the University of Pretoria. Topics include networking and support; the use of role models; confidence building; and post-care training using mentors and counselors.	in South Africa. The evaluation was an experimental design with a treatment group of 116 and a control group of 64. The information was gathered through three research questionnaires. The methodology involved factor analysis on the validity of measuring instruments and performing comparisons between treatment and control groups. The relevant outcomes were measures of gained skills and knowledge on running a business and increases in number of employees, turnover, productivity, and profit. *Highlights:* • There were statistically significant gains in the four skill-transfer factors (entrepreneurial characteristics, entrepreneurial orientation, business knowledge, entrepreneurial and business skills) between the treatment and control group; • There were statistically significant (at a 5 percent level) differences in effectiveness between the treatment and control group in relation to business improvement factors; • There was improvement in the number of employees and the number of customers for the treatment group (statistically significant) whereas this was not the case for the control group; • However, in business performance indicators (annual sales/turnover, value of capital assets, number of employees, number of customers per month, success of the businesses, probability of the businesses, satisfaction of the customers, and break-even point), both groups presented improvements before and after (mainly due to improvement in external factors of the economy). But they were statistically significant for the treatment group in 5 out of 6 indicators, while only 2 out of 6 indicators were statistically significant for the control group;	

table continues next page

Table E.4 Entrepreneurship Training—Practicing Entrepreneurs (ETPr) *(continued)*

Name	Country/region	Program	Evaluation	Reference
			• 98.12 percent of the treatment group were satisfied with WEP and indicated that they would recommend it to a friend or a colleague; and • 96.94 percent of the experimental group stated that WEP had helped them grow their businesses and 97.96 percent indicated that WEP had some effect on their businesses six months after the training.	
DDFET—Dutch Dairy Farmers Entrepreneurship Training	Netherlands	**Beneficiaries** Less than 100 dairy farmer beneficiaries per cohort in the Netherlands **Description** The program objective is to improve the entrepreneurial competencies of dairy farmers. In this training program, farmers develop and implement a strategic management plan, drawing on their strategic, opportunity, and information-seeking competencies. The training program consists of eight sessions. In these sessions, groups of farmers discuss aspects related to entrepreneurial competencies. Each meeting lasts about four hours, during which time a different part of the strategic plan is discussed, as are the previous day's assignments. Searches for information on whether the program is still under implementation did not yield information.	Evaluation Tier 2 The evaluation assessed the training's influence on farm characteristics and the farmers' entrepreneurial competencies using a case-control study methodology. Two groups of full-time Dutch dairy farmers were selected to participate in the study. One group (n = 75) participated in the training program, the second group (n = 180) served as a control group. The sample size was 164, of which 50 comprised the treatment group and 114 the control group. Two identical questionnaires measured the competencies of participating farmers at the start and at the end of the study (two and half years later). The outcomes were based on farm and farmer characteristics and entrepreneurial competencies. *Highlights:* • On average, all participants benefited from the program, irrespective of farmer, farm characteristics, or the level of competencies at the start of the program; • It was possible to improve entrepreneurial competencies of dairy farmers through similar training programs; and • Strategic competencies of dairy farmers had a positive relationship with farm size, supporting the general idea that when farms become larger, it becomes more important for farmers to be able to set, implement, and evaluate a strategy.	Bergevoet et al. (2005)

table continues next page

Table E.4 Entrepreneurship Training—Practicing Entrepreneurs (ETPr) *(continued)*

Name	Country/region	Program	Evaluation	Reference
FTDAP—Farmer Training Development Assistance Program	Honduras	**Beneficiaries** 7,500 smallholder farmers in 16 departments of Honduras **Description** The program aimed to increase the skills and productivity of farmers through four activities: (a) farmer training and development, (b) facilitation of access to credit by farmers, (c) upgrading of farm-to-market roads and (d) provision of an agriculture public grants facility. The program ran from 2007 to 2010. In addition to training, eligible farmers also received a limited amount of financial support to install better irrigation systems. The project goal was to increase employment levels by improving farmers' yield with improved technology and mixing crops to emphasize horticultural over basic crops. Implemented by Fintrac, FTDAP provided technical assistance and training to 7,500 smallholder farmers in 16 departments of Honduras. Eligible farmers also received a limited amount of financial support to install better irrigation systems.	Evaluation Tier 2 The evaluation assessed any changes in agricultural productivity or income through training and technical assistance. A rigorous impact evaluation was designed but it could not be undertaken due to implementation problems. The evaluation was based on a quasi-experimental design that relied on a model-based approach (modified regression-adjusted-propensity-score-based estimator). Two rounds of surveys yielded 7,262 completed interview questionnaires, of which 4,526 were from the baseline surveys (round 0) conducted in 2009 and 2010, and 2,736 were from the follow-on survey round (round 1) conducted in 2011. Outcomes were measured in terms of increased cultivation of horticultural crops, household income, and employment. *Highlights:* • FTDAP had a positive impact on activities related to horticultural crops, but a broader positive impact on household income and expenditures was not detected; • The results also showed that net income change from other crops was on average 11,360 lempiras (US$601) higher for program participants than for nonparticipants; • All of the income/expense components for other (horticultural) crops had positive effects; • There was no effect on the proportion of farmers growing horticultural crops; and • There was an effect on income, net income, expenditures, and labor expenditures for other crops.	NORC (2012)

table continues next page

Table E.4 Entrepreneurship Training—Practicing Entrepreneurs (ETPr) *(continued)*

Name	Country/region	Program	Evaluation	Reference
PBS—Production and Business Services	El Salvador	**Beneficiaries** Over 13,500 participants in El Salvador's Northern Zone over approximately four years **Description** The project's aim was to improve the business ventures—profitable and sustainable—of poor El Salvadoran farmers in the Northern Zone. From 2008 to 2012, PBS in El Salvador was funded by the Millennium Challenge Corporation (MCC) and implemented by El Salvador's Millennium Challenge Account. Over four years, 13,500 residents were provided technical and material assistance in industries like tourism, forestry, coffee growing, and produce. The program included three activities: Production and Business Services (PBS), Investment Support, and Financial Services. The PBS activity offered training and technical assistance, in-kind donations, and other business development services to small farmers and business owners. The program was administered primarily by FOMILENIO (the Millennium Challenge account) in partnership with different organizations. *Cost:* The cost of the PBS activity amounted to about US$57 million.	Evaluation Tier 2 The evaluation assessed the impact of PBS assistance on employment creation and producers' investment and income, household income, and intermediate outcomes. The methodology was a randomized rollout design, in which some producers were offered PBS assistance several months before other producers were offered similar assistance. The pool of beneficiaries was around 15,000 individuals. The sample size was 1,736, of which 518,593 and 625 individuals were distributed in dairy, horticulture, and handicrafts chains, respectively. In all three value chains, individuals were randomized into treatment and control groups. Treatment groups were offered PBS assistance in the first implementation phase, and control groups were offered PBS assistance roughly one year after the treatment group. Outcomes were measured in producer level and household level. *Highlights:* • The offer of PBS had a positive and statistically significant effect on employment in the handicrafts chain but not in the dairy or horticulture chains; • Among all artisans in the treatment group, PBS assistance resulted in 0.13 additional jobs (Intention to Treat Effect—ITT); • Among artisans who participated in the intervention, PBS assistance resulted in 0.19 additional jobs (Treatment on the Treated Effect—ToT). This difference was equivalent to nearly 50 days of full-time employment per year; • Only in the dairy value chain did the offer of PBS have a significant positive impact, around US$1,850 on dairy producers' productive income (ITT),	Blair *et al.* (2012)

table continues next page

Table E.4 Entrepreneurship Training—Practicing Entrepreneurs (ETPr) *(continued)*

Name	Country/region	Program	Evaluation	Reference
			with a p-value of 0.01. At over $3,000, this impact was even larger among individuals who participated in PBS assistance (ToT); • Across all three value chains, there was no significant impact of PBS on producers' investments and costs detected using the ITT and ToT approaches; • No statistically significant impact of PBS on net household income was found in any value chain; and • No impact of PBS on household consumption was found in any value chain.	
10KW—10,000 Women Program	India	**Beneficiaries** More than 10,000 businesswomen worldwide are expected to participate by the end of 2013. **Description** The program aims to provide support that otherwise wouldn't have existed for women's enterprise development in India's growing economy. Launched in 2008, the Goldman Sachs 10,000 Women Initiative works with over 80 academic and nonprofit organizations globally to create programs and coursework that is specific and relevant to each of its locales. In India, the program is available in several major cities and focuses on small and medium-size enterprises. Over the last four years, more than 550 women entrepreneurs have participated in the program across Bengaluru, Delhi, Hyderabad, Mumbai, and Pune.	Evaluation Tier 3 The evaluation assessed past participants' business development since completion of the program, using a quasi-experimental design, with participant interviews, surveys, literature reviews, and business expert interviews. Forty-one women responded to the surveys and interviews. *Highlights:* • Past participants reported newfound skills that strengthened their businesses' performance as well as an enhanced network; • Half of respondents saw their revenue double over 18 months, and respondents said their businesses grew by 6–10 employees; and • Several respondents talked about their increased confidence and their involvement in the community mentoring other women on business skills.	ICRW (2012)
CEM—Certificate in Entrepreneurial Management	Nigeria	**Beneficiaries** Over 600 business owners (and aspiring business owners) in Nigeria during its first six years	Evaluation Tier 3 The evaluation assessed past participants' employability, firm performance, and business skills.	Adiele (2011)

table continues next page

Table E.4 **Entrepreneurship Training—Practicing Entrepreneurs (ETPr)** *(continued)*

Name	Country/region	Program	Evaluation	Reference
		Description The program aims to train potential and practicing entrepreneurs in business management and entrepreneurial skills, with the ultimate goal of improving functional and operational deficiencies that are prevalent at small companies in Nigeria. Six years after its inception in 2005, CEM had graduated 600 business owners/managers from its program. It was launched out of the Pan-African University.	The program was evaluated in 2011 using a non-comparative retrospective design of an online questionnaire completed by past CEM participants (n = 192) and three focus groups of male and female participants from all class years. *Highlights:* • CEM has had a positive impact on skills improvement and on the capacity of participants as well as the performance of their businesses; and • 74 percent of participants saw an increase in revenue in their firms.	
CREA—*Capacitacion y Reclutamento Empresarial Americana*	Mexico	**Beneficiaries** 928 female entrepreneurs in Mexico's State of Zacatecas **Description** The program aimed to help female entrepreneurs enhance their basic business skills. Held in 2009, the entrepreneurship training program was offered to female entrepreneurs in a handful of localities in Mexico's State of Zacatecas. Led by university professors and graduate and undergraduate students, the women used practical examples in their intensive class over six weeks. Modules ranged from marketing to price setting, with a set curriculum of introducing the main concept, applying the concept to simple examples and using those concepts in their homework.	Evaluation Tier 3 The evaluation sought to assess the program's impact on women's businesses using a randomized controlled trial in a sample of 17 villages—seven treatments and 10 controls—of 928 women. The participants completed a follow-up survey several months after completion of the program. It must be noted that the randomized evaluation results have yet to be finalized and available results are preliminary. *Highlights:* • Those with the training saw a significant effect on weekly revenue as well as daily and weekly profit; and • The women who underwent the training also knew their profit levels.	Calderon, Cunha, and de Giorgi (2011)
DFCU—Development Finance Company of Uganda	Uganda	**Beneficiaries** Several dozen female entrepreneurs in Uganda each year	Evaluation Tier 3 The study evaluated the program's impact on women's networks, firm formation, and business	McKenzie and Weber (2009)

table continues next page

Table E.4 Entrepreneurship Training—Practicing Entrepreneurs (ETPr) *(continued)*

Name	Country/region	Program	Evaluation	Reference
		Description This program aims to help women entrepreneurs enhance their business skills and create a more thorough network. Small and microenterprise female business owners in Uganda took part in a comprehensive training program held at DFCU bank. The training focused on potential borrowers and took place over 12 days. The content included banking requirements, processes, financial literacy, separation of business and personal accounts, and the provision of opportunities for business networking and mentoring. The first training in 2007 included 51 women.	skills, using two evaluation methods. In 2009, the course was offered to 75 female DFCU clients. But low participation made the sample size too small, leading to the use of a different methodology for a subsequent evaluation. The second evaluation compared the change in firm outcomes over the 2007 to mid-2009 period for firms in the first training group in 2007 (treatment group) with the change in outcomes for firms whose owners started training in mid-2009 (control group). *Highlights:* • Among the treatment group, 72 percent said the training significantly improved their firm's performance; • Trainings made participants more likely to separate their personal and business finances, but there were no other clear business skills; impact; and • The training was not associated with greater access to finance or higher sales.	
ELP—Executive Leadership Programme	Northern Ireland	**Beneficiaries** About 10 business leaders each year in Northern Ireland **Description** Ireland's Executive Leadership Programme aims to aid senior executives from large and small companies in developing the knowledge, skills, and awareness to better communicate their values and move toward team-based leadership. In its first six years, 64 business leaders participated in the program.	Evaluation Tier 3 The evaluation assessed the program's effects on participants' skills and management education acquisition. This was a three-part evaluation—first, a survey of participants and businesses (n = 34); second, of these responses, 25 were probed for the program's impact on business skill development. Finally, three of the participants sat for an in-depth interview about the program. *Highlights:* • Evaluation indicated the program effectively mixed executive education and on-the-job training—specifically around skill acquisition and management education.	Leitch and Harrison (1999)

table continues next page

Table E.4 Entrepreneurship Training—Practicing Entrepreneurs (ETPr) (continued)

Name	Country/region	Program	Evaluation	Reference
GOWE—Growth-Oriented Women Entrepreneurs	Kenya	**Beneficiaries** 700 female entrepreneurs in Kenya **Description** The program aimed to improve participants' access to capital and mentorship and to enhance business knowledge and skills. Focused on female entrepreneurs in Kenya, the program involved (a) participants' access to finance at the African Development Bank, (b) training and business mentorship, and (c) improving the capacity of local business service providers to help with the delivery of services better targeted to beneficiaries. Running from 2007 to 2010 and implemented by the ILO, over 700 women participated in the training.	Evaluation Tier 3 The evaluation assessed the program's efficacy in training them. Evaluated in 2010, the methodology included focus groups and one-on-one conversations among past participants. *Highlights:* • The trainings were highly rated by participants, but there was a common belief that the program needed better mentorship and experiential learning; and • Past participants believed the program should have better follow-up around financing and should set training prices at market rates.	ILO (2010)
INT—Interise	United States	**Beneficiaries** In 2013, Interise anticipates 700 participants **Description** The objective of the program is to provide existing small employers with the resources they need to sustain and grow their businesses. Initially started as a regional program in Massachusetts in 2004, Interise is now a national program in the United States, imbedded in over 30 communities. Interise aims to help disadvantaged communities—its inaugural program in Boston focused on the city's lower-income communities. From these initial courses, Interise gathered data to better understand what aspects of its curriculum were most effective. By the end of 2013, Interise will be serving	Evaluation Tier 3 This evaluation assessed the social and economic impact of the program. Interise does an extensive evaluation of its program each year, and in 2011, an annual survey was sent out to past participants. Of the 451 alumni that received the surveys, 61 percent responded. *Highlights:* • 62 percent of Interise participants had added jobs to their companies or maintained all jobs; • 61 percent of businesses offered health insurance to their employees and gave out an average salary to new employees of about $41,000; • Over half of Interise participants also reported a growing business—with increased revenue (57 percent) and government grants averaging $325,000 per business (47 percent of the businesses); and	Interise (2011)

table continues next page

Table E.4 Entrepreneurship Training—Practicing Entrepreneurs (ETPr) *(continued)*

Name	Country/region	Program	Evaluation	Reference
		approximately 1,000 entrepreneurs per year. In addition, it offers entrepreneurs the possibility of accessing a national network designed to provide continued support and accountability as they implement their growth plans. *Costs:* Local partners set their own tuition rates, ranging from $500 to $2,000 per participant.	Nearly 80 percent of Interise participants reported being actively involved in the community—and the majority (58 percent) encouraged their employees to be active as well.	
MSETTP—Micro and Small Enterprise Training and Technology Project	Kenya	**Beneficiaries** Nearly 32,000 MSE proprietors between 1994 and 2002 **Description** The program aimed to provide skills training and appropriate technology knowledge for micro and small business owners, and to encourage technological innovation in this sector. Running from 1994 to 2003, MSETTP also aimed to increase entrepreneurial development of the private sector, as well as increase employment and incomes among informal-sector (Jua Kali) micro- and small-scale enterprises (MSEs). The beneficiaries were the Jua Kali workers in the manufacturing sector. The project was financed by a World Bank loan. A critical component to the program was the voucher training program, which subsidized skills and management training to workers in the manufacturing sector and developed a private market for training services. Nearly 35,000 small enterprises were trained under the program.	Evaluation Tier 3 The evaluation of the project aimed to compare changes in performance of trainees. The methodology was a performance evaluation— beneficiaries (both trainees and trainers) were surveyed on the project's outcomes. There was also an assessment based on project reports, legal documents, project files, and interviews with people involved. In 2005, the World Bank conducted a Project Performance Assessment Report to evaluate whether the expected results were produced and to disseminate lessons drawn from the experience. *Highlights:* • The tracer studies conducted showed that the program improved profits, sales, and investment in a significant proportion of trainees, relative to a control group. It also encouraged business start-ups; • Nearly 35,000 MSEs received training, compared to the project's official target of 32,000; • Four out of five trainees reported that the relevance and quality of the training they received under the program was good or excellent. Trainees surveyed reported that thanks to the training they improved the quality of their product (43 percent), introduced	World Bank (2005)

table continues next page

Table E.4 Entrepreneurship Training—Practicing Entrepreneurs (ETPr) (continued)

Name	Country/region	Program	Evaluation	Reference
		Costs: 10 percent of the cost of training was charged to the trainee, and this percentage increased with additional vouchers to the same individual.	a new product or service (71 percent), increased sales (66 percent), or found new markets (58 percent). A lower proportion (20 percent) reported that they enjoyed easier access to credit after receiving training; • The program encouraged some training providers to expand their training business (38 percent reported using their revenues to improve their training business), but the long-run impact of the project on markets for training services appeared to have been modest, as many trainers returned to their previous activities once the program ended; and • The efficiency of the project was negligible, mainly due to implementation problems.	
PAVCOPA—Agricultural Trading and Processing Promotion Pilot Project	Mali	**Beneficiaries** Merchants, producers, and processing industries in Mali **Description** The program objective was to help producers and processing industries and for merchants to improve the quality of their products and increase exports; as well as to bridge the gap between agricultural processing/marketing enterprises and financial institutions. Implemented as a five-year pilot program in 1991, as Mali faced severe economic and political instability, PAVCOPA had several components, including the "Access to Credit." This was done by organizing	Evaluation Tier 3 The 2003 World Bank report indicated the project never operationalized its monitoring and evaluation unit. Further, the statistics made available were prepared ex post by a monitoring and evaluation officer hired two months before the project's completion. No reliable quantitative information exists on the impact of project activities on the beneficiaries. *Highlights:* • PAVCOPA organized more than 100 negotiation sessions between private enterprises and the small number of financial institutions in the project, giving bankers an opportunity to familiarize themselves with the specific characteristics of local agribusinesses; and	Sangho (2003)

table continues next page

Table E.4 Entrepreneurship Training—Practicing Entrepreneurs (ETPr) *(continued)*

Name	Country/region	Program	Evaluation	Reference
		workshops and meetings between entrepreneurs and banks and financial institutions, and by organizing training and study tours on agricultural processing for banking and financial sector staff. Financed and implemented by the World Bank, the entrepreneurship component included workshops and training modules; study tours were supposed to cover the key industries: mango, green bean, and hide/skin subsectors, among others.	• The project helped design and implement financial schemes that opened up alternative financing opportunities for producer groups (e.g., the importation of potato seeds) and got micro-credit institutions involved in agribusiness activities.	
WETVBI—Women's Virtual Business Incubator	Tanzania	**Beneficiaries** 500 businesswomen in Tanzania **Description** The pilot program aimed to improve women's existing businesses by teaching participants business and production skills. The program trained 500 women in Dar es Salaam; it included a virtual incubator, tailored resources and support, a market focus and the development of a mentorship network. The women underwent entrepreneurship and business management training, technical training around production skills as well as specialized technical assistance and mentoring.	Evaluation Tier 3 The study assessed the efficacy of training and mentorship on business skills and firm production. Five hundred women were divided into two possible trainings—one with mentorship and technical assistance, the other without. An additional 250 women in the control group received no training. All 750 women were given a baseline survey before the trainings and a follow-up survey in 2011 after the program ended. Results are pending.	Bardasi and Holla (2010)

References

Adiele, M. 2011. "Certificate in Entrepreneurial Management (CEM) Training Programme, 2005–2011: Impact Evaluation Report." Lagos, Nigeria: Enterprise Development Center, Pan-African University.

Almeida, R., and E. Galasso. 2007. "Jump-Starting Self-Employment? Evidence among Welfare Participants in Argentina." Policy Research Working Paper 4270, Development Research Group, World Bank, Washington, DC.

Attanasio, O., A. Kugler, and C. Meghir. 2009. "Subsidizing Vocational Training for Disadvantaged Youth in Developing Countries: Evidence from a Randomized Trial." Discussion Paper 4251, Institute for the Study of Labor, Bonn.

Bardasi, E., and A. Holla. 2010. "Impact Evaluation of the Tanzania Women's Virtual Business Incubator." World Bank, Dakar.

Bauer, K. 2011. "Training Women for Success: An Evaluation of Entrepreneurship Training Programs in Vermont, USA." *Journal of Entrepreneurship Education* 14.

Bergevoet, R. H., G. W. Giesen, C. M. van Woerkum, and R. B. Huirne. 2005. "Improving Entrepreneurship in Farming: The Impact of a Training Programme in Dutch Dairy Farming." Paper presented at the 15th Congress of the International Farm Management Association, "Developing Entrepreneurship Abilities to Feed the World in a Sustainable Way," Campinas, Brazil, August 14–19. http://www.ifmaonline.org/pdf/congress/05Bergevoet%20et%20al.pdf.

Bikhazi, R., and N. Kabbani. 2010. "Assessing the Impact of the ILO Know About Business (KAB) Entrepreneurship Education Programme: Lessons Learned from the Middle East." International Labour Organization and Silatech presentation.

Bjorvatn, K., and B. Tungodden. 2010. "Teaching Business in Tanzania: Evaluation Participation and Performance." *Journal of the European Economic Association* 8 (2–3): 561–70.

Blair, R., L. Campuzano, L. Moreno, and S. Morgan. 2012. *Impact Evaluation Findings after One Year of the Productive Business Services Activity of the Productive Development Project, El Salvador.* Washington, DC: Mathematica Policy Research. http://www.mathematica-mpr.com/publications/PDFs/international/el_salvador_impact.pdf.

Blattman, C., N. Fiala, and S. Martinez. 2013. "Generating Skilled Self-Employment in Developing Countries: Experimental Evidence from Uganda." *Quarterly Journal of Economics*. http://papers.ssrn.com/sol3/papers.cfm?abstract_id=2268552.

Blattman, C., E. Green, J. Annan, and J. Jamison. 2013. "Building Women's Economic and Social Empowerment through Enterprise: An Experimental Assessment of the Women's Income Generating Support (WINGS) Program in Uganda." enGender Impact, World Bank's Gender Impact Evaluation Database. http://www.poverty-action.org/sites/default/files/wings_full_policy_report_0.pdf.

Botha, M. 2006. "Measuring the Effectiveness of the Women Entrepreneurship Programme (WEP) as a Training Intervention on Potential or Start-Up and Established Women Entrepreneurs in South Africa." Doctoral dissertation, Economic and Management Sciences, University of Pretoria, Pretoria.

Brannback, M., J. Heinonen, I. Hudd, and K. Paasio. 2005. "A Comparative Study on Entrepreneurial Opportunity Recognition and the Role of Education among Finnish Business School Students." Åbo Akademi University. http://web.abo.fi/~mbrannba/MIE/brannback156.pdf.

Bruhn, M., and B. Zia. 2011. "Stimulating Managerial Capital in Emerging Markets: The Impact of Business and Financial Literacy for Young Entrepreneurs." Policy Research Working Paper 5642, Development Research Group, Finance and Private Sector Development Team, World Bank, Washington, DC.

Calderon, G., J. Cunha, and G. de Giorgi. 2011. "Business Literacy and Development: Evidence from a Randomized Trial in Rural Mexico." Capacitacion y Reclutamiento Empresarial Americana Mexico (CREA Mexico), The Department of Economics, Stanford University, Stanford, CA.

Charney, A., and K. E. Libecap. 2000. "The Impact of Entrepreneurship Education: An Evaluation of the Berger Entrepreneurship Program at the University of Arizona, 1985–1999." University of Arizona—Eller College of Business and Public Administration, Tucson, AZ.

de Mel, S., D. McKenzie, and C. Woodruff. 2012. "Business Training and Female Enterprise Start-up, Growth and Dynamics." Policy Research Working Paper 6145, World Bank, Washington, DC.

Drexler, A., G. Fischer, and A. Schoar. 2010. "Keeping it Simple: Financial Literacy and Rules of Thumb." Discussion Paper 7994, Centre for Economic Policy Research, London.

Elert, N., F. Andersson, and K. Wennberg. 2013. "The Impact of Entrepreneurship Education in High-School on Subsequent Entrepreneurial Performance: A Longitudinal Study." The Ratio Institute, Sweden.

Field, E., S. Jayachandran, and R. Pande. 2010. "Female Entrepreneurship? A Field Experiment on Business Training in India." IMFR Researcher, Working Paper 36, Centre for Micro Finance, Chennai, India.

Frank, H., C. Karunka, M. Lueger, and J. Mugler. 2005. "Entrepreneurial Orientation and Education in Austrian Secondary Schools." *Journal of Small Business and Enterprise Development* 12 (2): 259–73.

Gielnik, M., M. Frese, A. Kahara-Kawuki, I. Wassawa Katono, S. Kyejjusa, J. Munene, and T. J. Dlugosch. 2013. "Action and Action-Regulation in Entrepreneurship: Evaluating a Student Training for Promoting Entrepreneurship." *Academy of Management Learning and Education*, October 3. http://amle.aom.org/content/early/2013/10/03/amle.2012.0107.abstract.

Gine, X., and G. Mansuri. 2011. *Money or Ideas? A Field Experiment on Constraints to Entrepreneurship in Rural Pakistan.* Washington, DC: World Bank.

Goppers, K., and M. T. Coung. 2007. "Business Training for Entrepreneurs in Vietnam: An Evaluation of the SIDA—Supported Start and Improve Your Business (SIYB) Project." Swedish International Development Cooperation Agency (SIDA).

Ibarraran, P., D. Rosas, and Y. Soares. 2006. "Impact Evaluation of a Youth Job Training Program in the Dominican Republic." Inter-American Development Bank, Washington, DC. http://www.iadb.org/en/publications/publications-detail,7101.html?id=18088.

Idogho, P. O., A. E. Ainabor. 2011. "Entrepreneurship Education and Small-Scale Business Management Skill Development among Students of Auchi Polytechnic Auchi, Edo State, Nigeria." *International Journal of Business and Management* 6 (3).

IFC Monitor. 2008. "Do Programs Supporting High Growth Entrepreneurs Work? Evaluating the Endeavor-South Africa Project." Monitor 45322, Endeavor Global, International Finance Corporation, World Bank Group, Washington, DC.

Institute of Statistical, Social and Economic Research. 2012. *An Impact Evaluation of the MiDA FBO Training: Final Report*. Accra: University of Ghana.

Interise. 2011. "Interise 2011 Report Card: Creating Jobs, Growing Business, Building Communities." Interise, Boston.

ICRW (International Center for Research on Women). 2012. "Catalyzing Growth in the Women-Run Small and Medium Enterprises Sector (SMEs): Evaluating the Goldman Sachs 10,000 Women Initiative, India." ICRW, Washington, DC.

ILO (International Labour Organization). 2010. "ILO Evaluation Series: Growth-Oriented Women Entrepreneurs (GOWE)-Kenya Program." http://www.ilo.org/wcmsp5/groups/public/---ed_mas/---eval/documents/publication/wcms_142992.pdf.

Johannisson, B., H. Landström, and J. Rosenberg. 1998. "University Training for Entrepreneurship—An Action Frame of Reference." *European Journal of Engineering Education* 23 (4): 477–96.

Karlan, D., R. W. Fairlie, and J. Zinman. 2012. "Behind the GATE Experiment: Evidence on the Effects of and Rationales for Subsidized Entrepreneurship Training." Economics Department Working Paper 95, Yale University, New Haven. http://ssrn.com/abstract=2008446.

Karlan, D., and M. Valdivia. 2011. "Teaching Entrepreneurship: Impact of Business Training on Microfinance Clients and Institutions." *Review of Economics and Statistics* 93 (2): 510–27.

Klaper, R. 2004. "Government Goals and Entrepreneurship Education—An Investigation at a Grande Ecole in France." *Education+ Training* 46 (3): 127–37.

Klinger, B., and M. Schündeln. 2007. "Can Entrepreneurial Activity be Taught? Quasi-Experimental Evidence from Central America." Working Paper 153, Center for International Development at Harvard University, Cambridge, MA.

Klofsten, M. 2000. "Training Entrepreneurship at Universities: A Swedish Case." *Journal of European Industrial Training* 24 (6): 337–44.

Kolvereid, L., and O. Moen. 1997. "Entrepreneurship among Business Graduates: Does a Major in Entrepreneurship Make a Difference?" *Journal of European Industrial Training* 21 (4): 154–60.

Leitch, C. M., and R. T. Harrison. 1999. "A Process Model for Entrepreneurship Education and Development." *International Journal of Entrepreneurial Behaviour & Research* 5 (3): 83.

Macours, K., P. Premand, and R. Vakis. 2012. "Transfers, Diversification and Household Risk Strategies: Experimental Evidence with Lessons for Climate Change Adaptation." Policy Research Working Paper 6053, World Bank, Washington, DC.

Mahohoma, E., and M. Muyambo. 2008. "The Impact of Junior Achievement in Namibia." Junior Achievement Worldwide and Junior Achievement Namibia. http://www.docstoc.com/docs/51842795/JA-Namibia-Impact-Survey---REPOR.

Mann, P. H. 1990. "Non-Traditional Business Education for Black Entrepreneurs: Observations From a Successful Program." *Journal of Small Business Management* 28 (2): 30–36.

Mano, Y., A. Iddrisu, Y. Yoshino, and S. Tetsushi. 2011. "How Can Micro and Small Enterprises in Sub-Saharan Africa Become More Productive? The Impacts of Experimental Basic Managerial Training." Policy Research Working Paper 5755, World Bank, Washington, DC.

McKenzie, D., and M. Weber. 2009. "The Results of a Pilot Financial Literacy and Business Planning Training Program for Women in Uganda." Finance & PSD Impact Report 8, Lessons from DECRG-FP Impact Evaluations, World Bank, Washington, DC.

Moberg, K. 2012. "The Impact of Entrepreneurship Education and Project-Based Education on Students' Personal Development and Entrepreneurial Intentions at the Lower Levels of the Educational System: Too Much of Two Good Things?" European Summer University Conference, University of Southern Denmark, Kolding, August 19–25.

Nakkula, M., M. Lutyens, C. Pineda, A. Dray, F. Gaytan, and J. Huguley. 2004. "Initiating, Leading and Feeling in Control of One's Fate: Findings from the 2002–2003 Study of NFTE in Six Boston Public High Schools." Harvard University. http://www.nfte.com/sites/default/files/harvard-nfte_study_02-03_full_report_6-6-04.pdf.

Neill, C., K. Sreedhar, and K. Kapadia. 1998. "A Final Evaluation Report of the Women's Enterprise Management Training Outreach Program (WEMTOP)." EDI Evaluation Study ES98-3, prepared for the Economic Development Institute, World Bank.

NORC. 2012. *Impact Evaluation of the Farmer Training and Development Activity in Honduras: Final Report*. Chicago, IL: University of Chicago. http://www.oecd.org/countries/honduras/report-100512-evaluation-hon-farmer-training-and-development.pdf.

Premand, P., S. Brodman, R. Almeida, R. Grun, M. Barouni. 2012. "Entrepreneurship Training and Self-Employment among University Graduates: Evidence from a Randomized Trial in Tunisia." Policy Research Working Paper 6285, World Bank, Washington, DC.

Reimers, F., P. Dyer, and M. E. Ortega. 2012. "Entrepreneurship Education in the Middle East." Summary findings. https://www.jaworldwide.org/inside-ja/Reports/INJAZ_Al_Arab_Final_Evaluation_Report.pdf.

Rosendahl-Huber, L., R. Sloof, and M. van Praag. 2012. "The Effect of Early Entrepreneurship Education: Evidence from a Randomized Field Experiment." Discussion Paper 6512, Institute for the Study of Labor, Bonn, Germany.

Sage Policy Group and Nearing Group. 2010. "Economic Impacts of ACTiVATE at UMBC." Submitted to bwtech@UMBC Research and Technology Park.

Sangho, Y. 2003. *Mali Agricultural Trading and Processing Promotion Pilot Project (PAVCOPA): Implementation Completion Report*. Report 25884. Washington, DC: World Bank.

South African Institute for Entrepreneurship. 2006. "Business Ventures Full Impact Report" (accessed August 8, 2013). http://www.entrepreneurship.co.za/page/business_ventures_full_impact_report.

Valdivia, M. 2011. "Training or Technical Assistance? A Field Experiment to Learn What Works to Increase Managerial Capital for Female Micro-Entrepreneurs." Working Paper 2011/02, Banco de desarrollo de América Latina (CAF), Lima. http://siteresources.worldbank.org/INTGENDER/Resources/336003-1303333954789/final_report_bustraining_BM_march31.pdf.

World Bank. 2005. *Project Performance Assessment Report: Kenya Micro and Small Enterprise Training and Technology Project*. Report 32657, Washington, DC.

———. 2012. *Can Skills Training Programs Increase Employment for Young Women? The Case of Liberia*. Washington, DC: Adolescent Girls Initiative, World Bank.

Zhang, G., P. Cheng, L. Fan, and Z. Chu. 2012. "An Empirical Study on Impact of College Carve-Out Education on Entrepreneur Intention." Social Science Research Network (SSRN). http://ssrn.com/abstract=2034168.

Zia, U. E. 2007. "Building and Construction Improvement Programme: Entrepreneur Training & Employment Generation." Unpublished program evaluation of the Hope '87 End project. http://www.hope87.org/Documents/bacip.pdf.

Environmental Benefits Statement

The World Bank Group is committed to reducing its environmental footprint. In support of this commitment, the Publishing and Knowledge Division leverages electronic publishing options and print-on-demand technology, which is located in regional hubs worldwide. Together, these initiatives enable print runs to be lowered and shipping distances decreased, resulting in reduced paper consumption, chemical use, greenhouse gas emissions, and waste.

The Publishing and Knowledge Division follows the recommended standards for paper use set by the Green Press Initiative. Whenever possible, books are printed on 50 percent to 100 percent postconsumer recycled paper, and at least 50 percent of the fiber in our book paper is either unbleached or bleached using Totally Chlorine Free (TCF), Processed Chlorine Free (PCF), or Enhanced Elemental Chlorine Free (EECF) processes.

More information about the Bank's environmental philosophy can be found at http://crinfo.worldbank.org/wbcrinfo/node/4.

www.ingramcontent.com/pod-product-compliance
Lightning Source LLC
Chambersburg PA
CBHW060311240426
43661CB00059B/2725